A SEASON IN STRIPES

A SEASON IN STRIPES

Life with the Leicester Tigers

MICHAEL TANNER

MAINSTREAM
PUBLISHING

EDINBURGH AND LONDON

First published in Great Britain in 1998 by
MAINSTREAM PUBLISHING COMPANY (EDINBURGH) LTD
7 Albany Street
Edinburgh EH1 3UG

ISBN 1 84018 052 8

A catalogue record for this book is available from the British Library

Typeset in Giovanni Book
Printed and bound in Great Britain by Butler and Tanner Ltd, Frome

Contents

Author's Note		7
Foreword by Peter Wheeler		9
1	It's a Man's, Man's, Man's World!	11
2	Brace Gets the Fat Lady Singing	18
3	Heat and Dust	28
4	The Gospel According to Bob	38
5	Glaw-ster!	47
6	King of the Modern Game	58
7	Little Big Man	66
8	The Italian Job	71
9	New Kids on the Block	82
10	Bob and Dunc Steady the Ship	88
11	A Good-Value Day	98
12	Lunch with the ABC Club	106
13	Hail Reg!	118
14	Bench Fever	124
15	Shere Khan	133
16	Limmage's Lawn	142
17	Pooley's Fight for Fitness	151
18	A Litter of Cubs	161
19	Bob Bites the Bullet	169
20	Nobby Hits the Big Time but Pots Misses Out	176
21	Bob and Dunc Walk the Plank	183
22	We Play It with a Will	206
23	New Brooms	214

Dedicated to Dennis Haines,
former Tiger; inspirational coach; and valued friend

Author's Note

It is some 20 years (and as many lbs) ago since I spent a 'season in stripes', firstly as a player and then as a coach. Even in the 1970s the prospect of chronicling the way in which a 'professional' (with a small 'p') rugby club like Leicester functioned on a day-to-day basis was an intriguing one. The advent of 'Professionalism' (with a capital 'P') made that prospect not only more intriguing but also more appealing to publishers. Sincere thanks, then, to Bill Campbell and Mainstream for allowing the ambition to be realised.

Rugby football is now big business, growing bigger by the season, month, week and, so it seems, even by the day. Clubs don't come any bigger than Leicester Tigers: 118 years of rich history studded with great names and memorable successes; possessors of the finest club stadium in the country; one of only two clubs (Bristol is the other) whose players are identified by letters instead of numbers; and the sole English club granted an annual fixture with the Barbarians.

Today is tomorrow's history, and my sole objective in compiling this book was to record how Leicester Tigers lived and breathed – not necessarily how they played: there was to be no plethora of match reports – during the 1997–98 season. One hesitates to use the phrase 'fly on the wall' in view of recent TV documentaries but, in all honesty, that was the *modus operandi*; the only difference being the substitution of my eyes, ears and tape recorder for a roving camcorder. The key events, on and off the pitch, the personalities who helped fashion them (and, in turn, were influenced by them) are all within, the stories recorded as they unfolded. It was very much a case of *carpe diem* as far as I was concerned. There was no end-of-season editing, no recourse to the 20:20 vision of hindsight in order

7

to match the material to the outcome.

The book could not have been written in the manner intended were it not for the utmost co-operation of the Leicester management and players, and I extend a sincere and massive vote of thanks to all concerned at Oval Park and Welford Road. It would be remiss of me, however, not to specify one individual: during a period when even finding 30 seconds to grab a sandwich on most days was in itself a sleight of hand worthy of Paul Daniels, director of rugby, Bob Dwyer, somehow always conjured up minutes here and minutes there to satisfy the incessant demands of the dreaded, ever-pestering 'scribe' – thanks a bunch.

Finally, thanks are due to a couple of individuals outside the Tigers family who contributed mightily to the finished product you are about to read: Mike Batty, for selflessly supporting a book about a sport he barely tolerates or understands by maintaining the smoothest of information highways; and John Shotton for reading – and making valued suggestions to – the manuscript in between frequent visits to his physiotherapist and the Indian subcontinent!

Michael Tanner
Sleaford
Lincolnshire
May 1998

Foreword

In days gone by, number eights did not wear earrings, support for lineout jumpers was only required after midnight, a kick for touch was meant to go into touch, penalty tries were awarded once per season, and the only way referees got wired up was from the cross bar if they awarded a late try against Gloucester at Kingsholm.

It was also true that anybody coming down, or should it be up, from Oxford or Cambridge Universities with any sort of rugby reputation, was viewed with suspicion for two very good reasons. Firstly, they usually wanted to introduce a complicated system of lineout signals that would one day foil KGB deciphering experts, although in fact we usually found that if any were forwards they struggled to understand our standard front, middle and back signal. Secondly, nobody really regarded Varsity rugby as much more than schoolboy stuff augmented by a few potential internationals on a diploma course that carried a pass mark equivalent to the average number of times you were likely to win the Lottery jackpot in your lifetime, which in terms of privilege and opportunity most of them just had.

So it was with a measure of suspicion that I greeted Mike Tanner the second time he arrived at Leicester, not now fresh from the best education that being a promising scrum-half could buy, but with the idea of writing a book about a season at the club. Now Michael was not a bad scrum-half for someone exposed to all those superior attitudes at Oxford, and who might believe that playing in the Varsity match is the pinnacle of any rugby player's career, but what was he like as an author and could he be the first Oxford graduate who did not justify our suspicions?

Coming off of the back of Bath's experience with their documentary last year, we should have shown him the door and given him Harlequins' telephone number, but as he was probably going to write the book anyway, and as a past player with a feel for the club, at least if we talked to him he might get things half right. Judgement on what fraction he actually got right will depend on individual views of how they were involved in what happened during the year.

It was a difficult, challenging, exciting, frustrating, positive, sometimes frightening year of enormous change. From amateur to professional, members club to plc, Dwyer to Richards, £3 million to £4.5 million turnover. Everybody was affected by it but not all were comfortable with it.

At the time of writing change continues in the world of rugby, generally and at the club. We are looking forward to a new season with a better quality squad of players, who have committed their future to the club and are led by a coaching team that sets the highest standards and has the widest horizons.

No one can tell what will happen this year, as the Allied Dunbar Premiership becomes even more competitive and challenging. However, we can be sure that Leicester Football Club is now better financed, better structured, and better staffed to succeed than ever before.

The club is a kaleidoscope of people and activities set in an intense sporting environment on an open public stage of interest and comment locally, nationally and internationally. I hope you will find that Michael Tanner has captured some of this during an extraordinary year and to those who care for the club, I hope you will find something in this book that will draw you even closer.

Peter Wheeler
Chief Executive
Leicester Football Club plc
July 1998

1

It's a Man's, Man's, Man's World!

Once upon a time, pre-season training tended to commence on a balmy evening in late July with a (protracted) game of 'touch', some (interminable) lapping and a (nauseous) series of sprints conducted to a chorus of birdsong – prior to a fortifying pint or two in the club house bar. Not any more. Certainly not if you are a Leicester Tiger. For an evening in July read a morning in June; for the great outdoors read the sweaty confines of a gymnasium. Substitute James Brown for our feathered friends and, most definitely, replace best bitter with Lucozade Sport and you've got the picture.

Monday, 23 June 1997, sees a 50-strong squad of Tigers report for duty at Loughborough University. Only the sick, lame and the exalted – notably the club's record representation of six British Lions – are excused. Session upon session, day after day, the sinews, muscles and bones are cajoled back into action. To 'old sweats' like Dean Richards, who has seen it all and done it all at every level, this is akin to the Chinese water torture. Never one of rugby's zealots on the training front, 'Deano' reckons it's just plain ridiculous.

The Loughborough ordeal soon gives way to a three-week programme based at Oval Park, the club's training ground in Oadby, a ten-minute ride from the Tigers' Welford Road headquarters in the city centre, always known thus even though the postal address is Aylestone Road.

The training ground is actually the home of Oadby Wyggestonians RFC. For more years than anyone can remember, it used to be that the Leicester club trained on the 'Rec', across the Welford Road, in the shadow of Leicester Prison. Generations of Tigers commenced Monday and Thursday evening training to the click-clack of studs negotiating this busy urban thoroughfare. The treacherous slope, not to mention the canine (or even camel-derived when the circus had been in town) booby-traps that occasionally prompted lightning sidesteps from the most cumbersome of forwards, ensured this relatively confined recreational area was never good enough for a club that has always prided itself as being professional with a small 'p'. And, if the dog dirt didn't catch out the unwary or unsighted, the swings, slides and roundabouts just might. In addition, the 'Rec' (now Nelson Mandela Park) is owned by the Council and, following some difficulty when three Tigers toured South Africa with England in the 1980s, it became apparent the tenancy was far from secure. Consequently, the club struck a deal with Oadby Wyggs whereby it would lease and develop their ground in Wigston Road, Oadby. Draining the pitches, providing floodlights and all-weather surfaces, and improving the club house facilities cost in excess of half a million pounds. Oval Park, as it was christened, was formally opened on 6 December 1992 by M.R. 'Micky' Steele-Bodger, president of the Barbarians.

On a July morning – as the sun sends long shadows across its immaculate emerald carpet of grass – from the numerous state-of-the-art floodlight pylons, Oval Park is the very epitome of a professional training complex with a very large 'P'. Incorporated within the club house is a new gymnasium with which the players are to become intimately, and painfully, acquainted. Tuesdays and Thursdays are especially strenuous days with sessions on the weights. The rest of the week offers light relief by comparison. Monday features a 10 a.m. aerobic workout at the Pinetrees Leisure Centre (on Leicester's Frog Island) and a 6 p.m. wrestling/speed session at the Police Barracks in Enderby. After being granted post-weights lie-ins on Wednesdays and Fridays, it's a 4 p.m. trip to either Bradgate Park, Leicester's vast open-air playground to the west of the city, or Western Park – one of the city's green lungs – for more aerobics, possibly a *fartlek*. The week's activities are rounded off by a Saturday morning stint back on the weights. Sunday? A day of rest.

The signs of professionalism are to be seen at every turn. For instance, as the players arrive in dribs and drabs for another punishing weights session on a humid, mizzly Thursday morning in the fourth week of conditioning, they are presented with training vests and shorts (courtesy of new club sponsor Next) by Duncan Hall, the club's director of coaching development.

'Last year we didn't have enough gear to wear. This year we have five pairs of vests and pants for summer training and six sets for the winter. When you're a Tiger you've got to look the part. You wear club apparel. If you don't, you're fined! You're also fined if you're late!' says Hall as he rummages around inside one of the huge cardboard boxes, on which he had latterly been resting his feet, to finally extricate the correct sizes to lob in the direction of Derek Jelley. The prop is not late. It's purely Hall's way of making his point, laying down the law, showing who's boss.

The craggy, 41-year-old Australian has no need to overexert himself on that score. A pair of gnarled ear lobes betray the 15 occasions he inhabited the Wallaby scrummage during the 1980s and, although he seems a mite small for an international second-rower by modern standards, he has obviously kept himself in pretty good shape. Hall still looks as though he could handle himself if things turned nasty in a Brisbane bar and a 'stoush' suddenly erupted. It is easier for players to respect a coach with Hall's credentials. The players do respect him and, moreover, they consider him, as the Australians say, to be a 'bloody good bloke'.

Hall is an integral part of the rugby revolution sweeping through the Tigers. He came to Leicester after four years as director of coaching with Queensland, where he oversaw 12 staff and ran the entire show. At Leicester he does not run the show, Bob Dwyer does. But when Australia's 1991 World Cup winning coach cast the assistant bait in Hall's direction, he bit. 'I wanted to coach, but one of the problems with Queensland was that if you were an employee of the Union you couldn't coach the team. I had gone up the ladder, but had got further away from what I was good at. Coming here was a great opportunity. There are only four main jobs in Australia: Queensland, New South Wales, ACT and the national side. Most of them meant you had to move to Sydney – but I'd rather go anywhere in the world than Sydney! It's great to visit but expensive to live in! We've still some way to go with professionalism at Leicester. There's a lot still to be learned. It's really all about putting bums on seats. That's what creates income – and if we don't get income no one gets paid!' Clearly, globetrotting has not diluted that sardonic view of life which has come to be associated with the Australian male, and, with that observation, a glance at the clock – fast approaching 10 a.m. – sends him next door to monitor the progress (and punctuality) of his breadwinners.

In all honesty, cocking an ear or sniffing the air would suffice. Clanking, grunting, fetid torture chambers of this variety hardly demand visual confirmation of their inmates' activity. Abundant instruments of pain are dotted about a white breeze-blocked room measuring barely 30 feet by 30 feet. Only the incessant din of 'club' music and the various homilies and epigrams pinned to the walls distinguish this pain-racked environment from one, say, Guy Fawkes was obliged to endure in 1605.

'I'm a great believer in luck and I find the harder I work the more I have of it,' Thomas Jefferson assures hooker Dorian West, who is about to indulge in a set of inclined bench presses.

'I do the very best I know how, the very best I can,' Abraham Lincoln is telling Richards and Wells, 'and I mean to keep on doing so to the end.'

It is unlikely two such Leicester stalwarts need the hint or take much notice of 'ole Abe'. One sign, however, probably does attract the attention of each and every Tiger. Amid the many pearls of wisdom from American presidents, business tycoons and sundry geniuses, one quotation stands alone: 'There is one simple reason why we are so consistently successful. We practise really high standards.' Beneath these words is the name Sean Fitzpatrick, All Black. Enough said.

Today's session is a particularly heavy one: an hour and a half of push-press, bicep curls, power clean-high pull, hanging snatch below knees, and many more such mind-boggling excercises; two minutes respite between each repetition. Testimony to the benefits of this regime is to be found in the muscle definition of virtually every player in the squad. Even a scrum-half like Jamie Hamilton boasts the sculpted physique of a male model who could make money modelling swimwear (well, he was once a sea-scout in Australia). 'It's a man's, man's, man's world,' shouts James Brown, wholly appropriately, from the ghetto-blaster stuck in the far corner, beneath the charts prescribing the sequence of exercises. Differing needs for backs, front row, locks and back row are recognised by specific programmes. The backs, for example, carry out plenty of hamstring curls; the front row strengthen their necks using a harness weighted with 30 kilograms which they must raise from their chest 20 times. England internationals Richard Cockerill and Darren Garforth, recently returned from the tour of Argentina, commenced their work earlier than the rest and are into the third of four repetitions using this hideous contraption which possesses all the comforts of a scold's bridle. All that's missing is a rack and thumbscrew. 'Come on, Daz! One more!' bellows the bull-necked, shaven-headed Cockerill

– looking for all the world as though he's got the role of Magwitch sewn up should there ever be another remake of *Great Expectations*. Their recovery period is taken lying on the floor. A faint squelch is discernible from the carpet beneath the bearish form of Garforth and when he rises one can appreciate why: a huge prop-sized pool of sweat puddles the spot, reminiscent of those chalk shapes delineating the corpse that always seem to welcome one of Agatha Christie's detectives at the commencement of a murder enquiry.

Cockerill and Garforth may have returned to the gym-face but none of the six British Lions (Martin Johnson, Graham Rowntree, Neil Back, Austin Healey, Will Greenwood and Eric Miller); Scotland tourist Craig Joiner; or the much-heralded new signings (Waisale Serevi, Marika Vunibaka, Michael Horak, Fritz Van Heerden and Eric Rush) are present. Nor is Springbok fly-half Joel Stransky who tore the medial ligament in his left knee during the end-of-season Middlesex Sevens.

The mood is light-hearted rather than ultra-serious. All that changes with the appearance of a comparatively slight, bespectacled, middle-aged man sporting a yellow golf shirt and a pair of khaki 'stubbies' (shorts, to us Poms) whom some people think bears a more than passing resemblance to a younger Rolf Harris – minus beard but plus attitude. Bob Dwyer is looking every inch the British perception of the archetypal Australian, but Dwyer is no figure of fun. This is the Main Man; Numero Uno. The players are palpably in awe of him: from 34-year-old Richards, a veteran of 309 first-fifteen appearances, 48 internationals and two Lions tours, at the top of the ladder, down to 19-year-old rookie lock Tom Butler on the bottom rung.

Almost imperceptibly the noise level has dropped and the only sound now challenging James Brown's tonsils is the sound of bouncing iron and of voices exhorting colleagues to even greater endeavour. Dwyer drifts from group to group, enquiring about the progress of an injury here (John Wells's troublesome Achilles tendon), or eliciting a nervous laugh there. After delivering one such rib-tickler to Cockerill, the newly capped England hooker, who is proudly wearing a Cellnet-sponsored England vest, wanders off – to reappear seconds later clad in one bearing the name of the club's sponsor. Cockers, court jester supreme, can be a handful. It is safe to say he has got under more skins than a taxidermist: one training ground altercation between himself and flanker Dick Beaty led to the latter suffering a fractured cheekbone, and another fracas led to an enraged Dean Richards pursuing him round the field. He is given plenty of rope, which he tends to use to the full, but – like Magwitch – beneath the surface one suspects there beats a charitable heart and generous spirit. A photographer has just arrived from the *Leicester Mercury* to record the revamped weights room which Hall and the club's fitness and conditioning coach – the prolific try-scoring wing of the '70s John Duggan – have expertly transformed into a gymnasium during the off-season. There's no point in annoying the new sponsor before the deal has even officially been announced.

Dwyer's gaze comes to rest on the new spotty-brown carpet. 'Can you believe it took eight weeks to get this flooring? What is it about this country? What does it take to get things done?' The slowness with which the wheels of British commerce turn is one of Dwyer's *bêtes noires*: one year over here and Dwyer is in mortal danger of turning into a whingeing Pom. He relates one of his favourite stories testifying to the Old Country's mysterious way of doing things: 'My wife went to buy a car last November. She chose the model she wanted, went to pay up and they told her it would be delivered in March! What a joke!' Then, as suddenly as he came, he is gone. There is never a moment to lose, or waste, in the life of Bob Dwyer. He operates on distinctly high-octane fuel. If you didn't recognise all the symptoms of the hyperenergetic, driven high-achiever, you'd swear he was fuelled by something more narcotic than a diet of fresh air, exercise and boundless aspiration. One remains convinced that were a Geiger counter to be run across Bob Dwyer's chest the readings might well trouble the top of the scale.

As the players begin to finish their morning's work, the adjacent room belonging to the physiotherapist, Mark Geeson, begins to fill up with bodies. Besides the soothing ministrations of Geeson and his equipment, the physio's room is an ideal spot to wind down and catch up on the latest gossip. Craig Joiner has popped in for exactly that purpose. The heavily suntanned winger has recently enjoyed a week in Corfu after touring Zimbabwe with the Scottish development fifteen. He trades stories with Matt Poole, who is in the process of collecting his tickets for that evening's premiere of *The Lost World* at the new Odeon multiplex at Freemens Park, close to the Welford Road ground. Numerous local sporting luminaries, besides Tigers, are due to attend – including Gary Lineker. 'Is Johnno going?' asks Joiner. 'I dunno. But I doubt it. He had his op today,' says Poole of his second-row partner who has been plagued with a groin problem.

Joiner has been house-hunting. Last year he shared a house in Botchestone with Will Greenwood and Austin Healey but the trio are now going their own domestic ways. The burly figure of Dorian West passes through, an apple clenched between his teeth. The ebullient hooker's ill-fitting flip-flops attract instant ridicule: 'Athlete's foot!' explains 'Nobby' between mouthfuls. 'Impossible – you're nothing like a f***ing athlete!' comes the reply.

Hottest, and liveliest, gossip concerns the state of play on the comings-and-goings front. There's talk of an Australian scrum-half: 'Nah, he wants too much money.' Flanker Bill Drake-Lee enters and says goodbye to Geeson. 'You're going to Moseley then?' confirms the physio. 'Yeh. It seems all set now.'

Drake-Lee's medical records are pulled from one cupboard and placed on a pile in another. The stack is growing ever higher. It already contains the files of eight players, including Rory Underwood, Steve Hackney, John and Rob Liley and Aadel Kardooni – all crowd favourites and all departed for pastures new over the summer. The books must be balanced. The professional era has descended upon Leicester Tigers with a vengeance.

2

Brace Gets the Fat Lady Singing

Reaching Peter Wheeler on the phone these days demands the patience of a saint and actually getting to see him, even in the off-season, requires the credentials of Job himself. If he is not negotiating transfer details with a player's solicitors he's sweet-talking a merchant banker or sponsor.

Peter Wheeler always was one of rugby's movers and shakers. In a playing career encompassing 41 England caps (plus another seven for the British Lions) he gained the reputation – though he plays it down – of being the team's unofficial shop steward, the team 'fixer'. The 1997 incarnation of 'Brace', the snappier version of his England nickname, 'Wheelbrace', is a tad heavier engined than the all-action, ball-handling prototype of the modern hooker who, lest it be forgotten, was so good back in the '70s that it is he who would be wearing the number two jersey in Ian McGeechan's Lions dream team of the last 30 years, not John Pullin, Bobby Windsor, Brian Moore or Keith Wood. The blond-topped choirboy visage that once camouflaged the exceedingly tough nut beneath may also betray the slight ravages of time but the suspicion still lingers that Wheeler, when not playing hardball, can charm the birds from the trees if he has a mind to, and he does – frequently. Nowadays, England's Mr Fixit is fixing things for the Tigers. Wheeler's involvement should come as no surprise: five stints as club captain (including the three successive John Player Cup-winning seasons of 1979–81) and one season as coach (the inaugural Courage Clubs Championship of 1987–88) testify to that, but never in his wildest dreams did he for-see a time when Leicester would boast a chief executive or that he would be filling the role.

'I never envisaged doing the job. I never visualised that the game and the club would get into this position and need such a big organisation to run it. You felt that the game would go professional and start paying people, but you never really thought it through to see what that would mean. Nothing of this size. And, in fact, it was only 18 months ago that one saw it was going to be big and one was going to need massive attention and a lot of change.

'My involvement deepened significantly when I became president elect three years ago, because a number of others who should have been before me were not available. It coincided with everything starting to happen, the First Division clubs getting together and so on. Then things went open and everything was off and running. What accelerated things dramatically was the involvement of Sir John Hall and the other entrepreneurs who saw that we were not just going to be paying players a hundred quid. They suddenly injected £3–£4 million, lifted the game and made a huge step in next to no time. We saw here the way things were going – our players came under attack, if you like, to sign contracts for Newcastle, Richmond or Saracens – and that we had to make sure we did something to keep them. We needed to offer them something and we needed to get some money in to pay for it. So, very quickly, within four to six weeks, we recognised that we needed more than just an executive committee if we were to maintain our position in the game. We suddenly found that monthly committee meetings, with not very much happening in between, were inadequate – things needed to move quicker than that. It was difficult keeping 27 people informed about how things were developing and providing sufficient information on which they could make informed decisions. I was on the executive management committee which should have been given executive powers, but to do so would have needed a change in the club's rules and regulations. So, instead, it met on a weekly basis, with delegated powers, and reports to the general committee. And, in January 1996, I was appointed chief executive.

'I still think that without Sir John Hall's interjection we were in a better position than anyone else because we had a stadium that held 15,000 and a membership, at the time, of 14,000. If anyone was going to be well placed for professionalism we would, but the big leap forward meant that, almost instantaneously, a number of clubs leapt ahead of us. We suddenly found we didn't have the biggest ground because Wasps had QPR, for instance. We had to grasp the nettle and move very quickly if we were to save our players who were very attractive to other clubs.

'The second phase of our new management structure is now in place for this year. Last year it was difficult to realise the scale of increase, there was no template, we just had to do what we thought was right and we got a lot of things wrong in terms of scale – we actually needed double of everything. The increase in turnover from £1.8 million to £2.9 million needs to go up to £3.6 million this year. It's a lot of money and we have to go out and get it. All our systems were those of an amateur club. There were no job descriptions; no one had a contract, not even a letter of appointment. We could not stay as we were because we would not attract the best players and coaches. We had to generate income or we would decline.'

Where was the money to come from in order to finance this revolution? Rocketing expenses were obviously going to outstrip income. Wheeler rises from behind his exceedingly functional and less-than-chief-executive-style desk and, taking three or four steps to cross his unprepossessing and less-than-chief-executive-sized office, picks up a hefty red folder from a shelf: 'Leicester Football Club, Five-Year Business Plan 1997', it says on the cover. The club, currently registered under the industrial and provident societies acts, intends to become a public limited company with the aim of raising something like £3 million from shares issued to its members. There will be no sugar daddy, no Sir John Hall, Chris Wright or Nigel Wray, at Welford Road.

'We don't want to be owned by a rich individual or rich company. We wish to remain in the control of the members. Each one has a share, which is non-transferable and of no value – nominally a pound. We can borrow money under our rules and regulations, but we cannot raise money from the value that's within the club. In order to do that we have to convert the club into a limited company which would enable us to issue more shares. This gives us financial powers. At the point we convert, every member has one share in the new limited company, and we'll issue more shares – two and a half million – with a limit on the number one person can buy, in order to stop one person taking over the club. Safeguards will be put in place. No one person or group of people can own more than 20 per cent of the shares – we may need to reduce that to 10 per cent. No shares will be transferred without the approval of the new board. At a special general meeting on 11 September the committee will recommend to the members that the club be converted and suggest that certain people should form the board of directors. The make-up of this new board has been one of the most emotive subjects at the general committee, getting the balance between club protection, in the form of Bob Beason, David Matthews and Garry Adey, and bringing in someone from outside in business, because it's got to be a business to generate income. So, David Jones of Next has agreed to come in. If all goes to plan and the conversion is backed at a series of meetings we will commence trading on Ofex, the low-cost market outside the Stock Exchange. Up to 4.4 million shares at, say, 125p would raise £5 million. We are not raising the money to pay off debts or to pay players. We're really raising the money to get our financing right, to match our expenditure with our income. Because the rise in expenditure has been so quick and so steep we can't get the income up straight away but we can in 18 months' time. We lost £250,000 this year; we project a £15,000 loss next year; and the following year we get into profit. We can borrow from banks to tide us over that period, but we want to get things financially structured and use the value that's within the club to initially help us through. Our strategy is that we must fund a rugby operation that gets us into the top four in England. The other thing we need the money for is to improve upon the amenities within the ground, to help us bring in that income, for example, letting out rooms. At the present we let out rooms that are just rugby club bars. We want conference facilities, new entrances, car-parking, signs, catering outlets around the ground. A stadium like this is a unique venue and we must capitalise on it.

'Our playing costs are around £2.5 million, of which just under £2 million goes on salaries. We have a five-year contract with Next – our main sponsor – for not quite seven figures, between £400,000 and £750,000 per year, with minimum payment levels based on success. The Goldstar contract, which was the best deal in the country two years ago, was only for £60,000.

'We get £500,000 from being in the First Division, which is increased by another couple of hundred thousand if we get into Europe, and if you're successful in Europe you get the same sort of sum on top of that. We've a minimum level of guaranteed payment over the next five years from television and sponsorship, so we do have a guaranteed level of minimum income.'

The chief executive is now in full flow. But, as he knows perfectly well from his own playing days, success off the field stems from success on it. The hectic quest for the latter, a much tougher proposition with the onset of professionalism, has seen changes come thick and fast. Harsh decisions have had to be made; heads have rolled; egos have been bruised. Some of the blood is on Wheeler's hands.

'We took decisions that we thought were in the best interest of the club in the circumstances that prevailed at the time, and those we thought were going to prevail in the future. In some respects over 10,000 members can be a weakness because you have a vast cross-section of people all looking for basically the same things but in different ways. We're going through a massive change and people don't like change. We're doing things differently – and we're charging them more money!

'Most of that money goes toward paying players. We have a wage structure which we want to adhere to. You want to lay down a structure so that each player understands why he's getting such-and-such, whereas somebody else is getting more. We distinguish between world class, Lions and internationals; and some might have a bit more value because they're younger or maybe they're a goal-kicker. Last year we were flying by the seat of our pants, talking with players in an effort to get it right. We also spoke with people from football, rugby league and basketball, trying to get a feel of it, and trying not to make the mistakes they'd made, and then developing our own way of doing it.'

When talk turns to money the players keep their pay slips pressed tightly against their chests. 'It wouldn't take a rocket scientist to work out who ought to be the club's top earner,' concedes Wheeler. 'The most valued people in the world are, firstly, second-rows and, secondly, goalkickers and fly-halves.' Every contract differs, he continues. 'The win and appearance bonuses vary, too. Some people prefer to have a higher basic and lower win/appearance money; others prefer vice-versa.' When the *Mail on Sunday* carried a report on the salaries of certain home internationals it suggested Martin Johnson's total earnings from Leicester and England would amount to £250,000; other 'guesstimates' were Will Greenwood £185,000, Neil Back and Austin Healey £180,000, Richard Cockerill and Darren Garforth £140,000, Eric Miller £120,000 and Craig Joiner £75,000. Such figures were understandably ridiculed by the players concerned for being grossly inflated, yet they may not be that far from the mark. With match fees and win bonuses at £400-500 in each case, a basic first-teamer at Leicester is likely to earn between £30,000 and £50,000, for example, while foreign 'stars' like Stransky and Serevi may command something into six figures – even before any sponsorship and marketing deals are taken into account.

But can a 'family' club like Leicester, which Wheeler himself once described as possessing 'a sense of identity, a special, almost unique atmosphere,' survive the influx of 'foreign mercenaries' who may or may not truly develop, let alone earn, their Tigers' stripes?

'We are never going to be able to produce 21 first-class players out of Leicestershire. We want to keep the hard-core local but you are still going to need your Joel Stranskys. We need, as we always have at this club, world-class players.'

Certainly, the first team has long since lost its exclusively Leicestershire character, but in the last season of the amateur era (1995–96) the majority were either Midlands born and bred, or had played virtually all their senior rugby in the area. Will the Tigers forfeit that priceless 'identity' and succumb to the cosmopolitan flavour of, say, a Wasps or Harlequins where any local allegiance is baseless? Wheeler argued: 'Anyone who was down here for Rory's farewell day will not believe the club has lost its heart and soul.' In the opinion of many supporters, of course, Rory Underwood was one of the principal casualties of the on-field bloodletting; off the field, director of coaching Tony Russ and first-team coach Ian 'Dosser' Smith were other high-profile victims of professional culling.

'It's all about standards. When the game went professional our standards needed to be on a world level and in Bob Dwyer we have a guy who has taken a side into the World Cup final. That gives people confidence. There is an aura about him, he's someone who has done it and doesn't need to impress for the sake of impressing because what he's done speaks for itself. He doesn't duck any issues, he fronts up, as they say in the southern hemisphere, to problems. And there have been difficult ones. We've faced change, and when you are trying to push through change you rattle people along the way, they feel nervous, frightened. Obviously you have to listen to what they are saying, but you should drive through it and eventually you start taking them with you, providing you are clear about where you are trying to get to.

'I would hope the people we bring in will be the right kind of people to fit in with the club's heritage. It's the first time we've come up against this. It's a professional world and you've got to say, "Right, if next year is going to be more difficult and we want to improve on last year, where do we need to strengthen the squad and who's going to match up to it and who's not going to match up to it?" It's very sad to see players go. In the old days they'd have gone on playing and retired as and when. But they saw they weren't getting first-team rugby and they'd got an opportunity of a second career elsewhere.'

Joel Stransky epitomises the calibre of player who interests the Tigers. And Wheeler has not been idle in funding others. Since May's Pilkington Cup victory Wheeler has been shopping and after his very own 'Supermarket Sweep' it was a heavily laden trolley that arrived at the check-out. From the world-class section he had collected Fijians Waisale Serevi and Marika Vunibaka, Springbok Fritz van Heerden and All Black Eric Rush; and from the up-and-coming shelves came South African Under-21 cap Michael Horak and Bristol's Martin Corry, recently capped by England on the short tour to Argentina, and another young flanker, Paul Gustard, who had captained the England Under-21 party to Australia.

'I spoke with Serevi last year but he was contracted in Japan until November and then went back to Fiji to prepare for the World Sevens. Bob coaches the World fifteen for the Sanyo Cup, so we spoke to Serevi then and got his agreement before the game because we knew once people had seen him everyone would want him. Ditto Vunibaka. The Fijians are very family oriented and close people. It would be harder to make it work if we had only taken one of them and Vunibaka is generally regarded as one of the top five wingers in the world. Serevi is wonderfully versatile having played scrum-half, fly-half, full-back and wing for Fiji. There are probably a few question marks as to how he'll adapt to the discipline of fifteens as opposed to sevens, but you'd have to say he's the sort of player that people will enjoy seeing, and players will learn from him because he'll do things differently to anyone in the world. And the Middlesex Sevens is worth £50,000! We do have a problem with Vunibaka's work permit; the criterion is you have to have played for your country in the last 18 months, but at fifteens. What the labour board don't understand is that in Fiji you get promoted *out* of the fifteens side into the sevens team. Whilst Vunibaka was picked to play in the fifteens for Fiji he was pulled out of there to go and play in the World Sevens, which was actually more important.

'Fritz van Heerden is contracted to Western Province until October because of the Currie Cup. It depends on how well they do in the competition as to when he'll arrive, but our contract starts on 1 November. Eric Rush is still under contract to the NZRU, but we are trying to obtain his release, not least because he also holds an Irish passport. The valuable players are not necessarily the best but are those who can get European working rights or those who are not classified as an overseas player – which is useful for the European Cup where you can only play two overseas players. Michael Horak also holds a British passport; he's been playing rugby league in Australia for Perth Reds. He's a full-back or wing.'

Martin Corry's arrival has also met the odd hitch – exemplified by the morning's lengthy conversation with his solicitor. Bristol are not exactly overjoyed at the prospect of losing such a promising young player who also happens to be their captain. They are also talking about breach of contract should he depart.

'I spoke with Martin this time last year, along with his father. I was impressed with him, not least because he felt a lot of responsibility to Bristol as he was captain. He felt that if he left it might influence others and he didn't want to affect the club. He had all the sort of solid values that you want to bring to a club like this. But then he contacted us this year on the basis that he understood his contract to have been for one year and to have now expired. He wanted to come to Leicester after having got his cap against Argentina, and if he wanted to get into the World Cup squad he had to be doing something now, he couldn't go through another year without making progress and he felt Leicester was the place to do that. Through his solicitor we were aware that Bristol believed that he signed a two-year contract. I checked with the Rugby Union and they said he's registered on a one-year contract, so we said we'd be happy to sign a contract, on condition his Bristol contract is declared void. We've told his solicitor to get it legally determined.'

Wheeler is not a man to rest on his laurels. Many a club would look back on the first season of the professional era in which it had won one of the three major trophies – and come close in the other two – with considerable, and justifiable, satisfaction. Yes, Wheeler was pleased to see the Pilkington Cup secured but that was merely the beginning. 'This time last year I would have said that we were embarking on a three-year plan. We are improving in all areas but we haven't arrived in any of them. We haven't got near to arriving off the field. We had a measure of success in that we won the Cup, had a good shout in the league, until the fixture backlog knackered us, and got to the European Cup final – although we didn't feature much in the final itself. Lots of clubs would like to have reached the European Cup final! No one else did any of that and, if you take all three competitions together, we won more games than anyone else. If that's a measure of success, we were the most successful in the country. We are on a huge learning curve and we are slightly ahead of where we wanted to be at the start of last season. By last Christmas we were led to believe we were further down the road than we were but we are not yet halfway. We had to ask ourselves whether there was a fundamental reason why we lost those late-season games and forfeited the league. Now everyone's back full of vigour and freshness. The next stage is to improve on last year, both in how we play and in results. We aspire to play open, expansive, positive rugby but we need to be realistic. We felt we needed at least three years, as in a sophisticated game like rugby it takes a long time to change things.' The chief executive pauses for reflection, or is it breath? 'The abiding lesson of rugby,' he says leaning back in his chair, 'is that as soon as you think you've cracked it you are gone.'

Wheeler is currently working on the impending announcement of Next as the club's main sponsor. As befits a professional outfit, a press and media launch has been arranged for the morning of 14 August. By 10.30 a.m. the great and the good are assembling in the President's Lounge – the Crooked Feed – partaking of the distinctly upmarket canapés being offered by a bevy of waitresses. This is in distinct contrast to the players (decked out in the new kit) who have obviously been told to confine themselves to the fruit sticks. Wheeler is busily 'working' the room, which contains an assortment of local sporting celebrities such as James Whitaker, from the county cricket team, who has brought along the 1996 County Championship trophy, and Steve Walsh, Neil Lennon and Emile Heskey from Leicester City are accompanied by the Coca-Cola Cup, that was won this last spring. Bob Dwyer is in deep conversation with Mr and Mrs Serevi. Lions manager Fran Cotton, looking very spruce in grey double-breasted suit, and his business partner at Cotton Traders, the former England scrum-half Steve Smith (blue-suited but opting for tieless informality), are in attendance as the manufacturers of all the club apparel, both playing strip and associated leisure wear. Cotton makes a beeline for three of his successful Lions party, Healey, Greenwood and Back, who have taken possession of one of the sofas. An arm on Cotton's shoulder, the cry of 'I knew you could do it!', followed by a hollow laugh at such blatant misrepresentation of his views prior to the tour, announces Dwyer's entry into the conversation. There is little opportunity for further banter because on the stroke of eleven the distinctive opening bars of 'Eye of the Tiger' boom from the sound system. All eyes turn to the far end of the room where, at a table flanked by the Pilkington Cup and examples of the new shirts, Peter Wheeler and David Jones sit.

Wheeler gets up and begins by thanking everyone for coming, singling out his one-time front-row partner for England and the Lions: 'Franny's not done bad for a prop,' he says, listing Cotton's impressive portfolio of posts and achievements. 'I can't imagine where we're going to see him next – Tony Blair's Cabinet, I shouldn't wonder.' After receiving the sought-for guffaws, Wheeler introduces David Jones, 'the Joel Stransky of the business world, a man whose last-minute drop goals have clinched many a deal. It's good to have Next alongside us for the next exciting five years in the club's history. Next's shares went from three pounds to eight pounds with just their name on our shorts, so where they'll go now with it on our shirts I don't know!' More chortles. Now the serious stuff. 'But, until David's signature is on the contract, the fat lady isn't singing,' says Wheeler, directing Jones's attention to the document in front of him. Jones duly signs. Wheeler beams. 'She's singing!'

3

Heat and Dust

The physio's room is full to bursting and Mark Geeson is being rushed off his feet. Leon Lloyd wants his ankle strapped; Stuart Potter is complaining of a bad back as a result of executing forward rolls on rock hard ground; Derek Jelley requires some heat for his tennis elbow; and now Darren Garforth comes in, also plagued by a bad back: 'It's all this sprinting on hard grounds, Gees. I can't be doing with it.'

It is still only the last week in July but the blistering heat, stifling humidity and a surface akin to concrete have been exacting a collective toll on the squad now that it has moved outside to commence 'proper' rugby training every Tuesday and Thursday at four in the afternoon. Two tubs of iced water are set down on the touch-line for the players to replenish their water bottles at every opportunity. As they set off (still minus the Lions and overseas stars) on a series of warm-up laps of the pitch nearest the clubhouse, a sudden sharp shower breaks the heavy atmosphere. The relief is palpable and immediately finds expression in an increasingly light-hearted mood. Colin Bovell, one of the sprint coaches from Loughborough University employed to oversee the warm-up, directs them to the in-goal area for some stretching exercises.

The horseplay continues unabated. Leon Lloyd, the harum-scarum young wing (whose off-the-field adventures have seen him survive not one but two horrendous car smashes) and the patriarchal Dean Richards negotiate stomach curls whilst still managing to laugh their socks off; the rumbustuous Richard Cockerill, decked out in a fetching tiger-striped orange top, is needling his understudy Dorian West and soon finds himself being chased into the twenty-two. The players split into four groups for some short sprints where the emphasis is upon technique – leg-lift and so on – rather than pure speed. Some have heavier legs to lift than others and their efforts induce ritual dollops of sarcasm. Richards has targeted John Wells and a loud shout of 'Gobshite!' in his direction indicates Deano has scored a direct hit – much to the amusement of everyone else who, to a man, give vent to a girlish chorus of 'Oooohh!' Next on the agenda is a series where the emphasis is placed on sudden change of direction and subsequent acceleration. Now it's Duncan Hall's turn to chastise. 'You're like the *Bismarck*,' he informs West, 'you're changing direction half a mile away from the target!'

Bovell divides them into three groups and tells them to pair off in preparation for ten minutes on each of three contrasting activities. Within that time each man will work for 30 seconds and rest for 30 seconds. Richards and Wells are old playing and training partners and for the ensuing half an hour they will again join forces. First it is ten minutes on the tackle bag. Richards braces himself against the huge blue bag as Wells hurls himself toward it. 'One go to get up!' bellows Hall, just in case Wells harbours any thoughts of a rest. Bang on 30 seconds a blast from John Duggan's whistle signifies that it is now time for Richards to hit the bag. And so it goes on until the ten minutes are up. The second activity is a spell of ballwork under the auspices of Andy Key, a former Tigers back, who is the third member of the senior coaching staff alongside Dwyer and Hall. One man passes and loops round his partner to collect the return, repeating the manoeuvre back and forth as many times as possible between the goal-line and the twenty-two within the allotted 30 seconds. It is in the looper's interests for the receiver to adopt a very steady pace so that he doesn't have to run too hard. Wells and Richards have the tempo off to a tee. Nothing too strenuous here. Lastly comes ten minutes of punching, an exercise designed to increase hand speed but one catering to all rugby players' baser instincts. One man dons gloves and must land as many punches as he can on his partner who hides behind a protective tackle shield. Richards gets first go with the gloves and performs a passable impersonation of George Foreman, delivering great swinging haymakers with either mitt. Further down the line Matt Poole is jabbing away in the style of Ali, while the crouching figure of Richard Cockerill is frantically whipping in a succession of clubbing hooks (doubtless warming up for future contests with Regan, Greening *et al*) with the venom of 'Smokin'' Joe Frazier. The whistle sounds. 'How many?' Bovell asks Cockers; '94,' comes the deadpan reply. 'Bollocks!' is the unanimous verdict of the others.

Amid all this assorted mayhem Duncan Hall adopts the ringmaster's roving brief. He prowls from group to group, dominating proceedings with the kind of understated machismo displayed by one of those rugged, no-nonsense 'gun' shearers in an Australian outback movie. Hall doesn't so much talk as growl – and Dunc seldom smiles. 'So I'm told, and I'm not ticklish either! I've just got high expectations on the field. I always give praise where praise is due. Seeing players perform well gives me my satisfaction. There's a time to train and have a giggle and times to train hard – and there's got to be more of the latter! But I've had my moments. I remember when I coached in Canberra and we were coming home from one match in the team minibus on a three-hour trip. Pretty soon they'd all ripped their clothes off – all bar the driver – and were having a nude drink as we drove down the Hulme Highway. So I joined in. Fortunately, when we stopped for Kentucky Fried Chicken we put our clothes on. I was fined with everyone else. There are some things you have to do. I was just as bad as them!' So, there is a larrikin trapped inside big Dunc!

Hall's demeanour is complemented by a mordant wit: 'There are only two types of coach, those being sacked and those waiting to be'; and an equally down-to-earth approach to coaching rugby football. 'My way of coaching is on the very simple principles that the game is pretty basic. I think too many people bring too many complexities into the game for the wrong reasons. If we can do the simple things, win the ball, use the ball, retain it and stick to basic principles, go forward, support, continuity and pressure. Relate everything back to that and we will succeed. I'm a great believer in performance goals. If you can do the simple things on the field and perform to the goals you've set, then the scoreboard will look after itself. You want to win, but how are you going to win? You've got to score more points, so how are you going to score? You've got to perform. Leicester have played a certain way for a long time, so to blend the way they play to include the whole team may take a while but I want the guys to enjoy their rugby. At the end of the day you have got to win. We could have played the best rugby anyone's seen and lost. I played in the 1981–82 Wallabies team which scored nine tries to three and lost a Test series. We remember how we moved the ball, but we were vastly disappointed because we were not successful – and that's what people remember. So, while we want to play attractive rugby and for the crowds to enjoy the game, ultimately people do enjoy the win.'

Hall's CV screams 'all-Australian sportsman'. As a schoolboy he represented Brisbane's Nudgee College at rugby, swimming and athletics in the city's Greater Public Schools championships (winning the high hurdles title); only cricket didn't appeal, 'too boring, you just stand around all day.' At one stage he was even school cross-country champion: 'Every day before rugby training we ran three miles and did a circuit of weights, and halfway through the season they held the cross-country championship – so you couldn't help but win, you were so fit.' Later on he played water polo for Queensland and indulged a passion for surf-boat rowing. His rugby career began at the age of ten with its course seemingly predestined by that of his father, Duncan senior.

'I was put straight into the school team as a front-rower. They said, "Your dad played rugby league for Australia in the front row, so you can play there too". Dad started as a centre cum wing when he played in the "country" before he went to Valleys in Brisbane and moved up to second row and then front row. League is the big thing in the "country" and he never played union. He eventually made two tours to the UK, in 1948–49 and 1952–53, and he was ranked fourteenth in the list of best-ever Australian league players in a recent newspaper article; he's the only Queensland player to be included in the best post-war team. I had the odd game of league as a youngster, but the trouble there was they wanted me to take the ball up all the time. That's a mug's game! It wasn't what suited me.'

What 'suited' Hall junior was union and he progressed through the Queensland representative sides to make his senior début (as a flanker) against ACT having just turned 19. Elevated to the Wallabies bench for the visit of Ireland in 1979, Hall packed down at lock (alongside Steve Williams) for his first cap against Fiji in May 1980. It was in the engine-room that he spent most of his international career, butting heads with the likes of Bill Beaumont, Maurice Colclough and the All Blacks pair of Andy Haden and Frank Oliver – whose sister he married: 'I couldn't beat him so I had to join the family.' Not that he wasn't averse to moving back a row and playing number eight.

'But they always pick two second-row and only one number eight! So you always have a chance in the second row. I could jump at two and I jumped at four in a Test against France in 1981. I just grafted away. My game was a continuity game. I could get my own ball at two, I beat-up on the opposition ball, I could scrum well and I was like an extra back-row because I had very high fitness levels and good mobility. In 1984 when Alan Jones took over, he wanted very tall players and it was quite apparent that I was never going to play for Australia again, even though in 1986 I played every game for New South Wales. I had one year of captain/coach after that with Gordon, in Sydney. I enjoyed my playing career. I got 15 tests, 75 games for Queensland, ten for New South Wales; toured South America, North America, the Pacific Islands, the UK, France and Italy. It was good fun.

'I turned my hand to coaching and when I was at Queensland we did a lot of cross-training – netball, self-defence – which I passed on as suggestions to Bob, then the national coach. I mentioned to him that if he heard of anything going I'd be interested in getting back into the actual coaching-side proper because, although I was near the top of the tree on the technical side, I was not allowed to coach a team. Eight months later he rang me and told me about the Leicester situation. Over here is the hardest part of the world to coach because it's an 11 months of the year job. It was a long way to come with my family – my two children Gabrielle and Tobias are nine and seven – but I was prepared to take the risk. I think in life you've got to take a risk or you'll never know.'

Bob Dwyer first came across his strong right-arm-to-be back in 1982 and soon recognised a coach in embryo: 'Duncan was the sort of player a coach wanted and admired, a real salt of the earth type of bloke. It was obvious he had a future as a coach and I recommended him for a job with a new club in Canberra. They said to me that they needed a high-profile coach who could attract players but I told them I thought they needed a good coach who would develop the club in a strong, solid way that would stand the test of time. A high-profile coach might attract a few big-name players but success might only be in the short term. Anyway, they took my advice and in the first two or three years the club improved absolutely out of sight, from the jokes of the competition to semi-finalists. The next job he gets is very likely to be the Queensland Super 12. I'd be lost without him. I cannot do the job without him, full stop. I don't have anyone else that I have the same confidence in, that I know won't be asking me things every five seconds.'

A lupine glint comes into Hall's eyes back on the training paddock when the pack chosen to play in Rory Underwood's game the following Saturday gets down to some serious lineout practice. This is the dog-eat-dog environment once inhabited by Hall himself, a place of murky deeds, where every trick in the book is resorted to in the struggle for even the merest morsel of possession. 'Tall chin, tall body, quick movements!' Hall barks at Tom Butler as Dorian West arrows another throw in the direction of last season's England colt. With the aid of his two lifters Butler soars heavenwards to make the catch, but Hall is not satisfied with the 19-year-old's urgency. He moves in to show Butler how it should be done. A feint, combining a nod of the head, drop of the shoulder and a snappy dummy step with the inside leg, is the prelude to the actual jump. 'There, now you do it.' West's throwing arm is again cocked, the call is given, Butler springs into life and then into the air to make the catch. 'That's better! Now do it again!'

While this is going on at one end of the pitch, Andy Key is putting the back line through its paces at the other. Nothing spectacular: short passes, straight running, committing a defender and recycling the ball. After 30 minutes working independently, Hall brings the fifteen together for a 40-minute team run of semi-opposed rugby. The remainder have been reduced to circling the ground under the auspices of John Duggan. As the young hopefuls cut out the pace wilier souls like Cockerill and Poole are conspicuous by their presence at the rear. Some things never change. Professional or not, nobody in their right mind likes 'lapping'.

When the players eventually troop in, cook Liza Woodford is putting the final touches to their post-training meal. Tonight's fare is prawn and pepper pizza with baked beans or chicken chasseur and rice, with bread pudding to follow. Lasagne and spaghetti bolognese, says Liza, remain the firm favourites. The biggest eater? 'Oh, Anthony Parish without a doubt. He's the only one who comes up for seconds!' Parish needs the fuel. The 28-year-old wing who supervises much of the weight training is built like a brick outhouse and boasts a chest like the Incredible Hulk.

'They must eat within an hour, ideally within half an hour, of training,' says Lisa Piearce, the club's sports dietician/nutritionist. 'They must get carbohydrate straight away so that it gets back into the muscles. That, and fluid intake, are the main concerns. The carbohydrate is needed in the muscles to do any type of exercise, whether in training or in a match. They need good glycogen levels before each game or training session, to see them through. The fluids are to ensure they don't fatigue earlier through dehydration, because they only need to lose a small percentage of bodyweight for performance to be affected. To leave enough room for carbohydrate in the diet we try to cut down on the fat – which is difficult! We do give them guidelines, and we measure their fat levels with skin calipers taking measurements in millimetres from four skin-fold sites – biceps, triceps, back and waist. We add up the four figures and convert it to a percentage. Austin Healey and Joel Stransky have the lowest body-fat levels but the player who has made the greatest change to his body-fat level this season has definitely been Darren Garforth.'

Once the expected tryfest of Rory Underwood's match was safely out of the way (145 points are shared with the Invitation Fifteen) the mood becomes far more businesslike. A week later, on 2 August, a far stronger fifteen (containing Craig Joiner, Cockerill, Garforth and new signing Martin Corry) beats Llanelli 47–33 in the second part of a double-header initiated by the Extras sharing 44 points with Ebbw Vale. In both matches replacements were many and varied. Immediately afterward a party of 47 players and ten staff depart for a week's training-camp based on the campus of Limerick University – a far cry from the old weekends in Cromer; Martin Johnson (after a couple of weeks recuperating from his groin operation) and Niall Malone (following his honeymoon) would link up with the group on the Monday evening. With Joel Stransky back from South Africa and new boys Michael Horak and Waisale Serevi included, the only players missing were Eric Rush and Marika Vunibaka, whose registrations were still tied up in red tape.

In addition to the in-house staff, Bob Dwyer had recruited five specialists to advise on fitness and training: a biochemist and a consultant on recovery from the Australian Institute of Sport; two Americans from a company called SAQ (speed, agility and quickness); plus a sports physiologist. Before the players could ask why, Dwyer was telling them: 'All these things are very important for you to get a clearer understanding of what they can do to help you train harder, shorter, more intensely.' The camp schedule was an unrelenting sequence of weights, skills, fitness testing and full-scale rugby, made all the more demanding by a week of typically wet Irish weather. 'The rain wasn't a problem,' reasoned Dwyer. 'We could not have got through the work we did had the weather been the way it has been back here, where it was just too hot to train that hard. It was a very important week from an educational and getting-to-know-you point of view.'

Part of the latter resulted in the undoubted highlight of the week, Wednesday's 'team-bonding' session. One of the tasks involved teams of four constructing a raft to transport a fifth man across water. Dwyer picks up the story: 'Martin Johnson's team built a very good-looking raft but they had to improvise because the inflatable section burst. So they substituted an old canoe. It sailed pretty well without a load but as soon as they all got on, it sunk! They'd forgotten to check whether the bungs had been inserted!' Hilarity was also a constant companion to Waisale Serevi, whom Richard Cockerill took under his wing. The two frequently greeted each other with a Japanese-style bow and Cockerill would impose a fine whenever he caught Serevi speaking Fijian.

August continued to pass in a haze of prickly heat. On Thursday, 14 August, players are two days away from a triple-header at Welford Road: the Development Fifteen play Leeds (1 p.m.) while the Extras (3 p.m.) and Firsts (5 p.m.) face opposition from fellow Heineken European Cup qualifiers Caledonia Reds. It will be the first opportunity for the Welford Road faithful to run the rule over Waisale Serevi who will play at full-back. The sun is only just beginning to lose its burn as the evening session commences but everyone is on his mettle, for there are places to be won, an early-season pecking order to be established. Only the recuperating Johnson and Austin Healey, undergoing an operation to have his wisdom teeth removed ('That explains things,' says a dressing-room voice), are excluded from consideration. Forwards and backs separate for the bulk of the session. While Duncan Hall concentrates on the Extras and Development Fifteen packs using the awesome-looking, pristine Predator 65, a £2,500 all-mod-cons scrummage machine, Richard Cockerill, whose characteristic strutting gait makes him even more reminiscent of Benito Mussolini, leads the first Fifteen pack across to an older, gnarled, far less sophisticated, yet infinitely more evil-looking, scrummage machine fixed to a large peg in the centre of a circular pit full of coarse black grit. Although it cannot push back like the Predator, the machine is free to move left or right around the pit. With Johnson absent, Neil Fletcher, a 21-year-old 6ft 6in giant of 18 stone, late of Moseley, locks the scrum with Matt Poole; the back row combination of Corry, Miller and Back has a permanent look to it.

Il Duce is in charge. Cockerill is acknowledged as a fine scrum-mager and, indeed, was put in charge of all the scrummaging meetings on the England tour of Argentina. As the Lions demonstrated in South Africa by their prowess in this department, the scrummage has reasserted itself over the lineout: there are fewer lineouts nowadays and with lifting legalised, so many of them go with the throw. The legendary, all-international ABC Club that constitutes the Leicester front row prepares to bind. Cockerill raises both arms, the invitation for Rowntree and Garforth to close in and take a tight grip around his waist, their inside hands clenching a fistful of shorts and shirt. Once the ABC Club is happily bound, the locks and flankers engage; Eric Miller then completes the eight. The correct foot placements – not too splayed – and body positions – shoulders above the hips – are sought and found. Cockerill's voice rises from the bowels of this eight-plated human tortoise, at present quivering with latent power. 'Arms! Ready, ready! Squeeze!' is the mantra: 137 stones of muscle, bone and sinew catapults forward into the buffers of the scrummage machine with the noisy release of a herd of irate water buffaloes. Despite the obvious tendency for the machine to skew, the shove is so controlled it has remained straight. Cockerill calls for two more, and twice more the knees bend and drop, the backs straighten and the knuckles whiten as the tension is applied prior to the snap-shove. Satisfied, Cockerill tells the back row to disengage and, as the pressure comes off the wheezing shoulder-pads that had absorbed all the power coming through the front row, the locks follow suit, leaving the ABC Club to gingerly extricate themselves from the cushioned pads into which they'd became wedged. Young Fletcher's efforts are acknowledged with words of encouragement before Cockerill runs through the tactics for offensive and defensive scrums in various parts of the pitch. 'Wherever, we've got to have an early set and early crunch! Timing! Body shape!' The drive from eight pairs of legs during the first set has gouged an 18-inch furrow in the grit, so the machine is moved further round the pit into virgin territory. They form up once again. Only another 30 minutes to survive.

As Cockerill's pack confronts their silent, inanimate foe, the familiar figure of Martin Johnson, looking as mean, moody and businesslike as ever, pounds past in the company of John Duggan. 'He's a couple of weeks early,' confides the fitness coach, 'but he's so keen, a workaholic really. It's a question of striking a delicate balance between working hard and taking time off.' Johnson is adamant he will start his first season as skipper where he should, not on the bench or in the stand but wearing that striped jersey bearing the letter 'D'. Duggan is orchestrating two sets of 3 x 300 metres. Johnson is given 90 seconds respite between each run and three minutes between the two sets. They are not intended to be full-out sprints, but Johnson is not holding back an awful lot. There's no question he will be ready when the season proper starts against Gloucester in the Allied Dunbar Premiership on 30 August – and possibly even for the friendly against Bedford a week earlier.

Bob Dwyer, meanwhile, is running the backs who will take the field against Caledonia Reds. He is, of course, a backs' coach first and foremost. Some of his abiding principles – flat alignment, straight running, engage the enemy – are soon evident in the variety of options that are being worked off each of his midfield runners. Decked out in plimsolls, navy shorts and pale blue T-shirt with his spectacles dangling round his neck by their trademark cord, he does not so much look like one of the world's coaches as one of Bondi's finest. There is, however, not a 'tinny' to be seen. Dwyer is not one of those histrionic coaches who races around the field like a demented rhino causing more consternation than they cure. He strolls about sedately and says little, but the players hang on his every word. 'Let's not get in the habit of zig-zagging down the centre of the field,' he suggests after one over-complicated sequence. He is particularly attentive to his raw, but potentially match-winning, left wing, Leon Lloyd. 'Good, good, good!' he says, at the successful conclusion of the ensuing ploy which, as always, is finished with the ball being dotted down for the 'try'. The speed of both hands and feet and the changes of direction are bewildering to behold – yet it is fully 40 minutes before one pass is spilled. Craig Joiner appears suitably embarrassed. Dwyer lets it go without comment, there is no need. In one season at Leicester he has set out his stall, the standards have been set.

4

The Gospel According to Bob

Becoming a top-flight coach to a top-flight club is not necessarily about knowledge of the game or playing ability, and definitely not dependent upon the number of international caps you happen to have in your trophy cabinet. It's what is under the cap that counts. It is all about powers of communication and powers of motivation. As in any other form of education, successfully coaching rugby football depends upon the individual's ability to get across to his players what he knows in a succinct, positive manner whilst stimulating them into putting it all into practice on match days. In its long history Leicester has been fortunate to have had the services of two visionary and charismatic coaches. Future students of the game may perceive Chalkie White (1967–82) and Bob Dwyer as contrasting personalities but, in one regard, they are peas from the same pod: neither boasts an international cap but both are peerless communicators and motivators and, in consequence, both earned the utmost respect of their players.

Dwyer's arrival at Welford Road in the summer of 1996 was not without a degree of controversy. Tony Russ, director of coaching since 1990, had been acrimoniously sacked two months previously, and Dwyer's appointment cast a shadow over the future of first Fifteen coach Ian 'Dosser' Smith. Initially, it was announced that Smith would be retained in a full-time capacity alongside Dwyer, but no one was prepared to define his role. It was a pound to a penny that the new director of coaching (later revised to director of rugby) would prefer to install his own man. Within a month Duncan Hall was appointed director of coaching development and Dosser Smith was effectively consigned to the wilderness. 'We have trawled the world for the best and are pleased Bob has agreed to come to Tigers to further our professional set-up,' said Peter Wheeler. 'In this new era for rugby with its huge changes we must utilise every drop of experience.'

Robert Stuart Francis Dwyer had long been regarded as one of the world's premier coaches, despite lacking any comparable credentials as a player. Indeed, Dwyer hails from a rugby league background since his father, Ted, played first-grade league in Sydney for Canterbury-Bankstown as a second-row, and as a schoolboy, at Sydney's Waverley College, cricket was his favourite sport. Dwyer never advanced beyond Waverley's Fourth Fifteen and it was not until he transferred to Sydney High School, during his final year in school, that he ever wore a First Fifteen jersey. Things started to happen, however, once he began turning out for Randwick Colts after leaving school. The young flanker went on to play for Randwick for 18 years, making a total of 347 senior appearances.

But it was the intellectual challenge which rugby presented as a tactical game that increasingly appealed to the electrical engineering graduate from the University of New South Wales. In the mid-1970s he volunteered to be one of Randwick's three representatives at an innovative Australian Rugby Union coaching course and, in 1977, he became Randwick's first-grade coach. The 37-year-old Dwyer had never coached a rugby union team in his life. It did not take him long to prove that he could. In his first season Randwick reached the Sydney grand final. His side lost to Paramatta but the club returned 12 months later to win its first Sydney premiership since 1974 – and the first of five in a row. Dywer's Randwick fully lived up to its nickname of the 'Galloping Greens', for its runaway success was based on a highly fluid game. Two basic tenets of back-line play handed down to him by both his father and former Randwick centre Cyril Towers provided the key to realising this objective: stand flat and run straight.

'I don't work hard on back-line moves. We would have in our repertoire at Leicester 30, perhaps 50. What happens is you develop variations on them all the time. My philosophy is based around the premise that our fly-half, centres and perhaps blind-side wing have to attract their opposition – and maybe the open-side flanker as well. So we devise ways of making them think: "Is he coming, or is it him coming?" I say to the guys: "You've got to occupy them and if they hold off you've got to take advantage, that's when you take the gaps."'

At Randwick, of course, it helped enormously to have the three Ella brothers to put the strategy into effect. Dwyer was convinced the same principles could work at international level and wanted the opportunity to verify this belief. He decided to stand for election as national coach and in 1982's vote he dislodged the incumbent, Bob Templeton. The rest is history. During Dwyer's two spells in the job (1982–83 and 1988–95) the Wallabies won 46 and drew two of their 73 matches and became the only country to win the World Cup (1991) without home advantage. The loss to England in the quarter-final of the 1995 tournament and subsequent defeats in the Bledisloe Cup Tests against New Zealand brought cries for Dwyer's head and he was duly deposed. When the Tigers came a-courting (the Irish Rugby Union had also allegedly made an approach) Dwyer was assisting Club Racing in Paris. Dwyer's appointment was revealed on 30 May and on 8 June he drove through the gates of Welford Road (not for the first time: he'd been a member of the Randwick tour party that played the Tigers in October 1973) to set out his stall.

'It is a great opportunity to be in on the ground floor of a comprehensive development of a modern club. The next big advances in rugby will be made in the northern hemisphere. It has got the scope with the number of players, the quality of players and the marketplace in terms of attendances and sponsorship. I think it is a fantastic opportunity to be part of a developing level of the game. Leicester has not asked me here to perfect the rolling maul. To their credit, they have been very successful and they want to continue to be very successful – and they feel they want to change to be more successful.'

Dwyer's first season in charge brought success in the Pilkington Cup, a top-four finish in the Courage League (after contending for the title most of the season) and a place in the final of the Heineken European Cup, in which Brive produced a scintillating display on the day to brush the Tigers aside 28–9. What had he learnt about his players and his club from that initial campaign?

'I think the most important thing I found out about the club was that they had a fantastic team spirit which would give them victory where they would not otherwise have got it – a great burning desire not to lose. We won so many games in the last 20 minutes, especially in the first half of the year. That's a very important thing, and we've got to keep it.

'There's no more passionate set of supporters in the country and there is nowhere more tribal than Welford Road. In my years at Randwick we had a reputation for having a beer with the opposition and then heading back to Randwick "to pull up the drawbridge". We took it as a sign of respect. Consequently, I have no problem with the parochialism at Leicester. In fact, I feel pretty tribal myself. You work hard, you give and take, and it forges a strong bond. My view of the Leicester crowd is that they are fair and knowledgeable. They do not boo the opposing kicker and they will applaud a good passage of play by the opposition. However, they *love* only one side. The level of support is reciprocated in the way the players respond to the fans. There is a very relaxed natural acceptance by the players that the supporters are an integral part of the club, and they mingle freely. At Leicester there is the genuine satisfaction of being part of something that was always good, but which could become great.

'The people I want in the team are the people who look for plusses in other people. The people I don't want in the team are people who don't accept other people. I go to great lengths, albeit not too obviously, to ensure the positives are stressed. Instead of saying so-and-so hasn't got very good running lines I prefer to say so-and-so is a very explosive runner. If we do that everyone gets on famously. I also place a great deal of emphasis on the top players helping the lesser players. One, it brings the top player down to earth a bit. Two, it helps the younger player. Three, it helps the top player because he learns more from his teaching than the student, because it keeps him focused on all the principles that are important in his position. It creates a giving environment instead of a taking environment and that's a good environment to live in.

'Last season was a good stepping-stone, but we fell in a little hole in the league at the end. One thing Duncan and I learnt was that the English season is very tough, and the backlog for teams who are successful in all three competitions can be disastrous. We saw just how significant the effect of such a programme can be. Last season was probably one of the hardest spells of sustained rugby that the players and coaching staff have ever endured. We've learnt the lessons that attention to detail and recovery time are essential. In football, Manchester United suffered the same problems and were quite vocal about it, but when you add physical body contact, it's not hard to see that the rugby season is more draining. The potential for a clogging-up of the fixture list is huge, which is why we have sought to put together a group of 27 to 28 players, any 15 of whom we believe can play in the first team. We are going to be very careful in our preparation and workloads, and in our attention to over-training symptoms. Rest is going to form a more important part of the training than, perhaps, it did. If they train properly they can train less. What I want to achieve is a real uplifting of intensity and a reduction in hours.

'The European Cup final exposed our weaknesses. We really lacked pace throughout the team, certainly in the back row, and we lacked players with a really constructive capacity – Will Greenwood was the only one to create play. And we lacked pace at full-back, so we didn't threaten the opposition at all. We were overwhelmed by the sense of occasion to some extent. We thought we played our final against Toulouse, and I thought it too, so I can't complain about the players thinking it. We were in a very light-hearted state while they were in a very focused state. Now, whether we were light-hearted because fear of the occasion caused us to produce this external sign of relaxation, I don't know. We were also hit over the top of the head by an approach to the game which didn't have any bearing to the laws of the game. I am constantly reminded that one of the problems with my coaching technique is that I insist on playing within the laws. I keep on getting indications that it might not be an advantageous approach! There was plenty going on at the lineout, but we didn't have the sense to slow things down, widen the gaps and give the referee the opportunity to check it out. We weren't clever enough. But if anyone tries to do it to us again we'll know, won't we! "Excuse me, ref, we've had this situation before. Are you going to sort it out or are we?"

'Nevertheless, I feel last season was hugely successful. We won more competitive matches than any other club, won the Pilkington Cup, were second in Europe and finished fourth in a demanding Courage League. On balance I think we deserved to be second in the league but the horrendous backlog of fixtures cost us dear.'

The most controversial conclusion Dwyer reached was that some of his players were overpaid for what they offered and that he could sign better players for the same money.

'The nature of professional sport dictates that in order to strengthen your squad, which we must always endeavour to do, you must let some players go. We have to balance the budget. In some ways I was very disappointed to lose some of them. They had made a major contribution and are the sort of players in a non-professional era you would want to keep at the club. But, right or wrong, I thought they were not going to give us value for money in terms of the level of performance they could aspire to. So, it was a matter of making sure we had players who could take us where we wanted to go and, in some of them, we have aspiring players who only cost the club an amount commensurate with their current level of play. If someone rings me with a virtual world selection list and asks if I'm interested in Christian Cullen, Jonah Lomu, Ian Jones, Matt Burke or Zinzan Brooke, of course I am! Whether I would sign them at the prices mentioned is entirely different. In some cases players are overpriced and, in a lot of cases, we already have high-quality players in those positions. It is reasonable, however, to expect that players and supporters alike realise that it is the responsibility of the club's rugby administration to put on the field the best team it possibly can subject to monetary constraints.

'My philosophy was whether this player can play in the Super 12. Not can he be a star in the Super 12, but can he compete reasonably. I'm not under any misapprehensions that we can walk in and challenge Auckland next week. At Randwick we once played the All Blacks and the then president of the Australian Rugby Union said to me that only Randwick could have done that. Well, I want the same thing here. Players will either enhance their reputation as Tigers or will become part of some other club's plans. We have signed several high-profile players. In Waisale Serevi we have one of the most gifted rugby players in the world; his running and handling skills are bettered by no one in the world at the moment. Michael Horak is a full-back or wing of great potential who has come to us from Orange Free State via Perth Reds in the Australian Super League; Martin Corry is another who we look to for big things. The position with Eric Rush is still not clear. We wouldn't expect him until the end of October anyway, but it's still not certain that the New Zealand board will release him. Vunibaka also has problems, with getting a work permit. I don't think his absence will make much difference to Serevi as a rugby player. I think personally he'd like to have Vunibaka here because he likes him, he's a friend and he appreciates his rugby ability. But Serevi's a mature guy. He's been in Japan for a couple of years, and he's fitted in here like a hand fits a glove. But Fritz van Heerden will definitely be here as soon as the Currie Cup is completed. We've also given contracts to eight younger players who have been with us a while, whom we believe represent the future of the Tigers – Steve Beaufoy, Ben Wyer-Roberts, Dave Addison, Roly Edwards, Jun Shaw, Mark Jasnikowski, Nnamdi Ezulike and Marcus Briggs. That's a sign that we are looking after the bottom end as well as the top. I believe this puts us in a very good position. It will be necessary to have a strong second team, all putting pressure on for first-team spots, and enough players of the quality required to succeed at first-team level to compete throughout a long and hard season. We will need to include players from outside in the short term, but we truly see our long-term future in the development of talent through our schools, youth and junior policy.'

If 1996–97 was the beachhead, what are Dwyer's objectives as the second year of his tenure (his contract has an option for a third) begins to unfold?

'I'm interested in putting together sides capable of performing the whole range of techniques and skills, teams that can chew gum and walk simultaneously. Our goal is to examine all the things that have an effect on the players' performance and then say: "Okay, how can we isolate those things and how can we train those things, develop those things individually, and then put them back together again?" And, then, the player develops magically. We started last season by saying if we're bigger, stronger, faster and fitter we'll be off to a good start in terms of our progress. It was an introduction to our philosophy. Ireland was, in part, an educational process to support the various programmes that we've introduced, or are going to introduce, so that the players have quite a good education in terms of metabolism, biology, biomechanics, etc., which would have an effect on their training programme. It always seemed to me that if I understood what the programme I was performing was going to do for me and how it was going to do it, I was inclined to approach it more wholeheartedly. So, if I understood the biological process of energy build-up and systems, and how I could train the energy systems to store more energy or provide more energy more quickly, I could appreciate the development in that area. The guys are starting to come to terms with it.

'What we've been doing is to develop a programme which will develop the total player, and my philosophy of playing the game is to make sure the players are capable of playing every way, every pattern of play. It's the angles of run, it's the placement of the ball at the tackle, it's the body positions in contact, it's the positional play of support players – these are the basics. Unless we achieve this I'll not be happy, and I dare say even if we can play the game all ways I still won't be entirely happy! We want to strengthen our versatility and ensure the opposition cannot readily predict the game we want to play.

'I find it very difficult to get away from certain repetitions you have to do every time you practice. It's a bit like practising your scales. I can't come up with any other way of running but to put your left foot down, then your right and then your left. What we do is to come up with different ways of practising that without them knowing it: ball games, or something that distracts them from what we are trying to improve. Yesterday we had a touch football competition; it was the best touch football I've seen since I've been in England. It was a massive improvement on the past and we'd like to think it had something to do with the exercises we've been doing on leg speed, hand-eye co-ordination and quick hand movement. On Tuesday we had a game of touch gridiron, which has a heap of running in it and a heap of communication in it. That was designed to take the place of a cardiovascular session, in some ways even an aerobic session. But they don't know that. They just know they had a good time playing touch gridiron.

'What we're trying to create is an environment in which players will feel confident to try and achieve their potential, it's a very, very difficult thing to try to do. On analysis, my conclusion is: if you reach your potential and it is still not good enough you've got nowhere else to go, so people are fearful of giving things their absolute best shot, perhaps, subconsciously, because they fear they'll fail. It's just human nature. Players who want to win are a dime a dozen. The question is whether you really want to give it your best shot, whether you want to lay yourself exposed to the possibility of failure, and in order to do that you have to have a very, very supportive environment where the coaches are saying: "I'm not here to judge so much whether you're a good player or not, I'm here to help you. I am going to make a judgement every week who are the best players at the moment, but my reason for being here is to help you become a better player – and a better player and a better player. So, it may not be the judgement next month."'

Even in a club packed with internationals and experience like Leicester, however, Dwyer remains acutely conscious of the fact that he is all too frequently viewed as the man who should have all the answers.

'I have tended to be the person who imposes things. They may expect me to do it – which is a bit of a problem. I've always thought I was a very approachable bloke but I realise other people may not see me as approachable as I see myself. So players may be loath to approach and say, "Look, I've got this really good idea!" in case I object to the interference – which I wouldn't – or in case I think it's a dumb idea. So, in Ireland I sat down with the guys and said, "How do you think we should play the game?" and we went through various facets of the game on the blackboard: what do we do well, what could we do better? This season, two days after a game, we're going to talk collectively about what we thought we did well in the game, what we thought we didn't do so well, what we can do about it next week, and remind each other what we said in Ireland we thought was important and whether we still think it's important. There will be much more opportunity for the players to say, "We'll push in this direction." They did say in Ireland that it might be worth while playing a fraction deeper to see what we can achieve a fraction wider, and I'm happy to see how things go. And I said to them: "Don't forget the rolling maul! It's a very, very important weapon for the back line, because it gets forwards defending against forwards." It's attention to detail that counts.'

The new season is barely two weeks away: what can the fans expect to see for their money?

'We can't guarantee anything, of course, but I will promise you one thing: we are committed to playing better rugby this season and the fans will *love* it! Massive strides were made in the English game last season and I think there's more to come. I think the same amount of progress will be made this season as last, so by the end of the season the game will be virtually unrecognisable, a lot faster, a lot harder, a lot more skilful. I'm not making any predictions, except to say we will be looking to better our position in the league and play consistently better than last year. The team that wins the league will have to be an improvement on last season, and I see last season's top four as the best four again. And, if we play as well as I want us to play, then we'll have our share of wins. But we must aim for a place in Europe first: that's got to be our priority. The one thing we can promise is an extension of the all-round, fast-paced game we started to introduce last season.'

The first opportunity to gauge how 'fast-paced' a game the Tigers could play comes on 30 August when Gloucester's visit opens the Tigers' programme in the Allied Dunbar Premiership.

5

Glaw-ster!

When the Leicester and County Mission for the Deaf saw its centre for the deaf toward the top of Welford Road opened by HRH the Duke of Gloucester on 18 July 1961, it could not have envisaged the use to which the building would eventually be put on Saturday afternoons throughout the rugby season. The centre is literally just 'over the wall' from the home of the Tigers and serves as a wonderfully convenient team rendezvous on match days. Today, Saturday, 30 August, another scion of Gloucester is in town: the 'Cherry and Whites' are here to open Leicester's programme in the Allied Dunbar Premiership for which bookmakers William Hill make the Tigers 7–2 second favourites behind Bath at 9–4 – Gloucester are 50–1 shots.

The centre has one other priceless attribute on match days: 38 parking places, an expanse of tarmac that might as well be paved with gold. Understandably these spots are zealously guarded and every player and official must possess a pass to gain entry. At 12.30 p.m. the first car draws up, a spanking top-of-the-range silver Rover 400. 'You can tell the new boys or the big names,' says the attendant, 'they're the ones driving the new UAY registrations – last year's were FOM.' The occupant of the silver Rover is Waisale Serevi. One does not need to check the number plate to know it must be UAY. Next up is Graham Rowntree's Land Rover and, yes, would you credit it, he's forgotten his pass. 'But, I'm a player,' he offers softly with due humility and genuine modesty. The carpark custodian, Steve Benton, a member of Wigston RFC, is well aware of the fact and lets Rowntree off the hook, lowering the chain to allow him access. Richard Cockerill is beset by other problems. He wants his allocation of match tickets to pass on to his better half, who is waiting in his own Land Rover which bears the registration after Rowntree's (Garforth, naturally, owns the next). 'This is ridiculous! Not being able to get tickets till two hours before the game is f***ing stupid!' The immediate object of Cockerill's ire is likely to be Cliff Shephard, the first-team secretary who acts as bagman and general factotum.

While his colleagues make their way down the stairs leading to the bar that doubles as a team room for the 1 p.m. pre-match meeting, Cockerill continues to spit nails in the foyer. Word of his escalating displeasure quickly spreads. In this irritable mood, it seems Cockers resents being addressed by his christian name. 'Just call him gobshite,' volunteers Darren Garforth laconically, if not unhelpfully. Matt Poole also has things on his mind, namely the threat to his very place in the team. During the previous evening's match preview on Leicester Sound, mention had been made of the imminent arrival of Fritz van Heerden, and how the Springbok lock was liable to alter the shape of the team upon displacing Poole. 'Yes, his gut's not as big as yours,' suggests the ever-sympathetic Garforth. After light-heartedly proposing a policy of non-co-operation with Leicester Sound, Poole finds solace in taking the rise out of Jamie Hamilton's decision to wear the most garish of the club fleeces, a riot of colour sporting lurid blue, red, green and yellow bands. Almost everyone else favours the short-sleeved dark blue polo shirt, which has more conservative thin hoops in the club colours of red, green and white, with the Tiger-head logo on the left sleeve. Serevi sits oblivious to all these verbal skirmishes until engaged in conversation by the ever-sociable Craig Joiner, who asks him about the size of the crowds in Japan. 'You'll notice a difference today!' he assures the Fijian.

The side contains precious little in the way of surprises. In the course of winning all three pre-season warm-ups, against Llanelli, 47–33; Caledonia Reds, 31–29; and Bedford, 34–17; Bob Dwyer had slid 34 prospective first-team players under the microscope. The pack virtually picked itself, with Martin Corry and Eric Miller inheriting the back-row gauntlets worn with distinction for so long by John Wells and Dean Richards. Martin Johnson not only succeeded in making this game but had also led the side at Bedford. Dwyer's initial answer to the 'where-shall-I-play-Serevi?' conundrum was to put him at full-back against Caledonia and Bedford, but today he would be on the wing. Dwyer thinks it will give him more space in which to conjure up some magic. Craig Joiner wins the other winger's jersey ahead of Leon Lloyd, while Michael Horak (who had been playing wing) wears letter 'O' at full-back. There is still no sign of the Vunibaka/Rush embargo being resolved. At centre and half-back respectively are the established partnerships of Will Greenwood and Stuart Potter and Joel Stransky and Austin Healey – despite the last-named having missed all the pre-season games in which his deputy, Jamie Hamilton, scored four tries. Niall Malone is the back who misses the boat completely.

At precisely 1 p.m. the badinage dies down and a hush envelops the room, by now containing all 21 players and replacements, as well as Cliff Shephard, physio Mark Geeson and Duncan Hall. Bob Dwyer has entered. Physically, Dwyer cuts a slight figure but there is something in his mien – the combination of wiry bouffant hairstyle, bristling moustache and professorial spectacles, perhaps – that makes him appear somewhat larger and infinitely more intimidating. Then again, perhaps it is just the aura which a World Cup-winning coach carries around with him. Whatever the source of this electricity Dwyer has no need to call the meeting to order, his presence is sufficient. He takes the backs off to one side, leaving Hall in charge of the forwards.

Martin Johnson, seated to Hall's left, begins by reciting all the lineout calls (a noticeable influx of Australian club names) and tactics (the lobs and the drives) quietly and matter-of-factly, before handing over to Richard Cockerill for the scrums. 'Early set! Run there and then rest. We don't want to be binding when they're already set,' he demands in an equally restrained manner. 'And Eric, don't have it at the back too long. If it's there, pick up and go!' The Irishman nods, and then reminds everyone of the shunt, the eight-man drive. Cockerill runs through the tap-penalty moves, particularly that involving the two props – famously called a 'Chris Evans'.

Ex-Bristolian Martin Corry, sitting the other side of Hall, has something to say on the subject of his former West Country rivals. 'Let's have plenty of talk, defensively, around the fringes of the rucks and mauls,' he implores, 'and watch out for Greening in particular.' One can almost feel Cockerill simmering at the very mention of Greening's name. The dynamic Gloucester hooker was, of course, his rival on England's summer tour of Argentina and, indeed, succeeded in getting the selectorial nod for the first Test. It was only due to Greening being concussed that Cockerill came off the bench to win his first cap. Sparks could fly this afternoon.

'Anything to be said about the ref, Ed Morrison?' asks Hall. 'He's from Gloucestershire!' mutters Poole, before Neil Back, doubtless eager to introduce a sense of perspective, adds soberly: 'He's good. He likes to talk. He's done a lot of southern hemisphere matches and likes the game to be played their way.' Back's interjection pleases Hall no end. 'Good. That's the way we want to play it. Remember, it's our first competitive game, their second – they beat Bristol last week. Get yourself into the game early. Get your confidence going early. Right from the kick. Don't give them an even break.' That said, he goes in search of Dwyer and the backs. Briefly left to their own devices, the forwards contemplate the bruising rigours of an afternoon sharing the trenches with the 'Cherry and Whites'. If it cuts up rough, runs the general consensus, no one need fear taking more than one punch before 'help' makes its 'presence' felt.

Dwyer is now at the helm. 'Let's remind ourselves of what we've talked about, this week and pre-season, about how we want to play. One: no penalties! Certainly not in midfield, and certainly not for talking back to the ref – that is out of the question. Two: we want to get most of the throw-ins. We don't want the ball to go into touch needlessly. If your line of running is taking you toward touch, drop down or drive infield early. Three: let's have depth behind any runner coming out of defence. Anything else?' A moment's silence before someone offers aggressive tackling. 'Yes! We've done a lot of nursing in the tackle. We've only made a couple of decent tackles so far. Get low and drive into the tackle. Lastly, then, never forget that passion and aggression win more games than anything else. This is a game of collisions. Fight to make ground and fight to stop them making ground. It is an absolute necessity for us to play aggressively so everyone who plays against us is afraid of us. After ten minutes I want to see them with their eyes wide open wondering what the hell's going to happen next.'

Dwyer's delivery is decidedly low-key, calm and measured, but the weight of his carefully chosen words rests like a hand on a detonator. His side is primed. It's approaching 1.30 p.m. Time to leave. The group strides the 100 or so yards to the ground with a purposeful gait, eerily reminiscent of that employed by the mobsters in the opening sequence of *Reservoir Dogs*. Let's go to work.

Once inside the home dressing-room beneath the Crumbie Stand, all hands reach toward the pile of programmes laid out on the small brown table sitting in the middle of the room which, judging by its scratched and battered countenance, has clearly seen better days. 'How dare they put Greening in our programme?' protests Cockerill upon discovering the profile of his arch rival on page 42. The Gloucester side has undergone a dramatic change from the one that had severely dented Leicester's hopes of winning last season's league title by inflicting a 32–30 defeat at Kingsholm on 8 April. While six of the pack and both halves remained, the back line has been totally replaced by imported signings, testimony to Gloucester's liaison with Arrows Formula One boss Tom Walkinshaw – and his chequebook. In the centre Australian international Richard Tombs is paired with Western Samoa's Terry Fanolua, and the wings are occupied by the Saint-Andres, Raphael and his elder brother Philippe – the latter has captained France on 29 of his 64 appearances (a record for a wing) and is the scorer of 30 international tries.

The atmosphere in the dressing-room is changing perceptibly as the last programme is thrown into a kit-bag. There are no homilies dotting these walls. No windows, either. The place boasts all the conviviality of a holding cell on Death Row, its occupants, however obvious and grating the metaphor, akin to a troop of caged tigers. Yet freedom is not uppermost in their minds. Disturbance is. Whenever someone goes next door to be strapped or treated by Mark Geeson the door is promptly shut. If the door is left ajar it is slammed shut. If the culprit happens to be a non-player the door is kicked shut with an unrestrained venom which makes one wonder how many hinges are broken each season. In the wild, their feline cousins, unlike lions, tend to be solitary creatures, so perhaps it is understandable that so much Tiger testosterone in such a confined space begins to generate an edginess that could comfortably slice bread. 'It can get very volatile in here but it's only banter, really,' confides Cliff Shephard, among whose many roles is that of whipping boy and butt of all dressing-room invective. There was a time when the 62-year-old was on the other side of the fence. Back in the 1950s and '60s he pulled on a first-team jersey on 140 occasions, scoring 36 tries from his position on the wing. These days he is forever to be seen scuttling to and fro with a fixed smile on his face which scarcely tallies with the impression he gives of carrying the cares of the world on his hunched shoulders. As he fusses over the contents of the drinks bottles on the table, Cockerill continues to bait him about the tickets. Then Austin Healey joins in, demanding to know where the embrocation is. 'I'm not the physio,' pleads Shephard. 'I didn't ask you if you were the bloody physio,' rails Healey, 'I just asked where the f***ing embrocation was. If you can't do the job properly, f*** off and we'll get someone who can!'

Austin Healey would be a rank outsider to figure prominently in any popularity poll conducted among the Leicester staff. He is the club's problem child, a mixed-up kid and habitual attention seeker. His in-your-face persona is to few people's taste, and he came to Welford Road in 1996 accompanied by a stinging endorsement from the press officer of his previous club, Orrell: 'He's a great rugby player but he's trouble. If you could cage him until 3 p.m. on Saturday and put him back at 4.30 p.m. you'd be okay.' In Healey-speak, the 'Scally' from Merseyside gets up more noses than a Vick inhaler. Healey's brand of 'humour' is customarily so close to the bone as to cause splinters and although there is a Dennis the Menace gleam in his eye, one glance at his victim's face suggests such jibes can wound.

At around 2.20 p.m., 40 minutes prior to the scheduled kick-off, the team will go out onto the pitch for an extended warm-up under the aegis of John Duggan. Until then each individual follows his own preferred method of preparation. Barely a peep emanates from any of the backs. Martin Corry sits in one corner, legs and arms akimbo, head raised and eyes closed, seemingly in a state of deep transcendental meditation. In the opposite corner is Graham Rowntree, who is inserting his contact lenses, surely a liability for a front-row forward. 'They all know I wear them but no one targets them over here. I lost a couple last year against Toulouse – the French go for your eyes anyway!' One or two others find it impossible to keep still for long. Johnson, clad only in shorts and socks, gives the finest impersonation of the caged tiger, patrolling his territory silently and menacingly, whereas the hyperactive Cockerill is fast bubbling himself up toward boiling point. He suddenly disappears into the toilet and a violent bout of retching ensues. Some seek the greater space and comparative solitude of the shower-room: Michael Horak is bouncing a ball off the tiles and Serevi, who has kept himself to himself throughout, sits against the wall, applying embrocation to his thigh and calf muscles. Will Greenwood is lacing his boots when, snap, the inevitable happens. 'I knew it! I just knew that was going to happen. Cliff! Got any laces? No, what d'you mean, no! Anyone got a lace?' Darren Garforth to the rescue. Having retrieved his polythene bag of assorted boot/kit paraphernalia, the prop checks the tightness of his own studs. He's wearing Mizuno boots, like Healey and Craig Joiner – most of the players favour Adidas – Serevi, ever the individual, sports a pair of Japanese-made Bluesole.

Around two o'clock the match referee, Ed Morrison, enters the room, all bonhomie and dapper of dress, right hand clasping a cup of coffee. 'What-ho, boi!' he exclaims, adopting an exaggerated West Country yokel accent upon spying Martin Corry. 'At least there's one man in here who'll understand me!' Nobody laughs. Bob Dwyer ushers Morrison into a corner and begins grilling him as to his interpretation of the new law relating to 'bridging' at the ruck.

The place is now a hive of activity and positively claustrophobic, leading one to ponder whether the room has shrunk or whether each player's physique has swollen, along with the ever-rising levels of tension. John Duggan calls them out for the warm-up. Wearing lilac-coloured training vests they file out of the dressing-room and, crossing the walkway beneath the seated section of the stand, make their way through the gap onto the terracing and click-clack down the dozen or so steps to the playing surface. Having shaken hands with each of his three new boys and wished them well, Bob Dwyer brings up the rear in company with Duncan Hall. The pleasantly warm and crystal-sharp sunlight comes as a welcome relief after the suffocating ordeal of the dressing-room. Halfway down the steps Dwyer is stopped by a lady supporter of mature years who regularly presents him with a box of Maynard's Wine Gums: he has, after all, been voted the club's best-looking official! The squad commences its usual Oval Park warm-up in the in-goal area beneath the Alliance & Leicester stand, before splitting into forwards and backs and running through basic unit drills.

Then the afternoon's first setback comes to light. Joel Stransky's kicking tee has gone missing. The only one that can be found is a very flimsy plastic version which Stransky immediately pronounces hopeless. 'It's far too light and sits up on the grass,' he moans. 'Anything can disturb it when I run up to the ball.' Setback number two quickly follows. As all the players, bar Stransky, eventually head back into the dressing-room for the final 20 minutes before kick-off (accompanied by today's mascot, 11-year-old Tommy Clark from Hitchin), Bob Dwyer is stopped dead in his tracks by the news that the game has been put back 15 minutes owing to crowd congestion outside the ground. The coach goes ballistic and the air turns blue. With his team's game-preparation geared to peak at 3 p.m. all but completed, he somehow has to reduce the adrenalin for 15 minutes. Stransky, too, is far from content. Still sitting on the replacements bench at the side of the pitch he weighs up the potential harm to his goalkicking that could arise from using the substitute tee. Confidence is king in the world of the goalkicker and right now

Stransky's confidence is under siege. All of a sudden Duncan Hall appears carrying two brand-new heavy rubber tees of the type Stransky prefers. The South African's eyes brighten. Without fuss or ornament Hall had dashed down to Oval Park (a good 20-minute round trip on a Saturday afternoon) to fetch suitable replacements. Such swift attention to the minutest of details is what separates the top coaches from the merely good coaches. 'Nice one, mate,' says Dwyer with a complimentary nod of the head.

By 3.15 p.m. some 11,159 paying customers (there are a few empty seats visible in both the Members and the Alliance & Leicester Stands), including a fair few travelling representatives of Gloucester's famous 'Shed', are vociferously awaiting the opening of hostilities. Dwyer and Hall take their seats in section 'O' of the Crumbie Stand, to the right of the committee box. Behind them sit the obligatory quartet of club doctors, while a bit further back are the rows reserved for press and radio. In front of Dwyer and Hall sit the six replacements (Overend, Lloyd, Hamilton, Jelley, West and Moody), as well as the injured and despondent Neil Fletcher. 'I really wanted to play against Gloucester,' he says in his best Brummie accent, 'but I pulled a hamstring against Bedford – same leg as the shin splints I've had trouble with – and I failed a fitness test on Thursday. I'm really sick about it cos I can run on it now. I'm going for an hour's run after the match, when the sun's gone down.'

Ed Morrison's whistle instantly diverts Fletcher's attention towards the pitch and he turns just in time to see Martin Corry rise to catch Mark Mapletoft's kick-off and be unceremoniously upended before his feet regain *terra firma*. Amid great, rolling, raucous chants of 'Glaw-ster! Glaw-ster!' from the travelling 'Shed', Mr Morrison's arm goes up to signify the first penalty of the match. Stransky rifles the ball in the direction of the clubhouse and sees it fade into touch.

The opening 15 minutes is all Tigers, with the pack clearly intent upon administering a severe dose of Hall's 'don't-give-them-an-even-break' policy. They might have gone ahead after five minutes had Stransky's penalty-kick from almost halfway carried a few more metres, but the South African makes no mistake with two further opportunities from wide out on the left side of the twenty-two in the eighth and thirteenth minutes. Duncan Hall's dash to Oval Park is already paying dividends. Not that the coach has any time to pat himself on the back because he is too busy recording every error made by his side. One such, an offside, gives Mapletoft the chance to make the score 6–3.

So far next to nothing has been seen of Serevi, apart from when he had strayed among the forwards as they awaited a restart and found himself 'politely' told by Cockerill to go away and join the backs. The little Fijian is about to rectify the situation. In the space of 120 seconds he brings the crowd to its feet with two sparkling pieces of bravado at either end of the pitch. Deep in his own twenty-two he takes a long pass from Horak (who had done superbly himself in fielding a high kick under extreme pressure) and, dodging several Gloucester attackers with a hypnotic display of twinkle-toed footwork, that blends the best of Houdini and Michael Flatley of *Riverdance* fame, he plants the ball serenely into touch. Play quickly sweeps upfield and receiving a pass from Will Greenwood, Serevi, running left into the Gloucester twenty-two, drags the covering defence towards him before choosing the second perfectly to whip the return across his body to the supporting centre. Greenwood ploughs on and then finds Horak charging up alongside, and it is the full-back who thunders over for the try near the posts with two Cherry and Whites on his back. Afterwards he said: 'To score in my first game was the ultimate. It was just luck. I was in the right place at the right time, although we talked all week of supporting each other. I just supported Serevi, saw one player in front of me and went for the line.' The conversion's a formality, 20 minutes gone, 13–3 to the Tigers.

The remainder of the first half, however, departs from the script. Gloucester's very own diminutive alchemist Mark Mapletoft – rated by many as the best of the English fly-halfs – proceeds to run the show. In a five-minute spell of wizardry, Mapletoft conjures up 13 points by means of every conceivable score. First, he lands a second penalty, which is followed by a sweetly struck drop-goal. Then he pulls the white rabbit out of the top hat. From a scrum wide on the left, he executes a clinical loop round Fanolua that eliminates three Leicester defenders and enables him to goose-step the last couple of metres to the posts without feeling so much as the breath of one Tiger on his neck. The successful conversion gives Gloucester a 16–13 lead.

Hall's pen is in danger of running dry, and Dwyer's voice is now beginning to be heard more frequently. 'He must have got injured diving over the ball and hitting his head on the ground,' is the less than sympathetic reaction to an injury sustained by one Gloucester forward. 'Surely, it's a penalty not a scrum – that wasn't accidental, it was a tennis serve!' he bellows at a Gloucester back's vain attempt to intercept a pass and snuff out a dangerous Leicester attack. Then, spotting Ed Morrison lifting whistle to mouth, he shoots away toward the dressing-room to wrest maximum advantage from the newly instituted ten-minute half-time interval.

'I told them they had lost concentration, that's all,' he reports. 'We started well but slackened off the pressure. They'd stopped talking to each other, lost concentration and got jittery.' Dwyer hands round his wine gums, shuffles his papers and resumes his seat.

Dwyer is forced to wait just five minutes before Stransky kicks his third penalty to level the scores. He is soon out of his seat again – along with two of the doctors – when first Austin Healey and then Neil Back, who has been poleaxing everything in a Gloucester shirt, pick up knocks. Back's dislocated finger is instantly remedied while the scrum-half limps back into the fray (though he is later replaced by Jamie Hamilton). The coach seizes the opportunity, however, to remove Matt Poole and send on Lewis Moody. The visitors are beginning to exist on crumbs but although traffic is becoming distinctly one-way, heroic defence on Gloucester's part, and a slight anxiety over the final pass on the Tigers' part, are combining to thwart the home side.

With 11 minutes remaining, the Tigers are camped in the Gloucester twenty-two. A scrum on the left seems the perfect scenario for a Stransky drop-goal – he puts it wide. Inside a minute the fly-half gets the chance to atone after Greening is penalised for handling in a ruck. The touch-judges take an awfully long look at each other before raising their flags, this time the kick is good. The cherry-and-white dam finally bursts. Pressed back on their heels once more, Gloucester lose a lineout on their own throw as Greening completely misses his jumpers. Eric Miller snaffles the ball, Hamilton sends it left, Stransky does well to pick up a dodgy pass on the half-volley yet still has the composure to feed Greenwood with a short, slipped scissor pass that sends the centre tearing over at the posts. Two minutes later the match is done and dusted with a vignette of vintage Leicester forward play. A two-handed lineout catch by Johnson and the pack pile in behind him to initiate the driving maul from which Neil Back spins off to score. Just like old times. Final score: 33–16.

To concede 14 points in the last four minutes of normal time is an exceedingly dry cracker for Gloucester to swallow, and it shows. Two of Ed Morrison's final acts are to prise Rowntree and Cockerill away from members of the Gloucester front row following a couple of unseemly brawls. The scoreline may have flattered the Tigers: it certainly did less than justice to Gloucester. 'I thought it was a high-quality game compared with the beginning of last season,' said Dwyer, alluding to last August's opening defeat at Saracens. 'I was pleased with the performance. We had all the territory and possession in the second half. Although it would not have won the European Cup it was a good start. There were plenty of good points. We had a lot of options throughout the game and our set pieces were a big plus.' Nevertheless, Duncan Hall's biro had recorded 64 errors, which included 27 missed tackles, 17 turnovers and ten penalties.

Despite Neil Back winning the Man of the Match award, it was Will Greenwood ('Greenwood grows into centre of excellence' and 'Greenwood gives Tigers edge' in *The Times* and *Sunday Times* respectively) and Michael Horak who were to grab most of the headlines. 'He's one for the future,' said Dwyer of the 20-year-old full-back, 'and it could be England. He's eligible because his mother was born here. He's going to go a long way.'

Horak was keen to play down such issues. 'One step at a time – I've played only one first-team game. I've never thought about it. I would like to play for South Africa but every Test-playing country is very strong these days.

'I would be honoured to play at any level for England. It was wonderful to play well on my first game, out of this world. And to score was the ultimate.'

Horak's day is not yet done. Along with the rest of the side he is back on the pitch, in the clubhouse in-goal area, within 15 minutes of the final whistle for a recovery session. The players are not alone. The balmy evening encourages drinkers to spill out of the 'Captain's Bar' to watch, while the perimeter fence is lined with autograph hunters. Graham Rowntree is the first to walk across and sign a programme. 'Wais!' he calls, 'there's some people over here want to meet you.' A sheepish Serevi joins him, to be engulfed by youngsters desperate to capture this most prized of signatures. Ten yards away Neil Back is also a centre of attraction – for teenage girls whose eyes betray sentiments not entirely associated with rugby football. Martin Johnson's progress towards a blissfully hot bath is continually impeded by posses of boys and girls, but each and every plea for a photograph or autograph is accommodated. Several unofficial games of rugby involving youngsters of both sexes have broken out all over the pitch. A contented mother and son head for the exit, her replica shirt swearing allegiance to 'Deano', his declaring for 'Cockers'. The young and the old, the old and the new. The Tigers go marching on.

6

King of the Modern Game

A season playing club rugby in France for Cahors had told Joel Stransky precisely what to expect on a visit to Les Sept-Deniers in Toulouse. In their European campaigns to date, Toulouse, winners of the inaugural competition in 1995–96 and losers of a memorable semi-final to the 1996–97 renewal at Welford Road by a scoreline of 37–11, had yet to lose a home game. On 20 September the Tigers came to fulfil their Heineken European Cup Pool A fixture as underdogs (the bookies were giving Toulouse a 15-point winning margin), and took their proud record (22–17) in an explosive match marred by allegations of eye-gouging by the home side. Stransky landed six of his seven kicks at goal for a haul of 17 match-winning points. Each and every kick had been launched to the tune of assorted klaxons and horns and, as Stransky ran for cover at the final whistle, he was repeatedly spat upon, and actually slapped round the head by one demented beret-wearing home 'supporter'. Once again the goalkicker had reinforced his claim to be king of the modern game.

The modest, personable Stransky would be the first to stress that rugby matches are won by teams, not individuals but, even so, if ever there was a day when the Tigers needed their kicker to excel, it was this one. The opening pair of Heineken Cup matches had not gone to plan. Milan were duly dispatched 26–10 at Welford Road, albeit not in anything approaching vintage style: Tigers 'won' the first half 16–0 but instead of piling on the points after the break only managed to 'draw' the second half, ten apiece, due to any amount of errors, mostly of the unforced variety. 'I was disappointed in the extreme,' said a clearly irate Dwyer. Worse followed in Dublin where a massively motivated Leinster side beat them 16–9 amid a typical

Irish maelstrom of driving wind, torrential rain and fanatical support. Stransky's two first-half penalties with the wind at his back were never going to be enough; he missed two others, one a dolly in front of the post.

'We were lethargic, and it's very difficult now to qualify as of right for the quarter-finals,' Dwyer pronounced soberly. 'That was a good win by a team who wanted to tackle and wanted the ball. They are a good side. Their win wasn't all down to passion and fury. There were some very good parts to their play and their defence was very, very good. They never got flustered. We are now flying on one wing. If we win every match we can qualify, but it will be very difficult. We have got to beat Toulouse home and away – apart from the other games we have got to play against Leinster at home and against Milan away. When you have got players not at the top of their form and a game like Toulouse away, which is going to be a real cauldron, you are looking for experienced guys to carry you through.' Dwyer was concerned about the form of the man he rates alongside All Black Andrew Mehrtens as currently the best all-round number ten in the world. 'The others are either kicking fly-halfs or play like centres. Only these two have the capacity to play both ways.' Stransky had missed more than his normal quota of kicks in these two games and his general play had also been out of sorts.

'He seems to be very quiet and withdrawn. He's got a lot on his mind. It's only four months since he injured his knee – and an ankle injury and stomach bug last week did not help,' observed his coach, who further wondered whether Stransky was missing wife Karen and daughter Sabrina, still back home in South Africa. Stransky owed his coach a good one.

Duncan Hall harboured no illusions as the trip to Toulouse loomed: 'The object of rugby is to get to the gain line. If the backs are being put under pressure behind the gain line your forwards have to run backwards. Psychologically, running backwards all the time is difficult. We won the territory war in Dublin but not the gain-line battle, what I call the corridor of power. If you can get past that corridor you're going forward. When you defend, you want to keep them on the far side of that corridor. Rugby these days can be a battle of inches. Leinster were everywhere – a swarming, all-encompassing drift defence! But they only play six or seven games and that's it. They go back and play for their clubs and drink lots of Guinness – no disrespect, but that's what happens. We can't be up one week and fall in a heap the next. It would cost us too much.

'We really let ourselves down. You get disappointed for the players because they haven't performed to the best of their ability and for yourself because that's how you get enjoyment, by watching them play well. We've got our backs to the wall. Toulouse won the first three games in their championship, two away in the European Cup and this is their first home match – and they'll want revenge for last year's semi-final defeat. For our Lions who haven't been performing well it's a chance to really kick a goal. That's what it's about, testing yourself at the highest level. Better players should perform under adverse conditions. If we had a team of guys who only perform when the going is good we are not going to get very far. They can perform under pressure, they showed that last year. What we have to do now is get rid of the inhibitions and just play.'

Dwyer, too, left his side in no doubt as to what was required at Les Sept-Deniers. 'It's going to be a great experience. It's a great stadium, great team, great club. It's no good achieving victories against lesser teams. You want your victories against the best. This game is 80 per cent passion, 10 per cent intelligence and 10 per cent ability. If we get the first right and half the other two we'll kill 'em!'

Dwyer had laid it on the line and his team responded. 'It was a huge, huge match, absolutely full of tension from start to finish. The game was always in the balance. It's these matches that make all the work, all the years of playing and coaching worthwhile. We played with more passion, more hunger and more impact than the week before. At half-time, and 10–9 in arrears, Peter Wheeler turned to Dwyer and said: 'It will be a test of character – and when they have had those before, they have come through.' A converted try from Eric Miller and two Stransky penalties marked a monumental second-half revival that sealed victory. None had 'responded' more gallantly than the ABC Club of Rowntree, Cockerill and Garforth, who had endured a torrid afternoon against international props Christian Califano and Franck Tournaire and the pugnacious hooker, Patrick Soula. As a fully paid-up member of the front-row union Wheeler was so chuffed with their performance that when Rowntree and Garforth fancied a celebratory cigar at 2 a.m. the following morning, the chief executive drove around Toulouse in a taxi in search of a tobacconist willing to satisfy their craving. 'Nothing is too good for the front row!' he quipped, brandishing the cigars at the successful conclusion of his nocturnal quest.

Joel Stransky, of course, was due a good one. The boot that won the 1995 World Cup for his homeland and the 1997 Pilkington Cup for his adopted home town was only taking a short holiday. Goalkickers of Stransky's calibre do not stay in a slump for long.

'I think I missed five or six on the trot a few years ago. I had a back problem, and the back is the balance of the body. If your back's not right you don't have equilibrium, really. I was having traction twice a day for three weeks. I really lost my technique and it took quite a while to recover it. I did miss a few then, but you never get into a very long missing run because you're bound to have an easy one sooner or later. At the other extreme, I once kicked 22 straight: 11 in one game, six in the next and the first five in the next – all in the Currie Cup.'

It's 11 a.m. the day before the Heineken Cup return with Leinster. There's now a definite nip in the air at Oval Park and the squad needs little invitation to hasten inside for a massage and shower once training is concluded. Stransky resists the temptation. He remains out on the pitch firing off a few kicks at goal from the vicinity of the halfway line. As Tim Barlow and Michael Horak take turns at hoofing balls back to him, Stransky tries to find the right words to express the science of successful goalkicking.

'Every kick should be the same. I pick a spot behind the poles, up in the crowd somewhere, a sign board or a tree. If the wind is blowing, coming right to left real hard, say, I would give it a bit of leeway, choose a different line and then select my new spot. I always aim the ball at that spot, aim to strike the ball just right of centre on the seam and walk back in the middle of the panel that's facing me – four steps and a fraction, it's always exactly the same, for long or short kicks. I might just take a step or two and chip it over if it was a real easy one right in front. The sweet spot is always the same. If you were playing in horrifically windy conditions you might vary it slightly up or down. If you had a howling gale behind you, you hit it a fraction lower and put it up in the air a bit more; or if you were kicking into the wind and you didn't want the wind to get it, you might hit it 0.5 cm higher. Generally, I would aim every time to hit the same spot.'

Retrieving another ball which Barlow has sent spiralling back to him, Stransky gives it a spin to select the best-looking panel for contact. 'I think these Gilbert balls are very good. I'm 30 now, so I started kicking with the old leather balls! These are not just good for kicking but passing too. It's the weight, the feel, the finish. The only time it gets slippery is when it's very hot and it's sweaty. I played a season in France and the French Adidas ball is really fantastic to kick.

I'm sponsored by Adidas and wear their World Cup boots. There's definitely something in their Predator boot. A place-kicker can kick the ball 10 per cent longer; on punting it's difficult to say because you kick the ball almost on your ankle joint, so I don't think it makes much difference there.'

Thwumpf! The satisfying sound of boot making perfect contact. Almost without looking up Stransky knows that one has bisected the posts. This particular morning conditions are well-nigh perfect for goalkicking. Those 'conditions' always include the length of the grass. 'From a kicking point of view it makes your tee sit at different levels to where your foot goes in. If it's a bit long your foot goes in deep and the tee is maybe one and a half to two inches above that. I remember one day when we had the grass over our feet. Then, you don't get any roll on the ball when kicking out of hand or bouncing one toward the touch-lines. Also, it makes the game a bit slower, makes the legs a fraction heavier, makes the players more tired. I've never kicked well at Twickenham. The grass shifts with you and affects your non-kicking foot. But you must never blame the grass or any conditions. You must adjust.'

Of course, however much Stransky attempts to replicate his match-day routine he cannot compensate for the lifeless atmosphere of Oval Park. No crowd, no game situation, in short, no pressure. How much of the goalkicker's success lies between the ears? Technique is one thing, but what about the psychology of goalkicking? 'I don't think about the pressure or my role as the goalkicker before the game. I would say every bloke in the team is just as important. It's my job. It's just like saying, "Is Austin Healey going to worry about whether he's going to pass the ball straight 20 or 30 times in a game or Richard Cockerill throw the ball in the right place 20 or 30 times?" We all have our individual jobs, that is part of my job, it's my responsibility, it's a responsibility I accept, it's a job I do well, it's a job I enjoy. If I started worrying about it, I couldn't do my job.

'But when you want to do something perfectly, like kicking, you have to have a routine, a set concentration pattern so that every kick is as close to being the same as possible – like Neil Jenkins with his twiddling fingers and deep breaths. You focus on your own concentration thing. I have a good friend who's a motivation specialist in Cape Town. He tried to get me to visualise the ball going through the posts before every kick. I couldn't. I said to him, my theory is that if you visualise the ball going through the posts you forget how to kick it. I would rather visualise kicking the ball perfectly, and then I know it will go through the posts. I concentrate on how I'm going to run up, where my first step's going to go, the next step and right through to kicking the ball. I know if I do that right it'll go exactly where I want it. It's just like a golfer visualising taking his club back to making the best point of contact.'

As if to prove his point another 'thwumpf' sends a third consecutive 45-yarder between the sticks. It's always good to end on such an upbeat note. His body is beginning to feel the chill of cooling sweat. Collecting his tee, he walks toward the clubhouse. Had he always been a goalkicker, a natural?

'I started when I was 16. I changed school at that stage, to a great team, a much stronger school but we didn't have a kicker. My old school – Rondebosch Boys High School in Cape Town – had two great kickers. Then I went to Maritzburg College, traditionally a very, very strong rugby school. We were messing around at training one day, having competitions, some team game, and I was in the team that the kicker was not. I was kicking them from everywhere and he wasn't making them. From that week I took over the kicking and did it for every team I played for. So, it just sort of happened. Guys at that age are pretty competitive. We'd go to training early and have competitions, and I just used to win. Then I put some time in and came good. I had been a centre up till then but that's when they switched me to fly-half.

'It's really a combination of swing and eye that makes a goalkicker. You can't teach someone from scratch, you've got to have some talent in the first place. If you take someone who doesn't have a good swing but he's got a great eye for the ball and still hits it pretty well, you can turn him into a good goalkicker. Blokes like Leadbetter can turn blokes with average swings into fantastic golfers and kicking is the same but, in the same breath, if you don't have anything to start with you can never progress to become a kicker. It's the same as any sport where there is contact with the ball – tennis, golf, squash or football to a certain extent – it's all about levers. I had a science teacher who sat down with me and worked it out scientifically. He worked out the best angles for me to take the ball back to convert a try, where the margin of error was least. He told me it's like the pendulum of a clock; the pendulum stops at the back, swings through to the bottom – which is where you make contact with the ball – and follows through right to the other side. A golf swing and a tennis forehand are exactly the same.'

Barring Stransky's entry to the physio's room are the ample forms of Cockerill and Garforth in conspiratorial-looking conversation. 'What's he said to Wig?' says the prop. 'Wig', alias Graham Rowntree, has been benched by Bob Dwyer for tomorrow's game against Leinster in favour of Perry Freshwater. Apparently, Dwyer has always had it in mind to play the New Zealander now and again but the mobile 17-stone Under-19 and Under-21 international from Wellington had been injured. Sitting alongside Rowntree would be Waisale Serevi, paying the penalty for the missed tackle which cost a try in Toulouse. Leon Lloyd will play on the left wing and Tim Barlow stays on the right after a good game in Toulouse. Craig Joiner (groin) and Will Greenwood (thigh) are still troubled by injury, which presents Niall Malone with his first opportunity of the season. A doubt also surrounds Neil Back, who has just undergone a fitness test on an ankle: if he doesn't make it, 21-year-old Paul Gustard will make his début.

Stransky himself is due to go for an X-ray on his neck once training is over. And he wants to get home to Thurnby to catch the Ryder Cup on TV. But showered and dressed he makes time to relive *that* kick – the kick which won the 1995 World Cup for South Africa. His distinctive, gently husky voice seems to sound more and more South African with each recollection of that famous day in Johannesburg. 'I think I was pretty lucky, for two reasons. One, the call; and two, the position. It was a case of what was the best position for me to stand in to avoid the pressure. I called it. Francois Pienaar was screaming some back-row move, and I was screaming: "Just get me the ball back!" I got Joost van der Westhuizen to tell Rudi Straeuli, and he held it. It was on the wrong side of the field for a drop-goal and their fly-half and scrum-half could have pincered me, but I stepped inside the fly-half and Bachop, the scrum-half, tried to knock the pass down. There were only seven minutes to go and when you're that deep into extra time everyone is very tired. You certainly don't want to get out of that area. It was a scrum on the twenty-two. If we'd played it back in we might have got a penalty and in any event we'd have stayed in their twenty-two – which is the right thing to do, keeping up pressure when a side is tiring. From that point of view a back-row move would have been the safer option. If I'd missed, we'd probably have been back in our own half from a long twenty-two fighting for the ball.'

Contrary to expectation, premeditated drop-goals are not so commonplace as we imagine. 'I think you'll find that you go through your whole career as a fly-half and very rarely get set up for a drop-kick. Most are instinctive because the fly-half's job is always captain of general play – he's the bloke who makes the split decisions, very much someone who makes his decisions spontaneously in the heat of the moment. There aren't many times where you would say, especially in the modern game, let's go for the drop-goal. Most times you'd say let's go for the try. You shouldn't really lose the ball, it might stop you from scoring. It's only a last resort when there's no way through. About 70 per cent of drop-kicks miss, I'd say, because the margin of error is huge.'

At least Stransky has nothing to fear from the home fans. 'Crowds can put you off, as much as you say you shouldn't let them. The most annoying is when it's quiet and some guy makes a noise just as you're going to kick. When everyone's making a racket, like they were in Toulouse, you adjust to it. You do get some funny comments from the Shed at Gloucester. One or two have been brilliant and made me laugh. There's always someone who's paid his money and has things to say!'

With an average of 14 points per game in his first 17 starts as kicker – at a strike rate of three out of four – Stransky is unlikely to hear the rough edge of anyone's tongue at Welford Road.

7

Little Big Man

Over a hundred years ago, at a time when the civilisation of the American Plains Indians was at its zenith, a young Sioux warrior belied his smallness of stature to earn the respect of his fellow braves in combat. In recognition of a heart and spirit out of all proportion to the body containing them, the Sioux christened the young buck Little Big Man. In his Pacific homeland Leicester Tigers' most surprising import of 1997 is referred to as Bati Balavu – the bravest of the brave. To the rest of the world he is known as the Suva Sorcerer, the Peacock, the Fijian Magician, Wais, Woz, Wizza, Small or Little Man. However apt the aforementioned, the name that best epitomises Waisale Serevi's attitude toward, and ability to play, rugby football is surely Little Big Man.

For as long as anyone can remember the 5ft 8in pocket dynamo that is Waisale Serevi has dazzled the rugby world with his bulging box of tricks on the sevens field. The South Sea Islanders took to sevens like cream to peaches. They pay the abbreviated game more respect than anywhere else, and the symbol of Fijian expertise and supremacy in the sevens arena is Serevi. The little man's mercurial footwork, deft change of pace, mesmeric sleight of hand and outrageous hitch-kick has regularly reduced world-class defenders to clodhoppers and inspired a hat-trick of Fijian victories (1990–92) at the Hong Kong Sevens (each one instigating a national holiday), and, fittingly, it was he who skippered Fiji (scoring 117 points) when the World Cup Sevens were annexed in March 1997 – his eleventh consecutive appearance in the Hong Kong tournament.

Serevi hails from Gau, a small island of less than 4,000 inhabitants, which lies to the south of Veti Levu, the largest of the

Fijian islands, on which Suva, the capital, is located. Gau may constitute a mere speck on the Pacific horizon but its people are rugby crazy and it provided no fewer than five of the side that won the 1992 Hong Kong title. Waisale Serevi Tikoisolomoni grew up in Suva, where his father was a council engineer, and his precocious skills quickly brought him to the attention of the national selectors. George Simpkin, former director of rugby in Fiji, quite simply considers him the greatest natural talent he has clapped eyes upon. Serevi made his international début in 1989 at the age of 21 as a fly-half against Scotland and has accumulated 18 caps altogether (a paltry number reflecting his worldwide sevens commitments), filling every position behind the scrum except centre. His last appearance, on the wing, came in July 1996 in the 43–18 loss to South Africa in Pretoria. By this time Serevi was playing Fifteens for Mitsubishi Motors in Kyoto but his crowd-pleasing persona made him a natural choice for the World Fifteen which contests the end-of-season Sanyo Cup with the English League champions at Twickenham – in 1996 he kicked five conversions in the 41–30 win over the Tigers, and in 1997 he ran in three tries against Wasps. Coach to the World Fifteen was Bob Dwyer.

'I tried to get him for more than a year but he was under contract in Japan. When the chance eventually came I took it, because I figured that if a genius is available you should sign him and then worry about where you are going to play him. He's more of a rugby player than a positional player. I have no worries about him. I don't hold with the view that good sevens players are often no good at Fifteens. The view in intelligent rugby countries like New Zealand and Australia is that there is a total interchange between the two games, and you only have to look at the success of guys like Christian Cullen to see the proof. I do not see why Serevi cannot make the transition. He's as fit as a trout and his ability to beat a man and create space is the same whatever the code. Perhaps he won't have so much room to manoeuvre but I think he will make a big impact.

'He's a real live-wire and reminds me of a pinball, bouncing about all over the place. The guy has terrific vision, agility and split-second reactions which allow him to create and take opportunities. He poses a threat to defences all the time because they never know in which direction the ball is going to leave his hands. He does so much off the cuff, but he is not just an asset for his talent. He has tremendous enthusiasm and that is a great and infectious quality. Within a week of his arrival we were playing the best touch rugby I have seen since I've been here: everyone was bidding for his services in their touch team!'

Dwyer's quandary over where to play Serevi was never going to be resolved easily. Attacking genius, yes, but Serevi was no defender and opponents were sure to target him for bulldozer treatment. In the pre-season games against Caledonia Reds and Bedford he was tried at full-back but when the phoney war ended and the real thing began against Gloucester in the Premiership, Dwyer switched Michael Horak to full-back and put Serevi on the wing. The decision backfired somewhat. Serevi saw insufficient ball to set either the side or the crowd alight; down in Toulouse a missed tackle cost the Tigers seven points and he was taken off. 'Wais needs to know that sometimes he has to put his body on the line,' his coach explained. There were even mutterings of the 'I wouldn't pay him in washers' variety, emanating from the men in suits and blazers. This seemed a strange attitude to adopt. What is to be gained by criticising a player for defensive frailties that are freely acknowledged? Far better to accentuate the positive and concentrate on the qualities he was brought to Leicester to express: the cache of attacking weaponry at Serevi's fingertips. The Fijian's 'minder', Richard Cockerill, sprang to his defence: 'He's been criticised but he's not bothered. He's come here to better himself and see if he's up to 15-a-side. He's a living legend in rugby terms but you couldn't hope to meet a nicer bloke. We take the mickey and he joins in – he doesn't think of himself as any sort of superstar. He's happy to come and train with the boys – last week he turned Leon Lloyd inside out, and Leon's no slouch.' Nevertheless, for the following Saturday's visit of Leinster, Serevi found himself on the bench and Lloyd found himself in the team.

However, Lady Luck was to deal Serevi not one good hand but two. Thirteen minutes before the break, with the Tigers leading 12–7, Serevi came off the bench to replace the crocked Michael Horak; then eight minutes later Joel Stransky hobbled from the field nursing a dead-leg. Serevi moved to fly-half and celebrated immediately by kicking a penalty, his first points for the club in a competitive match. In the second period he kicked another and converted two of the four tries the Tigers put on the board en route to a comprehensive 47–22 victory. Of far greater significance were the aces he was constantly drawing from from the bottom of the pack, evading tackles and flicking passes at will, just as if he were wearing the white jersey with the palm tree badge in Hong Kong. The role of playmaker had brought out the best in him and the little puppeteer pulled the strings for two of the tries. The press went to town. 'Super Serevi lights the Tigers' blue touchpaper,' said the *Mercury*; 'Serevi broadens Leicester horizons,' declared the *Daily Telegraph*. Bob Dwyer confined himself to saying: 'He went well. He has a great deal of subtlety in his play.'

Serevi would get a second opportunity to demonstrate that 'subtlety', because Stransky failed to recover in time to face Toulouse in the return match the Tigers needed to win if they were to progress into the quarter-finals of the Heineken European Cup as automatic qualifiers. Toulouse, smarting from two successive defeats at the hands of the Tigers, would be desperate for revenge and Welford Road was going to be no place for faint hearts on – or off – the pitch. 'If we thought they were hell-bent on revenge after last season's semi-final defeat for the match in France,' mused Dwyer, 'heaven knows what they're feeling in the build-up to this one!'

Serevi the Sorcerer did not disappoint, but the Tigers did, losing 23–22 to the last kick of the game. 'Serevi shines – but Tigers lose their fizz' (Leicester *Mercury*); 'Serevi serves up a hot dish for Leicester'(*Daily Telegraph*) and 'Toulouse late try steals Serevi's thunder' (*Sunday Times*) were the headlines that best put the afternoon's events in a nutshell. The Tigers led 14–6 at half-time having scored two tries: Serevi made the first for Will Greenwood and scored the second himself, converting the pair. Both tries were sheer stanzas of rugby poetry, bearing the unmistakable hallmarks of Fijian genius. Quite simply, Serevi brought the house down. The first came after he had caught his own chip over the advancing Toulouse defence one-handed and slipped the ball to Greenwood. His own try profited from another quick rucked ball, on this occasion in the shadow of the posts, which he capitalised upon by selling a hugely extravagant dummy and dancing across the line without a finger being laid on him.

Serevi's bravura performance had won him his spurs. To many ardent Tigers fans he was now a living god. Henceforth, whenever Serevi walked past any of his adoring disciples after a match they were apt to drop to their knees and adopt the reverential pose of cinema's Wayne and Garth in *Wayne's World*, crying out: 'We are not worthy!'

Serevi had also endeared himself to his team-mates. After the victory in Toulouse the coach journey back to the team's hotel was understandably a lively affair. The singing was long and loud with solos using the coach microphone being the order of the day.

Eventually the finger pointed at Serevi. The Fijian's eyes, those large, luminous pools set in the kind of open, friendly and childlike South Sea Island face that so captivated early navigators, became even more startled than usual. Bashfully he made his way to the front of the bus and picked up the microphone. Instead of turning to face his captive audience he stared straight ahead, through the windscreen and out into the darkness. 'This is a traditional Fijian song of considerable piety,' he explained, 'which is sung before our games.' The lengthy introductory speech then gave way to a faltering performance that was to singing what Pavarotti is to rugby football. Riotous applause greeted its conclusion – only it wasn't concluded. Continuing to gaze into the blackness beyond, Serevi began what was clearly a second, equally lengthy, verse. The reactions became even more hysterical. But he was not finished yet, not by a long chalk. There were three more verses to come and by the time he croaked out the last note, most of the bus's occupants were unsure whether to use their handkerchiefs to wipe the tears of laughter from their eyes or stuff them in their mouths in order to stifle fits of aching, gut-busting sobbing. It had to be experienced to be appreciated. People were laughing so hard they were incapable of making a sound. Finally, Serevi stopped, and turned round to a warm and tumultuous reception. It was a moment of bonding. The moment Serevi became a Tiger.

Earlier that day, just prior to kick-off, the sad news had arrived of the death of Graham Willars from stomach cancer at the age of 57. Player, captain, coach, president, Graham Willars was a Leicester Tiger nonpareil. No one who came into contact with Graham George Willars – however lengthy or brief the association – ever departed without fond memories of him. At his memorial service there were as many mourners outside Oadby's St Peter's Church as could be seated inside.

The Leicester family had lost an irreplaceable Tiger in Graham Willars, but it could just have gained a promising recruit in Waisale Serevi Tikoisolomoni.

8

The Italian Job

Place: the Post House on Leicester's Narborough Road. Time: approaching 6 a.m. on Saturday, 12 October. A bleary-eyed party of 22 players and seven officials congregate in the pre-dawn gloom ready to board a coach bound for Birmingham Airport and flight BA8370 that will deliver them to Milan's Litane, en route to Brescia, base for the club's sixth and final match in Pool A of the 1997–98 Heineken European Cup to be played the following afternoon in nearby Calvisano. The Tigers have already qualified for the next phase of the competition but, owing to the home defeat by Toulouse, not as automatic Pool winners, and they must win by enough points in Italy to ensure their play-off game for a quarter-final berth takes place at Welford Road.

By 7.30 a.m., suitably fortified by a full English breakfast at the airport's Novotel Hotel, the day's 'duty-boys' – Matt Poole, Michael Horak and Niall Malone – are helping Cliff Shephard manoeuvre the team's vast array of luggage through a specially reserved check-in. The jumbo-sized blue kit-bags, emblazoned with the names 'Leicester Tigers' and 'Cotton Traders', take some managing. Blue is the colour of the day: the squad travel in their blue fleece jackets with the red trimmings. It seems a pity that team unity is no longer displayed on this sort of trip by the wearing of club tie and blazer – which they all possess, courtesy of Next – but those days are most definitely gone, for the moment at least. Club president Garry Adey and honorary treasurer Bob Beason nod in agreement. Adey, a ball-wrestling number eight who won two caps for England in 1976, has other things on his mind, however. 'Have I still got blood on my face? I've had this terrible nosebleed. I can't think why.' Assured he

71

looks every inch a presidential figure, it is suggested to him that the ailment must result from nervous excitement at the prospect of a weekend away with the 'boys'. Completing the party are John Duggan, Mark Geeson, Duncan Hall (plus wife Anne) and David Finlay, one of the club's honorary physicians. Adey owns up to one further worry. 'Has the club got "wipe-out" insurance cover if the plane crashes?' he mutters, surveying the personnel around him.

At a separate check-in, Tigers' own version of the 'Barmy Army', some two dozen in strength, is getting into the spirit of things. Vociferous among them are the 'Woodies', representatives of the Woodmans Stroke pub in Rothley. Watch out, Brescia! With the coming evening's vital World Cup qualifier between Italy and England live on television, some sports bar or other looks like having its hands full. There is also a media presence: Chris Goddard from the *Mercury*; Bleddyn Jones, once a Tigers fly-half exhibiting all the neatness associated with Welsh number tens, who now combines being head teacher of Great Bowden Primary School with commentating on all the club's matches for BBC Radio Leicester; and Central TV's Dennis Coath, plus cameraman. The conspicuous absentee is Bob Dwyer. He has been attending a rugby conference in Lyon, alongside Pierre Villepreux and Jean-Claude Skrela, and intends rendezvousing with the group at Litane Airport.

Pretty soon Captain Tim Mitchell is wishing his passengers 'Good Luck!' in their forthcoming match whilst informing them that they are cruising at 550 mph above the English Channel. Few take much notice, since they are now either asleep or plugged-in to 'walkmans'. In-flight breakfasts – egg, bacon, Welsh rarebit – have been summarily refused, although the constant need to take on liquid, little and often, has ensured the aircraft's entire supply of Evian water has run dry within 30 minutes of take-off. Richard Cockerill, as usual, has energy to burn. He wanders the aisle and decides to rouse Leon Lloyd and James Overend from their slumbers.

The two youngsters can't be bothered to protest and Cockerill aborts the mission. He resumes his seat and begins talking to Dorian West, who is in the row in front of him. 'You've got a good life, Nobby,' he teases. 'All these trips and no work to do at the end of them.' The reserve hooker does not disagree but, at the age of 30, West is concerned what the immediate future holds for him at the club, 'I've got one more year of my contract after this season. What then? Coventry?' The subject turns to another much beloved of rugby players in transit. A magazine is produced, one of those magazines preoccupied with photographs of the female form and its remarkable aptitude for sexual gymnastics. 'Get your mind on the game!' Cockers is told. Yes, but what game?

After a smooth flight and speedy disembarkation, the party tumbles out into an exceedingly bright and sunny – for the time of year – Milanese afternoon to be reunited with their coach, who, having been up since 4 a.m., has had to hang around the airport for two hours. The transfer to Brescia is not expected to take more than an hour or so: it's a straightforward 90-kilometre journey due east along the Autostrada della Serenissima. The scenery either side of the autostrada makes for a fascinating contrast. To the far left an unbroken vista of green-clad Alpine foothills crowned with a bright azure sky; to the right an unbroken vista of factories and offices that could be Oadby's industrial estate.

By 2 p.m. everyone is crammed into the foyer of the Radisson SAS Hotel. Located on Brescia's Viale Europa, the hotel is not one of the world's most handsome, possessing all the architectural splendour of an Eastern Bloc community-housing project. Brescia is a beautiful city, but this part of town, the north side, is dominated by buildings – including the nearby hospital and Brescia University's faculty of law – that are equally dull. The players choose their own room-mates: Martin Johnson and Matt Poole are a fixture; as are Cockerill and Rowntree. New boys Serevi and Horak stick together, while Martin Corry shares with fellow back-rower Eric Miller. James Overend gets Austin Healey.

The remains of the day are given over to rest and recuperation and eating. The younger, fashion-conscious members of the team, led by Tim Barlow and Leon Lloyd, raid the trendier Brescia emporiums (and even Bob Dwyer succumbs to temptation and treats himself to a sumptuous leather jacket), but after supper and the soccer it's a quiet night for all. Only the next morning is it known that the Milan club had (allegedly) organised a reception – they insist a letter had been sent to Leicester giving details – but no one at Welford Road professes any knowledge of it.

Early risers on match day – well, up by 9 a.m. – catch Cliff Shephard in a slight paddy. Yesterday's temperatures were in the high 70s Fahrenheit and today's are forecast to be the same. Fluid intake will be vital, and Shephard has just discovered that there are no shops open where he can purchase supplies of mineral water. He decides the only option is to commandeer the Radisson's entire stock. The hotel staff immediately comply. Shephard hands over

L278,000 for the 40 1.5-litre bottles and gets down to the task, along with John Duggan, of transferring the water into the players' individual squeezy bottles.

Horak and Serevi are first to breakfast. Not many bother, favouring the extra hours in bed and the hot brunch at eleven. Duncan Hall, however, is up and about. He's been for a run around the neighbourhood, contemplating Milan's likely approach to the game. He once spent a season playing for the University of Florence, so he should have some insight into the Italian psyche. Milan are out of the competition and are not expected to win, but will they throw in the towel at the first sign of pressure or will the recent upsurge in the national side's fortunes, for example, generate some patriotic pride in performance that will make them determined to exit the European Cup with a bang instead of a whimper?

'They've a lot to play for,' reasons Hall, recovering his breath. 'The Italian side has come on a lot with Georges Coste coaching them, and Manuel Ferrari, another Argentinian, works with Milan. They will be difficult to beat at home. They beat Leinster over here and only lost to Toulouse by five points the other week. They'll be looking for a notable scalp. It can't be ours. We can't be complacent. We need the win for a home tie in the play-offs. A draw or a loss will be a bad result for us.'

Martin Johnson is likewise concerned about his side's attitude to the game. 'We have to make sure our performance is the best we can produce. It might need to be for us to win. It might not. We might be able to win by not being at our best. You just don't know. We are going into the unknown, but I do know that playing against Italian or French sides is difficult because they are so much better at home, so much more passionate.' It's 10.15 a.m. and the skipper is kitted-out for a quick run through all the lineout variations and drills. He gathers his pack around him and heads for a patch of scrubland beyond the hotel lobby, beside the Europa Sporting Club (and not far from a porn cinema). A passing crocodile of Sunday morning cyclists executes a double-take at the sight of Messrs Johnson, Poole and Corry being alternately jack-knifed into the wide blue yonder by their posse of lifters. After 15 minutes Johnson and Hall express satisfaction. The forwards are primed for brunch: pancakes and pasta are devoured at a rate of knots but the baked beans – or the nearest thing to baked beans the hotel can muster – are accorded the thumbs-down.

All that remains before boarding the coach to Calvisano is one last team meeting. Bob Dwyer presides. He pinpoints every conceivable area of possible complacency: the dead nature of the tie; a small crowd; a featureless ground; the absence of big-match atmosphere. 'Use all these things as your focus. If there's nothing coming down from the crowd onto the pitch, focus on that and use it to motivate yourself. No negative comments from anyone – stop them at source. No 50–50 passes! Get in close and *behind* the ball! We let ourselves down last week, so, let's take two steps up today, instead of the one last week and one this week. And, don't forget to take on water – short and frequent, not in long gulps! Okay? Right, let's go.'

Cliff Shephard and John Duggan are already loading up the bus as the squad emerges into scorching sunshine. Hardly anyone is aware of Shephard's early morning efforts on their behalf. Why should they? It's part of his job after all but, with the temperature now climbing toward 80°F, Shephard's 'water divining' will prove priceless. The drive to Calvisano, a mere village of 5,000, consumes about 30 minutes, and first impressions of the Stadio Communali di Calvisano endorse the memories of Joel Stransky, who played here once for San Dona during his two-season sojourn in Italy. 'Things have changed a bit since then but even then Milan were the strongest team in Italy. They had heaps of money because they were sponsored by Berlesconi, and always were a professional outfit. They always had a top coach and brought in the best players in Italy as well as some from overseas.' By UK standards the facilities are junior club level. Calvisano operates on a budget of only £¼ m: there is one tiny stand and both ends are wide open to the elements – which today is principally a strong wind blowing all the way from the Alps. The 'Barmy Army' has taken up residence and is in surprisingly good humour considering several of its members had arrived early in expectation of buying lunch in the clubhouse only to be turned away. 'Les Leicester', alias Les Allen, has also made it and is preparing to climb into the bulky Tiger costume in which he parades at every game, home or away. Allen has driven down through France with his wife and daughter because his outfit is so heavy and inconvenient to bring by air. In today's heat he is quite liable to fry but the former prop ('I played a bit in the army but I was no bloody good!') is undeterred. He loves being part of the Tigers extended family.

The Milan line-up shows four changes from that beaten 26–10 at Welford Road. It is packed with internationals (six of them will play for Italy against France in the Latin Cup the following weekend), some of whom, like Calvisano wingers Ravazzolo and Vaccari (reportedly offered a £100,000 contract by Bath last season, yet surprisingly sitting on the bench to start with), prop de Carli and flanker Racca have been imported from other clubs specifically for the Heineken Cup. Winners of Italy's Palmares Serie A four times in the 1990s, Milan had met the Tigers twice prior to this season, both games going Leicester's way, 40–24 (1992) and 53–7 (1993). The recent clash at Welford Road, however, did not go so smoothly, and Bob Dwyer's customary post-match sang-froid had been sorely pressed. 'We were just dead. The frustrating thing was that we made errors when we tried to pick up the pace of the game. There were a lot of points there for the taking and we didn't do it. I was disappointed in the extreme.'

Dwyer's current headache concerns injuries: in the week leading up to the Toulouse match there were 21 players on the injured list, including 12 with first-team experience. Thankfully, the situation has improved but Craig Joiner (groin) and Stuart Potter (calf) are still *hors de combat*, so Leon Lloyd and Niall Malone replace them. Joel Stransky's dead-leg has healed sufficiently for him to reclaim the fly-half berth, pushing Serevi out on to the wing. Dwyer and Hall, however, have been evolving some ploys whereby Serevi and Healey swap places at certain attacking scrummages, on the right side of the field for instance.

'It's aimed at giving Serevi early use of the ball because of his ability to confuse defences,' explains Dwyer. 'It also gives Austin an opportunity to show his running skills. We desperately need someone to start making dents in the opposition defence out on the wing.' Dwyer had conceded defeat in the quest for Eric Rush's release (the NZRU was retaining his registration so he could captain its sevens side in the 1998 Commonwealth Games) and Vunibaka's work permit saga was no nearer resolution. Neil Back, too, is out – his ankle continues to irritate and he craves a week off. The shirt goes to Lewis Moody, who thus makes his seasonal début. Back sits on the bench in case of emergency. 'The difficulty for us is motivation in a match we don't have to win in a stadium lacking atmosphere,' confides Dwyer as he inspects the pitch. 'The portents are dangerous but we have to overcome such hurdles. If we don't win here we're not going to go much further in the European Cup anyway.'

The dressing-room walls soon reverberate to the rhetoric of Richard Cockerill, whose inherent pugnacity makes him Mr Motivator *par excellence* in the minutes prior to kick-off. 'It was a shit week after losing last Saturday. We're not going back to the hotel losing again. Don't expect to f***ing win! Let's f***ing break them in two! No standing off! Clean those f***ing white shirts out, bollock them out of the way and they won't do it again!' As the studs rattle the dressing-room floor Johnson fires the parting shots. They are, as usual, few but, as usual, they pepper the bullseye: 'We've got to be meaner, f***ing hard,' he snarls. 'No mistakes today!'

Kicking off into the wind, in front of barely 1,500 spectators, the Tigers start as if they really do mean business – that is until Leon Lloyd throws a 50–50 pass which is returned with interest. A pained expression crosses Dwyer's face at the realisation his counsel had been superseded by youthful inexperience. Within seconds, however, Lloyd releases the youthful *joie de vivre* that tends to co-exist with inexperience, and demonstrates the cutting edge his coach has been demanding. He collects a Serevi pass in the left-side tramlines with all of 50 metres to the Milan line but, after swerving outside his man, a blistering turn of foot takes him clear of his pursuers; one final in-and-out shimmy bamboozles the covering defender and Lloyd is in for the opening score.

Dwyer could not have wished for a better start. What happened next was definitely not on the agenda. Now was the moment to turn the screw. Another quick score might well knock the stuffing out of Milan. But, caught napping at a swiftly taken tap-penalty, the Tigers are swept back 60 metres by a flowing move which results in an equalising try. 'We have so much trouble establishing cruise control,' mutters Dwyer edgily. 'Switch on!' he bellows in exasperation.

A Stransky penalty restores the lead and settles nerves a tad. Not for long. It's as though the Milan pack have suddenly cottoned on to the fact that the visitors – despite their thunderous overture – are a few beats off tempo. In a moment of blinding revelation Milan begin to realise they want to win more than their opponents. Consequently, they begin to play as if they can win. Their rampaging pack lays siege to the Tigers' line, entrenched in the right-hand corner – Serevi's corner. Yet another drive sees Milan's impressive Argentinian scrum-half Fabio Gomez run to the short side. He has two men free outside him. Only Serevi stands in the way of a seven-pointer that would give Milan the lead. Either Gomez will run through Serevi to score himself or, more likely, he will use the overlap to get the score. Serevi knows this. The situation is crystal clear. He has only one option. He goes for the interception – and gets it.

The Milan try-line awaits 97 metres away in the distance. The initial impetus from the interception gives the Fijian acres of open range to exploit, but by halfway he has the full-back, Williams, to contend with. He is level with the Tigers bench and Dwyer and the replacements are on their feet. They sense what Serevi will try to do next, as, probably, does Williams, though he will be helpless to stop it. Serevi slyly decelerates and jinks off his right foot to dupe Williams into thinking the attack will come on his inside. The instant Williams turns his back ready to counter an inside thrust, Serevi veers to the outside and unleashes his trademark hitch-kick, à la Campese goose-step, which leaves Williams for dead. The last line of defence is the covering winger, Marcello Cuttita. The Italian international has worked wonders, not only to get back but also get across the field to confront Serevi. In so doing, however, he has little or no control of his approach. In effect, Cuttita is walking a tight-rope. Serevi has got his number. He leans toward Cuttita to create the hesitation and, as the winger instinctively falters, he instantly hitch-kicks once again to whip past on the outside with poor Cuttita diving at thin air. The Barmy Army is going barmy – and with good reason. The Suva Sorcerer has given yet another masterclass in the art of broken-field running. Stransky drills the conversion through the wind and between the uprights. Instead of being 14–10 down, the Tigers are 17–7 ahead.

Nevertheless, before Dwyer can summon the breath to call for 'Control!' Milan are back in the game. Self-belief is no longer a problem. They surge back to the Tigers' end and mount drive after drive: three times they get the ball over the line only for referee Didier Mene to rule against a try. At the fourth attempt, well into time added on, flanker Silvio Tassi does manage to convince Mons Mene that the ball has been grounded. The half-time whistle blows with Tigers' advantage cut to five.

Francis Lagleyze's failed conversion of the Tassi try is one of five kicks (three conversions and two penalties) he misses during the match. The 12 points that go begging are made to look the difference between a famous Milan victory and a famously spurned opportunity, because whenever Joel Stransky is given the office he pots goals like a man inspired. He notches his fourth successful kick of the afternoon ten minutes into the second period when adding the extra points to a powerhouse 25-metre solo try from Martin Johnson. At 24–12 it is not unrealistic to assume the Tigers, with the wind at their backs, are on the verge of finally breaking Milan's resistance. How wrong can you be? Milan, not Leicester, engage overdrive. In the space of 20 minutes they cross for three tries (only converting one), against a lone Stransky penalty in reply, to grab a 29–27 lead with the scoreboard showing less than eight minutes to go.

The replacements bench is not for those of a nervous or delicate disposition. Paul Gustard has gone on for the injured Eric Miller (Martin Corry nurses a cut eye that will require three stitches – on his 24th birthday too), but the remainder are desperate to get a piece of the action. 'You burn adrenalin, just watching. It's so frustrating,' laments Perry Freshwater. James Overend is positively champing at the bit as he jig-jogs up and down the touch-line. 'Tell him you want to go on,' Neil Back says with a nod in Dwyer's direction. 'Tell him you want to get on and smash them!' Suprisingly, in view of the enervating conditions, Dwyer has never had it in mind to make tactical substitutions and the tormented Overend is obliged to continue pacing his stall. Dorian West cannot fathom why the Tigers are not using the wind to gain and secure territory like the Italians did in the first half. 'Why don't they shoe the f***ing ball down here?' he asks no one in particular, before deciding enough is enough. 'SHOE THE F***ING BALL DOWN HERE!' he yells at the top of his voice.

Milan continue to rumble forward, relentlessly carrying the game to the Tigers. With only three minutes left, the Tigers momentarily break free of their shackles and Milan are penalised, about 35 metres out near their right touch-line. Stransky is in no hurry. This could be the final opportunity for either side to score. It is the preferred side of the field for him; he has the wind in his favour – but nothing beyond the posts on which to draw a bead at this most desolate of grounds. 'There's no stand, signs or trees so I picked out one of the little clouds,' he confesses later. The way Stransky had been kicking he could as likely have slotted this one with his eyes shut. He is a cool customer; a nerveless marksman. Over it sails, still rising as it bisects the poles with all the faultless symmetry of one of Stransky's approach shots on his home golf course. Although it transpires there is still time for a last-minute Greenwood try (converted, naturally) to make the final score 37–29, Milan know the game is lost as soon as they see Stransky's penalty take flight. They end up outscoring the Tigers five tries to four but lose the kicking duel – and therefore the match – 17 points (four conversions and three penalties) to four.

The Tigers had got out of jail. 'Tame Tigers fail to find the vital spark,' Chris Goddard told *Mercury* readers. Bob Dwyer, too, was not impressed. 'We have got to play a lot better. This is not good enough at all. I'm sure we can win our play-off but we are going to have to pick our game up. Once again Joel played great. He tackled everything and his kicking was fantastic. Had they had Joel they would have won, simple as that. It's not the sort of place where the guys are going to be motivated for a top performance, but we have to contend with whatever is put in front of us. We went into an early lead and then thought this is going to be easy. We relaxed, let them back in and after that it was always going to be difficult.' And the scrum-half experiment? 'Could the switch become permanent?' asks a mischievous inquisitor. 'It's not out of the question. Serevi is the most accurate passer in the club, but I've not got a plan in mind to do that in the future.'

The crux of the game was pinpointed at the post-match dinner when the Milan president began his speech by saying: 'Pity Joel didn't stay at home!' Yet a win is a win whatever the style, and none to be celebrated more than one away from home. The players are in exuberant mood. When the Milan president had first got to his feet the respectful silence was shattered by the sound of a baby crying outside. 'Cockers, shut up!' booms the unmistakable voice of Will Greenwood to howls of appreciative laughter from his team-mates. Cockerill proves to be very much in the limelight this evening. The sponsors have donated a huge cup for the victors. It is decided to utilise the gift as a 'Man of the Match' trophy and the cup is duly awarded – somewhat tongue-in-cheek – to a visibly embarrassed Cockerill. Entrusting the impressive silverware to a member of the ABC Club, however, is not a prudent move because by 1 a.m., fuelled by the odd glass or ten of the local vino rosso, a burning curiosity to discover how the cup was put together ensures it has to be taken apart, a delicate process incurring a few dents.

Despite a night on the tiles – the younger element descend upon the Seconda Classe club in downtown Brescia – the squad convenes at 8 a.m. the following morning for a recovery session in the swimming-pool of the Europa Sporting Club which adjoins the Radisson. All, that is, except James Overend who has been allowed by his room-mate to continue sleeping off a monster hangover. The kindly soul who contributed to Overend committing such a cardinal sin was Austin Healey. Retribution would not be long in coming, and vengeance was sweet indeed.

Picture the scene. Litane Airport is packed to the rafters as the group prepares to check in. The players reach for their passports.

'God, Molly, were you in *Grange Hill* when that photo was taken?' mocks Healey, seizing the damning evidence from a red-faced Niall Malone. What's Austin's picture like then? A pause. 'Oh, come on, not the oldest joke in the book!' protests Healey. 'Who's nicked my passport?' Prime suspect James Overend denies all knowledge, as does suspect number two, Richard Cockerill. 'Someone must know!' bleats Healey. Disinterest reigns. The culprit refuses to show himself. The passport's whereabouts is well known but it's Healey's turn to suffer now: it's pay-back time for the lovable 'Oz'. The check-in queue shortens and Healey sits on his bag by the desk, head cradled in hands like a naughty schoolkid dispatched into the corner. Still the cavalry fails to materialise. Everyone heads for the duty free shop. With just the Halls and the Dwyers remaining, Healey explains his predicament to the check-in staff. Boy, is he being made to squirm. A security officer is called. Earnest conversations in Italian commence behind the desk. Bob Dwyer, sympathetically, starts warbling 'Always look on the bright side of life'. Then, a deadpan Duncan Hall gives Dwyer a surreptitious nudge and winks toward the blue book sticking out of his pocket. Hall has had the missing passport for some time. Even the belligerent Healey will think twice before trying to land one on Duncan Hall. The passport is slipped to Dwyer, who leans across the counter and suggests helpfully: 'I bet he's dropped it on the bus. I'll go and have a look.' Dwyer's search for the bus – now halfway back to Brescia – and the 'missing' item consumes all of 45 seconds. 'Here you are, Austin. Looking for this?' he grins, waving a Briton's most prized possession. Healey smiles wanly. He slouches forlornly away to join the others. He must grin and bear it. The perennial biter has been well and truly bitten. Oz has got his comeuppance.

9

New Kids on the Block

Leicester Football Club has long been regarded as a 'family' club; one with a strong sense of identity. Certainly, for any aspiring player keen to further his career prospects there was no better place than Welford Road to test himself by training, competing and playing with the best in the business. And yet, however valid those considerations, over-riding them is the acute sense of belonging that comes when a player joins the Tigers. Leicester is a club where people look out for each other, both off and on the pitch.

The four newest Tigers are Michael Horak, Martin Corry, Paul Gustard and Waisale Serevi. Horak is a 20-year-old full-back cum winger who has arrived at Leicester off the back of playing rugby league with Perth Reds in the Australian Super League; previously he had represented Orange Free State and South Africa Under-21 at union and South Africa 'A' at league. The son of a northern Transvaal scrum-half, the Johannesburg-born Horak learnt his trade at the noted rugby academy of Grey College in Bloemfontein – which also nurtured the talents of recent Springboks such as Ruben Kruger and Pieter Muller. The 6ft 2in fair-haired, blue-eyed Horak also holds an English qualification (indeed, he was soon called into the Under-21 squad) because his mother came from Bedford and did not move to South Africa until she was 15. Bob Dwyer first heard of Horak from a coaching contact in Perth; Joel Stransky was then entrusted with sounding out South African judges.

Martin Corry is a 6ft 5in and 17 stone 8lb back-rower born in Birmingham. Educated at Tunbridge Wells Grammar School, he played lock for the 1992 England Schools 'Grand Slam' Fifteen before attending Newcastle Polytechnic. Spells at Newcastle and

Bristol, where he was captain in 1996–97, led to appearances as a flanker for England Under-21, Emerging England, England A and, ultimately, to a full cap on the recent tour of Argentina alongside Cockerill and Garforth.

Paul Gustard is a 6ft 4in flanker who, at the tender age of 21, already tips the scales at 17 stone 3lb. A Geordie by birth (father Steve was a swashbuckling centre/wing with Gosforth) as well as education (Newcastle Poly, like Corry), Gustard progressed from England Colts and England Students, not only to make the Under-21 side from junior club Blaydon, but to skipper the side on its 1997 tour of Australia. When he's not at Oval Park or Welford Road, Gustard studies law at the Leicester Poly, or De Montfort University as one should say nowadays.

Waisale Serevi is the nearest thing to an attacking genius that rugby football currently possesses and he is, without a shadow of a doubt, most definitely a one-off.

On the morning after the Milan game, the quartet sit around a table in the foyer of the Radisson chatting about their initial impressions of life with the Tigers and their hopes for the immediate future.

HORAK: The people really look after each other, care for each other, at Leicester. Everyone knows each other. You go to many big clubs and everyone doesn't know each other. Here, you get a sense that they do.

CORRY: That's a good point, because when I was up at Newcastle as a student and about to leave, I felt I could play my best rugby with this kind of club, not a London club who play and then bugger off. I chose to go to Bristol because I felt Leicester, with Deano and Wellsy there, gave me no chance of first-team rugby. I thought I'd go to Bristol for a few years and then, when I felt those two were a bit older and my game was a few years further on and I could compete for a first-team place, that would be the time to come. It was very much in the back of my mind that the clubs I felt I could go to were the Bristols and Leicesters where there is a club atmosphere and a club environment, as opposed to superstars just coming to play the game and going off. It was a toss-up between the two. I loved my time at Bristol but I think Bristol can only take me so far. If I want to be the best I have to play for the best. There's a lot of good back-row players here and if I'm not good enough to get into the Leicester side I won't be good enough for England. There's no hiding place at Leicester.

SEREVI: I knew Leicester very well after playing against them in the Sanyo Cup. I knew about Bath and Wasps and Harlequins but Leicester are a good team and once I decided that I wanted to prove myself at the 15-a-side game, Tigers were the team for me. I played in front of big crowds in Hong Kong but here I can hear people shouting and screaming in the stand and I think I must play and lift my game so people enjoy the game and Tigers win. The attention does not worry me. When I'm in Fiji everyone recognises me and I have to hide in my car as everyone wants to talk to me and ask me how I am doing. It has been good to get away from the pressure.

GUSTARD: I always wanted to come to Leicester from when I was young, and nearly came here to university when I was 18 but decided, for better or worse, to stay in Newcastle. I went to Blaydon and then the opportunity came to join Leicester. I had a few offers. Bob Dwyer was a big thing. I rang him to say I'd like a chat about coming but we kept missing each other and I began to think he wasn't interested. I was getting frightened because I'd set my heart on coming here. But then we spoke and he explained what they were trying to do. I was totally impressed and anything else I'd heard from other clubs faded in comparison. I signed before Martin but, for me, it was coming to play with what I regard as the best club, best supporters and best players – people like Deano, Eric and Backy – rather than go somewhere like Quins where they had a lot of international flavour to their back row but, as Michael and Martin have said, they were not such a family club as Leicester.

HORAK: It's the small things. You're really conscious of a sense that no one feels they're better than anyone else. There's no sense of superiority at Leicester, whereas in other clubs if you're not in the cliques you're out of it. Here everyone talks to you and makes you feel at home. But sometimes I can't believe the things you guys laugh about!

GUSTARD: We're a lot more advanced now, more subtle – especially the ABC Club, they're into sarcasm now!

CORRY: Everyone likes to think there's a stand-up comedian inside them somewhere. But some blokes think they're funny and they're not.

GUSTARD: I was at Blaydon, a junior club, where everyone knows everyone and no one feels they're better than anyone else. Everything was a little bit more light-hearted, I suppose, than a senior club and jokes were flying around in training a lot more. When I came to Leicester I didn't expect the same but when the time's right, people are easy-going, so everyone can feel comfortable with one another. The training's still spot-on and hard, even so.

HORAK: But at big clubs, if you get there and you're not in the first team, those blokes don't mix with you. They're an élite. Here it doesn't matter if you're in the Youth or Development, everyone is friendly with one another.

CORRY: That sense of feeling welcome at Leicester is unique in my experience. 'Gussy' was spot-on with what he said about junior clubs. We've all come from junior club backgrounds and that's what we're all looking for – a junior club environment where everyone plays because they love the game and they love playing for that club. That's the key. When you take the field you've got to be prepared to die for your team-mates. If you don't socialise with your team-mates – go out on the 'lash' with them – you don't get that team spirit.

SEREVI: I have signed for Leicester for two years and I am prepared for what's coming. With three competitions we face up to 40 games a season in all kinds of weather. I have played in Japan and at half-time I was so cold I ran off the pitch and put my hands in hot water! The cold will be a big challenge – they will train out there and I'll be in here! It is a very big challenge, the biggest of my career. I hope by the end of my time here I will have shown people that I am not just a sevens player. That is important to me. I want my Fifteens to improve. I want Leicester to improve on where they left off last season. Playing fly-half for Fiji I struggled, because our forwards won so little ball but at Leicester they dominate at scrum and lineout, so I hope to see as much ball as possible. I enjoyed playing fly-half against Toulouse. I was lucky to play fly-half because I knew coming to Leicester we have got the best fly-half in the world, Joel Stransky. He has got everything. Playing fly-half for Leicester is good because you get lots of ball. It's different to Japan. There we had to go to work from eight to five, and then went training at night. Here it's more professional, we just train. That's good. I am very fit, I have always kept fit. I haven't found training a problem, I'm enjoying it. Everything's been good.

GUSTARD: It's a bit different for me because I'm still studying. I'm in my last year at the Poly doing law and I structure my university timetable around my training.

SEREVI: I don't get bored. I train, I do the washing, the cooking – chicken and rice is the same here as it is in Fiji and Japan – and I go to sleep. I'm a teetotaller and a Methodist – I have found a church to go to. Michael comes to my house. We go shopping. I miss my family. If they were here tomorrow I'd be happy. They come at the end of the month. I miss my little girls, Una who is three and Asinate who is two. They are in Suva with their grandmother. My wife Kara is a captain in the Fijian peace-keeping force in Sinai. When I went to Japan in 1992 several Fijians followed me. Now I've come to England maybe many more will come too. It would be nice if a work permit could be sorted out for Marika Vunibaka so that I could have a fellow countryman with me at Leicester.

HORAK: Wiz and me are always together because all the boys have got girlfriends or are married. We don't mix with the 'Dream Team' – the students! They share everything! I've not found the normal man in the street to be so friendly over here as in most big cities, like in Australia. The first night Wiz and me got to Leicester we wanted to go and eat a kebab, and walking down the street the first bloke we bumped into was coming out of a pub. 'Excuse me, do you know where a kebab house is?' we asked him, and he said, 'Piss off!' Those were the first words said to us in Leicester!

CORRY: On the coaching side, the structure and personnel we've got at Leicester is head and shoulders above anything I've experienced before, purely because it's so well organised and is planned so far ahead. It's not done on a day-to-day basis, it's done a month ahead. They're not just filling in time, everything's done for a reason and a purpose. The Leicester structure is so far advanced of anything else in England and it's one of the main reasons I came here: because of the set-up, you can only improve.

GUSTARD: I came here to play first-team rugby, not stay in the seconds. My primary aim is to develop as a player, and with the help of Dunc and Bob and the players I've come on in leaps and bounds.

HORAK: In the Free State we just loved to throw the ball around. It's warmer and drier and that's all we ever want to do. We'd watch the Five Nations on the TV and see Rob Andrew kick all the balls away. Basically, it would be just chasing, if you were a back. Every South African boy wants to play for the Springboks, but in this day and age it's about playing Test rugby – if I could play for England it would be a huge honour. I'll take it one step at a time. What I like about Leicester is that we are starting to throw the ball around. Everyone enjoys it, everyone gets the ball, everyone has fun and that kind of game plan means you've got to know who it is supporting you and where they are running. At the beginning of the season you didn't know this. As time goes on you recognise the calls, you don't even have to look. By the end of the season it'll be a different team, you'll see.

CORRY: Yes, you learn how other people play the game. Take Wiz, for example. You run a straight line behind him because you know that after he's done all his wiggles, he's going to end up back on his line and he'll make something for you. It's the same in the back row. Eric and Backy play completely different games, and it affects how you support them. It takes a while to settle in and then it becomes second nature. Then you know the where and the when of how to support them. You create an option for them.

HORAK: There's something in a bloke's eyes, too. You know that Backy likes stepping off his left, so just run there. At the start of the season you're just like a bunch of cattle running around, wanting to help but not quite knowing how.

SEREVI: I don't want to kick! Give me the ball and I just want to run and play my natural game. I started playing rugby aged ten. The skills came naturally to me. I want to play for Fiji in the 1999 World Cup. The last two years we've had New Zealand coach Brad Johnstone. He wants us to stay playing normal Fijian rugby because we don't have the big forwards like at Leicester or in England, or in South Africa, New Zealand and Australia. In Fiji it's very hard when we have our scrums because the scrum-half has to run away because our scrum goes backwards and ends up with the number 15 at the back! We have improved a lot on that, and in the lineout. Our coach wants us to let the ball go to the wing and support the wing with the loose men because we have some loose men who can run. We want to open up the game, don't come close to the fringes, play it out wide and be prepared to run. At set pieces we do have calls with targets to run, like at Leicester, but in second phase lots of Fijian players can, one on one, beat easily any defender in the world, so they don't stop us from running. Before, it was just people running all over the place!

HORAK: My game is pretty bad at the moment. I felt I was all right in the first two or three games but since then I've gone a bit quiet. I'm not one of those guys who just wants to be okay. I want to be one of those the opposition feel they have to watch out for.

The conversation is suddenly curtailed as everyone is told to board the bus for Litane Airport. Whether Horak has the credentials to become another Tiger to be feared remains to be seen. Right now, he is content – like Corry, Gustard and Serevi – to be just another new kid on the block within the most closely knit community in English rugby.

10

Bob and Dunc Steady the Ship

Six days after the Italian Job the Tigers turned their attention back to the Allied Dunbar Premiership – and received a right old pasting. The fact that this 25–6 hammering came at the hands – and ground – of their near neighbour, and traditionally most bitter enemy, Northampton, made such a caning all the more humiliating. 'There was not one area where we shaded it,' said a downcast Dwyer. 'We got dusted all over the park.' This constituted the worst result against the Saints since the 26–7 defeat of October 1973, and led Chris Goddard to opine in the *Mercury*: 'It's probably fair to say that if this had been a horse race the stewards would have ordered a dope test. Even the best sides can be beaten on an off day but their transformation this season from racehorse thoroughbreds to candidates for the knacker's yard is now complete.' Oval Park was not going to be overrun with happy bunnies.

It was time for some soul-searching and Monday's team meeting heard any amount of plain speaking. There were plenty of questions to be answered. Had preparation been hindered by the Sunday game in Europe and a day travelling home when the side should have been resting? Was it prudent to hold a day of fitness testing only 24 hours later? Then, on the Wednesday, the England contingent rushed off to Bisham Abbey for a squad session. Were the big names jaded after the summer tours? More worryingly, perhaps, was it more a case of other teams finally catching up with the Tigers and working out how to beat them? The food for thought was considerable. 'It's a bit difficult looking each other in the eye at the moment,' conceded Martin Johnson. 'It's worrying when it happens, but one shaky performance doesn't make us a bad team, just as one good one doesn't make you a good team. We were outplayed. It's a sobering experience and not one we experience very often. All we can do is pull ourselves together and go for it next week against Bath.' The skipper concluded with a typically Johnson rallying cry: 'Let's just go out there and give them a good hiding!'

The feeling that everything was not tickety-boo was fanned by the diverse noises emanating from Oval Park – even Joel Stransky publicly admitted the players had spoken with Bob Dwyer about the length and extent of training. In the one corner was Graham Rowntree: 'Team spirit is okay. It's just the morale that is down. You can see it in people's faces. We had a cracking training session last Friday but on Saturday you could see people had lost confidence. I wouldn't say everything fell apart but everything we tried to do wasn't coming off. People didn't start bickering but did start looking at each other. We've not got to the stage where people are shouting at each other. We are just lacking a bit of confidence, in fact a lot of confidence. We have not played that well for weeks. Training has gone well but we are getting into a rut and starting to worry about things. The pressure was piled on because of qualifying for Europe and we just lost a lot of confidence. We are not pulling together. The pressure is there and when things are not going well that's when you feel it. That's why we have to pull together. We decided we have to be more positive and look forward. The game has changed. Every game is now a qualifier for one thing or another. When things are not going well the pressure increases and that's when it comes down to yourself. We have been around for a long time, we have all been in pressure situations. You have to lift yourself out of it and that means sitting down with everyone and seeing what bits are not going right and saying what we can do. With the amount of experience and quality players we have got, if we can't sort problems out we are not going to go anywhere. But we have a great squad – I wouldn't swap anyone – and a captain who leads by example. There's only a few things we have to put right and we'll be back on the winning trail.'

In the other corner was the volatile and voluble Austin Healey who was quoted in the *Mercury* as saying: 'On and off the pitch there's too much arguing. There aren't enough people getting down and doing their jobs. Not enough hold their hands up when they make a mistake.' Then, on the day of the crunch Premiership game with Bath at Welford Road, the *Daily Telegraph* carried a feature on Healey in which he said: 'A lot of us, including Johnno and Backy, were complaining about feeling tired even before the game last week, and after 20 or 30 minutes I felt absolutely shattered. I'm definitely finding it a bit wearing, especially after playing all last season and then going on tour with the British Lions. Will Greenwood says he feels like his brain is turning into mushy peas, and I feel the same. You get on the pitch and don't feel as mentally sharp as you were when you were an amateur. In the old days, you'd switch off simply by going to work, or in my case university. Now you seem to have a rugby ball in your hands seven days a week. When I was at college and the weekend came around, it was a case of, "Brilliant, we've got a match." Now it's more like: "Oh, right, yeah, we've got another game." Someone said to Louise, my girlfriend, that the reason we're playing poorly at the moment is that the team is spending too much time together, and it could be true. Since I became a professional rugby player she reckons our sex life has decreased by about 100 per cent. It's not her who complains about feeling tired it's me. I flop into bed and go straight to sleep. Team spirit's okay but it could be better. Personally, I think we need to have a few more team-building things instead of train, train, train. Get away go-karting or something; or paint-balling and shoot each other in the face. A lot of us think we're getting stale just from the monotony of what we do all week. One of the lads said the other day: "We work our arses off in a game, come off and get bollocked. Then we work our arses off again in training and get bollocked again." I said to Bob Dwyer recently: "Why not surprise us one of these Monday mornings? Like, okay, today we're off to play five-a-side soccer." He said: "When you get the basics right, then we might surprise you." I feel old at 23!' Healey's team-mates were unfazed. They are accustomed to taking his utterances with a Siberian-sized pinch of salt.

Bob Dwyer was prepared to concede ground in some areas but not all. 'I would say there's no doubt we were psychologically tired but that should not detract from a very fine Northampton performance. Somewhere in there there must be a lesson for us in how to remain psychologically fresh in a trying period. It's said that no one is playing particularly well at the moment but the Lions tour didn't do any of our players any good at all. The lack of an off-season for our representative players didn't do them any favours. Players need an off-season. They need rest and recuperation, and then to build up for the new season – ideally four months to rebuild muscle tissue. You can't do that while you're playing. We have download weeks for R&R and then we pick up. Last week was a download week, but it wasn't supposed to be a download week in performance. The Premiership is tough, undoubtedly the toughest club competition in the world. The French might argue theirs is equally tough but it isn't. The winners this season will lose four games minimum. The standard has improved all across the park. The promoted teams, Richmond, Newcastle, each field about eight internationals. If you meet someone on a good day, then anyone can beat anyone. Add the European Cup for the top teams and it's a tough, tough competition. I don't think lack of confidence is right. I think the constant pressure eats away at the concentration levels and you become mentally tired. We talk about being mentally tough and some are much better at producing a performance week in week out because they take responsibility for their own mental and physical preparation and performance. The obvious ones are Johnno, Backy and Joel.'

Duncan Hall avoided the public debate. After the Donnybrook débâcle he had voiced some misgivings about the players' mental approach. 'By the time we get to a game, the game should be 80 per cent mental, 20 per cent physical. I think we haven't had the percentages right. We have not had the right mental attitude.' Now he was prepared to expand in private. 'At their meeting the players identified three or four areas, from their own individual preparation to how they looked after themselves after the Milan game and never recovering, to having to spend 11 hours going to an England training session, to thinking it's going to be easy. Maybe against Northampton we were affected by the amount of travelling we'd done. But when you get to play the game on Saturday it's mental. You've done all the physical stuff. Mental tiredness can either be the lethargy from the amount of training, or the weather and those sorts of things. I don't think enough of the guys are mentally tired from thinking too much!

'All of a sudden guys have gone professional. They've done things a certain way year in year out. Education is a great thing but it needs to be done younger. I've tried psychiatrists and psychologists but you can dabble with danger. You've got to be careful who you invite in. To be a professional sportsman is a difficult job. Guys who have long-term contracts will think: "I'm pretty secure, off we go." Then expectations come in and it's, "Oh, this is not how I thought it would be." Some have managers who have them doing promotional activities but they want to have their own life and do their training. You think you've got all this time but you don't. It can be very frustrating for them. They've got to be organised. Some guys will get a whole lot of money, have a big spend, buy a nice house, car.

Everything is going fine, then they get an injury, they're not playing well and the pressure is on. In the old days rugby was a release from the stresses of employment. Go out, bash the hell out of someone and go back to work on Monday. Now it's their livelihood.

'Our performance has been up and down. There's not just one reason, there's a whole series of things. Last year we started reasonably shakily but got away with a few wins. Then after winning games in Europe we played some fantastic rugby in November to December. It took us time to settle down into a pattern of play. This year I think there's a similar pattern evolving, but some of the players are tired. We try to freshen players up. There are two important factors, one is rest, and having some part of the summer to rest; and the second is the off-season and pre-season where you need to develop your base running and your strength and your weights programmes so you can play the season. But with the season getting longer and longer and the rest shorter and shorter, the training is not being done at the right time of the year.

'From a forward's point of view I know myself that to play back-to-back seasons – all the scrums, mauls, rucks and all the physical, hard, driving things – is pretty demanding and it's difficult to keep coming up and doing it again. In rugby league they do a lot of ball and conditioning work but apart from a little bit of tackling, not much physical work. But in union you've got to practise collision things – hard scrums and a lot of ruck and maul so you can recycle. And everyone's got to do that. Then, on Saturday, we ask guys to be hungry and "up"! We do have to look, as professional coaches, at how to keep players fresh and how to moderate six training sessions a week so they can handle the trauma.

'The one thing the players agreed about this year's training pattern – how we split the work up – was that it is good. There's plenty of time for rest. It's up to the coaches and support staff to give them the right amount of training but they're not to know what they're doing outside of what they do here. The individual has, in the end, got to prepare for his own performance. We're always talking to the players, asking them: "Have you had enough rest and recuperation? How's your diet? How do you feel?", trying to identify guys with a problem early enough. But they have to help themselves!

'One thing that disappoints me is that not enough players spend enough time on their own individual skills. Years ago people would be out before or after training doing another 15 minutes on lineout throwing or kicking. Joel introduced a breath of fresh air last year by actually doing that. Serevi does his own practice; so does Michael Horak. Perhaps cold-weather players don't want to stay out so long. But if players only rely on what they do with the coaches they're never going to improve.

'We want to rest players but we also want to get the points on the board. Because we're in Europe it becomes very difficult to do that, so we don't have the luxury of being able to rest players. Some players get paid more than others, and you get paid more because you're a big game player or a better player. While you're searching for guys to come in underneath and provide competition, the big players cost you a lot of money, so they've got to play.

'What it all proves is that there are only so many games you can play at your peak. All the guys are trying hard to play for the club, because the club is their prime employer. It's a long season and you can't run your race in the first half of the year. We're now in a situation where we've coped with most computations that will happen, that can happen in any one game. Everyone's got a responsibility. It's all about learning. If you don't learn to improve it's a waste of effort. We won't be wasting the experience of Northampton.'

Dwyer and Hall were of one accord regarding selection for the Bath game: the players who got us into trouble had better get us out. Dwyer, however, was not averse to shuffling the pack. He still yearned for more of a cutting edge on the wings and still wished to capitalise further on Serevi's instinctive flair for the unusual and the unstoppable.

In midweek, Serevi was played at scrum-half in the second team's match with Coventry. Lips were sealed, but any visitor to Oval Park later in the week knew Dwyer was at long last going to take the plunge: Austin Healey would move to the wing and Serevi would operate from scrum-half – as he had on one occasion for Fiji, against Scotland and Gary Armstrong.

'Bob thinks Wais can do a lot of good things,' confided Hall. 'Those inside positions are playmakers. The problem was how good his clearing pass was, because the primary job of the half-back is really to get the ball from here away to there. Martin was apprehensive to start with, because as a forward, and I was the same, you like to feel secure, to know the guys behind you are safe. Martin's advice is sought – not all the time – when going through the positions and talking about about what we want to do. The captain at English club level is a very important role. You want to have communication and opinions about what's going on. The club wants to pick the guys in the best positions to do the best for the club.'

However thinly disguised, the subterfuge was maintained to the bitter end. Even when the Tigers ran out onto a gloriously sun-baked Welford Road pitch to confront Bath, Serevi still wore the right winger's letter 'N' shirt. If the Fijian's subsequent location at the heels of his forwards created a hum of surprise in the packed crowd, it failed to shock Bath – who had clearly done their homework and put two and two together. The match proved the fast, fractious and thrilling encounter – chockfull of fire and brimstone – one comes to expect when Bath and Leicester join battle. The two front rows were quickly at each other's throats, a stone-cold certainty given Mark Regan's comments in the press on the subject of his opposite number, Richard Cockerill. 'He is a good player but nothing special,' the England incumbent was quoted as saying. 'We don't get on that well.' The scrummage became a war zone. Cockerill was eventually yellow-carded, but to his immense satisfaction Regan was eventually substituted, as was England tight-head Victor Ubogu. By this stage the Tigers had painstakingly constructed a 33–22 lead to put the result in safe-keeping.

The first half, however, had been a see-saw affair. The Tigers fell behind 9–3 on penalties (one of them a direct result of a miscued Serevi kick at the base of a scrum), before a smartly taken tap-penalty gave Healey a sniff of the try-line, and he finished off with a pair of dazzling sidesteps. Serevi, having been instrumental in the build-up to Healey's try, now played the clown once more, by attempting another relieving kick from the base of a defensive scrummage when the wiser option was to feed Stransky. Bath's scrum-half, Andy Nicol, managed to tap the Fijian's ankle in the act of kicking and as the ball plopped free, flanker Richard Webster picked up for an easy score. The conversion put Bath 16–10 ahead.

Martin Johnson's knee-jerk reaction to Serevi gifting Bath ten points was an inclination to banish him back out to the wing. Thankfully, second thoughts prevailed for, after an exchange of penalties, the mercurial Fijian had a hand in a fabulous try which enabled the Tigers to wrest a one-point advantage, 20–19, on the stroke of half-time. The move started after Matt Poole – of all people – took a quick tap-penalty ('I'd never taken one in my life and hadn't a clue what to do!') on the Bath ten-metre line which was then driven on by Johnson and Martin Corry; Serevi subsequently sending in Stransky at the right-hand corner. Stransky made the steepling conversion from this widest and most difficult of angles for a right-footed kicker look decidedly run of the mill.

The South African's *tour de force* continued in the second period with two further penalties and a conversion (raising his points tally to 23) of a Greenwood try. The try, in the fifty-first minute, had given the Tigers an 11-point breathing space at 30–19. Serevi was again to be found at the heart of the move. Picking up from a Leicester scrum on the left, he ran laterally to feed Greenwood with a short, flat pass and ran round seeking the return. The Bath defence, warily eyeing the Fijian threat, were also looking for the return pass, but instead, Greenwood, who slanted his run to perfection, ignited the afterburners and chipping over the advancing full-back, collected the ball to stretch triumphantly for the line. An enthralling momentum cranked up by a game of sustained ferocity showed no sign of slackening, but desperately hard though Bath tried to breach Tigers' defensive wall not a brick was dislodged.

There were some very happy – and very relieved – faces in the home dressing-room. Dwyer's inspirational ploy had come off, but only just. 'I suppose after 20 minutes there were a few people doubting the wisdom of the switch, but overall Wais made a major contribution to the team performance. It certainly gives him plenty of touches on the ball and the timing of his pass is second to none in the world. He made that little bit of space and put that little bit of doubt in the defence's mind for Will's try. There's a few things he gives us we haven't quite seen yet. Austin had a stormer and his selection on the wing for England is not outside his capacity. He trained the house down and made a big contribution to the team preparation. I don't think he had any complaints. You'd have to ask him but it looked to me as though he was okay.'

Over to Healey. 'It's given me a fresh lease of life. I enjoyed playing. I knew I was dropped and moved to the wing early in the week but, instead of sulking about it, I took it as a chance to have a bit of fun, and that's what happened. I've spent too much time recently worrying about being picked for England, being picked for Leicester. I was bored with complaining. Now I'm just here to enjoy it. And if I can take that attitude into every game then I'll get chosen anyway. It may harm my chances of playing scrum-half ever again if I carry on playing like that on the wing. It's a lot easier playing on the wing – after 20 minutes I could still breathe – and I'll be able to go out tonight and get drunk without being completely shattered because scrum-half play does take it out of you. I want to go out there and have a laugh. I'll never go back to the serious days when it was do-or-die and my head was exploding.' Before a head can explode, says Confucius, it must first swell to unbearable proportions!

As the curtain rang down on October, neither Dwyer nor Hall could blot out entirely those little voices in the back of the head alluding to the inconsistency of their team. The two highs against Toulouse in France and now Bath, were both displays of backs-to-the-wall grit in the aftermath of the depressing losses to Leinster and Northampton. There could be no slipping back into lethargy for the visit of Glasgow in the Heineken European Cup play-off to decide who got the right to visit Pau on 9 November. The tie was viewed in most circles as a David v Goliath contest. 'Yeah, and David won that one!' snorted Hall to any suggestions of the result being a foregone conclusion. Dwyer, too, was anxious to quash such talk: 'A famous Australian rugby league coach used to say the most difficult games are the ones you are supposed to win. And we are supposed to beat Glasgow at home. But they did not achieve their consistently good record without being a good side. An average side might fluke a couple of wins but you can't win consistently, as they have done against good sides, without being able to play. I think the Bath game will give us a lot of confidence. We have suffered, more than most, in having a large number of Lions. It's taken them a fair bit of time to start finding their form. We've also tried to integrate a couple of new players which takes a bit of time. At times our form has been good, at others average. But it's a lot better than at the same stage last year. What we need to do is continue to improve and I think our performance against Bath, especially in the second half, will give us a lot of confidence to go on and play better.'

The Tigers would receive comparatively little assistance from the crowd, since Welford Road was not even half-full when Glasgow got the match under way. The opening 15 minutes offered no clues of what was to follow. At this stage the Tigers (who lost Matt Poole with medial ligament damage to his right knee in the first minute) led 14–5. Thereafter, Glasgow grew to appreciate how Custer and the 7th Cavalry must have felt at Little Big Horn because the game became a massacre. In demolishing Glasgow 90–19, the Tigers also dismantled the European Cup record book. Two new records were set: for most points by a team; and most points by an individual, Joel Stransky's 35 (three tries, ten conversions) being one more than Richard Dourthe registered for Dax against Edinburgh. Two other records

Darren Garforth endures the front row's personal version of a scold's bridle in the Oval Park gymnasium.

The Chief Executive: Prince Charming or the Prince of Darkness?

Messrs Wells and Richards sweat it out during the heat of August, as John Duggan maintains a watchful eye: six months later it is they who would be cracking the whip.

The first-team pack (Neil Back nearest camera) take on Oval Park's ugliest scrummage machine.

Darren Garforth and Perry Freshwater (back to camera) perfect their lifting of Martin Johnson, watched (from R to L) by Derek Jelley, Dorian West (partially obscured), Duncan Hall, Matt Poole, Paul Gustard and Eric Miller – who seems to be taking an inventory!

(L to R): Healey, Corry, Miller, Johnson and Potter check the programme for the Premiership opener against Gloucester.

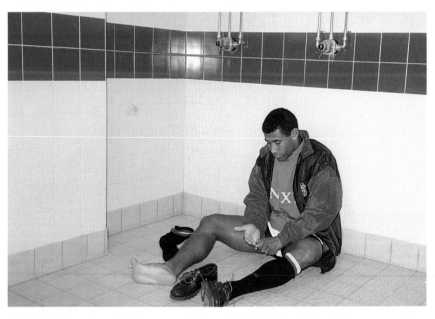

Waisale Serevi seeks the tranquillity of the Welford Road shower-room before his home debut.

The coaches' view: Hall and Dwyer discuss a training session.

The coaches' view: Hall (pen poised, as ever) and Dwyer dissect a game from their vantage-point high in the Crumbie Stand.

King of the modern game: practice makes perfect for Joel Stransky.

Wais signs: another young fan goes home happy.

New boys Corry and Gustard discuss back-row tactics amid empty milk bottles and banana skins, typical flotsam associated with the aftermath of an Oval Park training session.

Any patch of ground suffices for a quick spot of lineout practice on the morning of a match: Brescia's Radisson Hotel provides the backdrop as Garforth and Poole (obscured) launch Martin Corry; Eric Miller stocktaking once again!

Half-time against Milan at a featureless Calvisano: only 17–12 ahead, so Leon Lloyd, Will Greenwood, Niall Malone, Joel Stransky, Michael Horak and Austin Healey (back to camera) have reason to pay attention to the words of their coach.

were equalled: most tries (14) and most tries by an individual, Michael Horak claiming four. The club records, however, were made of sterner stuff: Liverpool St Helens were crushed 100–0 in April 1992, and Dusty Hare collected 43 points (two tries, three penalties and 13 conversions), in the 95–6 slaughter of Birmingham in September 1986. Stransky, who had once scored 46 for Western Province in a Currie Cup match, was suitably deferential: 'It would have been nice to have the record, but having been here such a short time and Dusty being a legend here, it's probably better that he keeps the record for now.'

Bob Dwyer had other things on his mind. He was not about to forego the opportunity of firing a few opening shots in the psychological battle with Pau. 'We really believed we could come to a dead halt. Glasgow had nothing to lose and everything to gain. We realised there was a genuine chance of failing to make the last eight, which would have to be considered a very unsatisfactory and unsuccessful European campaign. Now anything is possible. We think we are as good as any and better than most – it's a matter of whether we can produce the goods on any particular day as required. Pau will treat such a fantastic scoreline with respect because I'm sure Glasgow are not a bad side. They'll think Leicester are running into a bit of form.'

The Tigers were back on an even keel.

11

A Good-Value Day

Anyone who visualised the transition from Leicester Football Club to Leicester Football Club plc being a piece of cake is at best naïve and at worst a fool. Off-the-field change of this magnitude was hardly going to be all sweetness and light. To cite just one mundane everyday problem of the logistics involved, the pressure on the club's switchboard was such that penetrating the Welford Road iron curtain has even been known to drive the club president to the verge of apoplectic fury. Tempers were always liable to become frayed, voices would be raised and exchanges inevitably grew heated. Battered egos abound. The old way of doing things has, of necessity, been trampled underfoot by the way things must be done if the club is to go forward into the professional era on a sound administrative and organisational footing. 'There have been huge aches and we are creaking a bit because we're being asked to conduct a professional business in a professional manner with an amateur infrastructure,' admits commercial manager Keith Grainger, 'but we've already established one of the biggest and best systems around off the field. The club is starting to shape up and be in a position to buy the structure we need for the future.'

Grainger is one of several key backroom personnel whose efforts systematically oil the Tigers machine, ensuring it ticks over smoothly rather than stalls. At 10.30 a.m. on the Thursday prior to every first-team home fixture, for example, you will find Grainger and seven of his colleagues sitting at a table in Suite One of the Alliance & Leicester Stand discussing the strategies that will enable Saturday to pass without a hitch – or, to be more pragmatic, with as few hitches as are humanly feasible. Home games don't come much bigger than against Bath in the Allied Dunbar Premiership on 25 October.

Around the table with Grainger on Thursday, 23 October, are his right-hand woman Tracey Branson (sales manager), Claire Pitt (membership and ticketing supervisor), Helen Morrell (catering facilities manager), David Gaskell (safety officer – soon to be made stadium manager) and John Stew, representing Casils, who undertake the club's catering; chairing the meeting is Andy Key, a Leicester player man and boy, coach to the Extras and now recently arrived from British Steam Specialists to become Peter Wheeler's right-hand man or, to give him his exact title, general operations manager. The eighth – and missing – person is Tony Pike (promotions).

'Here he comes,' says Key, spotting Pike walking across the pitch. 'If Derek sees him, he'll shoot him!' he adds with reference to Leicester's proprietorial (and legendary) groundsman, Derek Limmage. 'I hope he's not wearing stilettos then,' chips in Helen Morrell. A breathless Pike eventually enters to take his seat (and punishment) between Tracey Branson and Keith Grainger. John Stew sets the ball rolling with a succinct report on the number of covers for lunch: 650 in all. Nearly half of these will be served in the 26 executive suites of the Alliance & Leicester Stand, while a party of a hundred from Price Waterhouse, the match sponsor, are taking over the Underwoods Suite; other meals will be served in the Barbarian Room and the Crooked Feed/President's Lounge, located in the clubhouse.

The privilege of match-day sponsorship is costing Price Waterhouse £110 (plus VAT) per person, for which they receive an extensive package encompassing: being greeted on arrival by a hostess and given a complimentary drink; an address by the club president; a silver-service buffet luncheon; reserved 'centre-line' seats for the match; company acknowledgements via pre-match advertising in the media, on the perimeter boards, in the programme and over the tannoy; the right to choose the 'Man of the Match' and present the award; the chance to meet the players and seize photo opportunities; afternoon tea; a souvenir gift; and – veritable gold dust – four carpark passes. For £85 (plus VAT) per person (minimum of 20 guests) Dunlop have taken up the matchball sponsorship: their package features slightly fewer perks, such as foregoing afternoon tea and the dubious privilege of meeting the club president! Smaller parties (minimum of four guests per reservation) wishing to partake of corporate hospitality packages can pay £75 (plus VAT) per person to enjoy a four-course table d'hote menu, half a bottle of wine, seats in the Alliance & Leicester Stand and after-match bar facilities.

There seem to be few complaints about the quality of the food Casils provide. 'The temperature of the meals was our major problem at the Toulouse game,' says Stew. 'The volume of food we're having to serve is such that we just don't have enough oven space. The reality is that we badly need another oven.' Obtaining a drink has also been posing occasional difficulty. 'Too many people staying near the bar,' declares Stew. 'It's not so much the service being slow, as bar space being minimal.' A new 'flow-system' is being tested to try and ease the log-jams. How thirsty fans will respond to the proposed 'queue here' signs is, however, open to question!

Demand outstripping supply is a recurring theme in meetings like this because everyone, it seems, wants a piece of the Tigers action. Nowhere is this negative equity more apparent than in the sphere of ticketing. At any Premiership game, for instance, there are only around 2,200 tickets not spoken for, out of the 16,248 ground capacity (4,427 seats in the Crumbie Stand; 4,112 in the Members; 3,209 in the Alliance & Leicester; and 4,500 standing in the Crumbie Enclosure). 'It's much harder to get a standing ticket than a seat,' says Grainger. 'There are only 200 per game for sale. The rest have all been sold to season-ticket-holders.' Quite simply, the club's fanatical following creates a membership rush every summer that sees the vast majority snapped up. The best seats in the house for the 1997–98 season went for £245 and the worst £145; the right to stand cost £120 (special rates available for families, senior citizens, students, juniors and the disabled).

This season's decision to place the sale of 'spare' tickets in the hands of the TicketMaster organisation has led to both Helen Morrell and Claire Pitt almost tearing their hair out at times. 'We've had hassle all week about tickets,' gripes Morrell. 'Ticketing is becoming a nightmare because we keep changing systems for different games.' Claire Pitt agrees: 'Members ask why they must go through TicketMaster to get tickets for games that are not in their "book", like Deano's testimonial and the Glasgow cup game. Members are going to get well wound up if we keep moving the goalposts on this.' Andy Key suggests an apology via the public address system. 'No, Saturday is not really the forum,' responds Pitt. 'Use the newsletter to apologise and then go through the system step by step to tell them what to do, for example, how to get tickets for the Tetley's Bitter Cup.' Morrell adopts a more forceful stance: 'I feel very strongly that we should not allow the members to feel they control decisions that management takes. We've been fire-fighting for 12 months, reacting to what they want.' Back comes Claire Pitt: 'We do have a disgruntled membership at present. A message would get every man and his dog in the office complaining about the announcement. It will stir them up again!'

Keith Grainger's main concern is to maximise revenue. 'TicketMaster was a commercial decision. We are doing our utmost to help the club's financial structure move forward and it brings more income. And another thing, I've noticed several boxes in the Alliance & Leicester with too many people in them. How are they getting in?' He asks Gaskell to tell Tracey Branson of any boxholders pulling a fast one so they can be warned that their licence is in danger. 'The trouble is,' retorts Morrell, 'everyone comes out of the woodwork for these big games.' Suspicions also exist of irregularities at certain turnstiles. 'Wherever there's tickets there's fiddles,' exclaims Grainger. Gaskell assures him that 'Operation Bingo' is in place to catch the suspects this coming weekend. 'It's our responsibility as a plc,' Grainger reminds the meeting, 'not to give too much away.'

The commercial manager has something else he wants to get off his chest. The players, he feels, are not fulfilling their obligations to sponsors as punctually or as diligently as they might. 'Yes, they have to warm down after a game, unwind, and if the game's not gone well it's not easy, but frequently they are not appearing at all. I think sponsors must be told not to expect players before 5.30 p.m. At the moment we're having to go round hoovering up players. Martin Johnson has a huge profile but I've not seen him do anything like this as yet.' Tracey Branson identifies Leon Lloyd, Craig Joiner and Austin Healey as three players who have made a conscious effort. 'I asked them after the first game of the season if they knew just how much the sponsors had paid to come and watch them. They were staggered when I told them £110. Now they turn up.' Grainger is only partially mollified: 'The big, imposing figures – forwards like Johnson – are much more eye-catching than someone like Craig Joiner who, though he is an international, is just a small and pretty lad like anyone else. We are a fat cat at present but we need to keep these sorts of people interested or they'll resign. They need to be spoilt, to feel they've had a good-value day.'

The club's commercial manager has been at Welford Road just five months, having come through a field of 200 applicants. It is not difficult to imagine why Grainger was appointed: his contributions to this morning are both exceedingly frequent and exceedingly incisive. The Geordie strikes one – and clearly sees himself – as a man with a mission; there does indeed appear to be something of the zealot in him.

After the meeting has broken up, Grainger is happy to reflect on his first few months at Welford Road. 'I was excited by the initial physical suggestion when you walk into the ground that it's a huge and established club. I said to Peter Wheeler that the strength of the club, i.e. its membership, could well also, potentially, be its weakness in the short term, in the sense that people might not be ready to accept the changes that they had to accept if the club was to stay viable and not go broke. Although the club has been established for years and years and done everything very well, the commercial people who were here before had done a very, very sound job, there still was an opportunity in each area – which was acknowledged by them – to improve the performances of each individual area by a few per cent, to increase the area's income up to the level it needs to be. The support of the committee has been very strong. The vast majority of the committee are aware of the commercial needs of the business and they've been supportive on most matters. The one thing they wouldn't concede was the use of the president's room on match days, which I felt more use could be made of.'

Grainger's CV commenced with eight years at Proctor & Gamble ('doing things like salesman and accounts manager') followed by a period as an area manager with Conoco. Then, more recently, and more pertinently, came a position with Newcastle United Football Club which entailed overseeing its sports club branch, namely ice hockey, basketball and rugby. The former player with Percy Park naturally gravitated toward the rugby side of Sir John Hall's sporting empire and his remit at Welford Road is to do for the Tigers what he did for Newcastle Falcons.

'Most businesses, particularly in sport, need a tripod to stand on. Firstly, a kit supplier; secondly, main sponsorship; and thirdly, a very supportive brewer. I can't claim a great deal of credit for Next, as that was well in place before I came; I'm working on the kit supplier; and the brewer has been renewed. So, the main sponsorships are very strong for the next five years.

'One of my ambitions was to create an average crowd of 12,000, and that's well on board. We've started to have major improvements in the programme, even though it's been an award winner for two years, and that's a big communication with the public. I'd like to think by the end of the season we'll also strengthen the in-house team, sales and support staff. We have a lot of staff from the amateur days who, for one reason or another, can't offer the commitment we need professionally.

'I've had 20 years' experience in retail and, without a shadow of a doubt, one of the strongest arms we can develop is the merchandising side of the business. We nearly trebled sales over the last year. It's starting to build as we've developed a distribution web and will continue to do so with the brand range that will come on board. Newcastle play to 36,000 fans and yet they sold 600,000 shirts last year! The Tigers shirt has been around some time and hasn't varied. I'm not sure I see the need to change that but I do see a need to support that core item with a better range of associated products, like coats and scarves.'

Sponsors, corporate guests, members *et al* thoroughly enjoy one of Grainger's 'good-value' days on 25 October, when Bath, the old enemy, are thumped 33–22. The club's two merchandising outlets – a booth under the Alliance & Leicester Stand and the shop in the clubhouse – do a roaring trade. Traditional items like shirts (home, away and training strip), scarves and bobble hats mingle with modern leisurewear, such as sweatshirts, T-shirts, fleeces and baseball caps. Sweaters and ties can still be found, but the range reflects the fact that the market for this kind of apparel lies with the younger generation. Indeed, for a mere £19.99, Tiger parents can dress their tiniest offspring in a natty baby-sized fleece sporting the club colours.

Sara Watson has managed the shop for the two years it's been open; previously she manned a small kiosk on match days for 15 seasons, a time when the grander items – be they sweaters or track-suits – still tended to come out of a cupboard in the honorary secretary's office. To witness the shop positively heaving with humanity on a Saturday afternoon suggests some dramatic enlargement is already imperative. Watson, and her seven match-day volunteers, are worked off their feet to cope with the endless crocodile of would-be shoppers who are directed round a one-way system that constitutes the only practicable method of servicing such weight of numbers. 'On a good day last year we'd sell £12,000 worth of goods,' says a breathless Watson, whom some might say is married to the club, 'but when Toulouse came the other week we sold £13,500-worth. The French supporters were in here buying two or three shirts at a time and half the team bought fleeces – both at

£39.99 each – and we couldn't get them out fast enough. And they were fighting to get the Tiger cuddly toys! The home shirt is still the most popular item. People seem to like them with the new Next label and the new Tiger logo has gone down well.'

Andy Key's management team likewise reports a pretty satisfactory day when it reconvenes at 9 a.m. on the Monday for its regular feedback and debriefing session. The food unit on the Alliance & Leicester concourse has recorded its best-ever sales (£1,400) and, John Stew suggests 'it is definitely on an upward curve now'. Keith Grainger agrees this is good news, even though it still amounted to 'peeing in the sea – we're only achieving 25 per cent of our potential in this area'. The new flow system in the main bar (the Tiger Room) fell flat: during the pre-match rush the instructions were ignored completely and a number of tables were obstructing the exit. It is felt more manpower is needed to regulate the flow if the system is to be judged fairly. David Gaskell's 'Operation Bingo' also proved a damp squib: 'Someone blew the whistle and they were waiting for us. Next time I'm going to tell no one. I'll just do it.' Gaskell's turnstile figures state Saturday's attendance to have fallen short of the capacity crowd reported in the press: the Crumbie Enclosure was clearly far from full. Not that Grainger sees any reason for complaint: 'It's good for us if the media report a capacity crowd because it makes a selling point to sponsors. Saracens, for example, only got 5,000 for their game against Gloucester, so we can say to sponsors, "Support us – we'll provide you with three times the crowd."' Whatever its exact size, the crowd posed no problems. Gaskell reports one man tripped up outside the ground and broke his wrist, while inside the ground was the usual trouble-free zone. 'The crowd itself is our best security,' he continues, emphasising his view with the tale of a drunk who did once start causing aggravation. Apparently, by the time the police reached him he was distinctly the worse for wear as a result of some brutal vigilante justice meted out by members of the Oadby Wyggs front row near whom he had foolishly decided to stand. 'He actually begged the police to rescue him!'

The players had more than fulfilled their obligations on the pitch but off it they were still to be found wanting. Only Graham Rowntree put in an appearance at the disco catering for youngsters and, according to Grainger, none of the five designated players materialised to mix and mingle with the day's sponsors. 'It was a fairly flat note to end the day on. Tracey had worked wonders to wine them, feed them, organise them, seat them – and then they're kept hanging around to meet these wonderful players who don't turn up. The biggest difference between Leicester Tigers and Newcastle Falcons is the lack of understanding, or the lack of commitment, to the off-the-field needs. They don't perform as well off the field on match days and it has a big bearing on long-term interest from sponsors. I don't know whether it's education or not. At Newcastle the players are trained at the club – here we don't see them all week. Perhaps it's difficult amongst ourselves to appreciate who does what. It's well overdue that we get everyone together to appreciate this. Commercially, in Bob Dwyer we've probably got someone who's as switched on as anybody, someone who knows the benefits of the relationship between players and sponsors, so I'm not concerned that it will happen, I'd just like to make it happen sooner rather than later. There's a need for it.'

However qualified the verdict, no day that generates £250,000 in turnover can be deemed to be anything other than a resounding success. As far as Leicester Football Club plc is concerned a match day like 25 October 1997 is merely a working template for the bigger and more lucrative days that the future needs to bring – and, furthermore, must bring – to Welford Road if the club's financial base is to be stabilised.

12

Lunch with the ABC Club

A biting wind whips errant leaves across the bonnets of assorted Rovers. The weather is at last on the turn as Oval Park's workforce labours beneath slate-grey skies. A bleak Monday-morning session is drawing to a welcome close and the reviving smells emanating from Liza Woodford's kitchen beckon the players just like the aroma of Bisto gravy used to entrance the kids in that old advertisement.

When it comes to eating, Leicester's ABC Club – as in the art of scrummaging – bows to no one. Graham Rowntree, Richard Cockerill and Darren Garforth sit themselves down to consume outsized baked potatoes buried beneath mountains of every salad topping on Liza Woodford's menu. Between mouthfuls, they ponder the week ahead which culminates in Sunday's Heineken European Cup quarter-final in Pau and the prospect of locking horns once more with some of the most fearsome scrummagers in the business.

COCKERILL: Every French side has a good front row. Just like in Argentina, every scrum they hit, they drive and there's no rest.
GARFORTH: Their whole game revolves around the scrum. There aren't many French sides that can't scrum.
COCKERILL: They're all hard-nosed. In England you get the odd pack that is aggressive and gets stuck in, but in France every single pack can all scrummage, even if they may not be the best of players elsewhere. They can all fight and they all get stuck in. There are no soft touches over there. That's what it's all about! There aren't many hookers who are probably as aggressive as me. Soula, at Toulouse, is certainly one of them. Dawesy was another and Moore occasionally – but more for England than Harlequins. He was never particularly interested when

he played for Quins. Dawe was very hard, very strong. Bath have now got Mendez and Regan but neither have filled Dawe's boots in any way.

ROWNTREE: South Africa have traditionally done well up front because they've always been very big. But if you look at the recent Tests against New Zealand, they were completely outplayed because New Zealand were technically superior. These days it doesn't really matter how big you are. It's such a massive technical aspect of the game nowadays, the scrum.

COCKERILL: Toulouse are probably the best front row I've played against – the two international props Califano and Tournaire, and Soula the hooker. Away to them this year was probably the hardest scrummaging we've faced. They were good, well drilled. But to say we struggled is a bit harsh, we just struggled in three or four scrums, admittedly pretty important ones. We were a bit lazy and didn't concentrate enough, which is down to me because I'm the one who controls the whole hit. We've spoken about it. Our pride has taken a big dent because we pride ourselves on what we do in that department. It's important to us. Against Toulouse we were second best but, saying that, it's the only time in six years it's happened. It will happen occasionally but Toulouse were better than any English front row we've come up against.

GARFORTH: And these boys we're playing against next Sunday aren't the easiest, you know.

ROWNTREE: But they both scrummage illegally! They either stand up when the pressure goes on, or at Toulouse, the tight-head Franck Tournaire would bore in at an angle and push upwards to split me and Cockers. If we did that over here, we'd get penalised off the park. They do it and all of a sudden it's hailed as great scrummaging. If we got them down here on a Tuesday night for a head to head we'd soon see who are the better scrummagers!

Just over 12 months have passed since the Tigers travelled to the Municipal Stade du Hameau for a pool match in last season's Heineken Cup. Pau led 14–6 at half-time but, gradually losing both composure and concentration, they resorted to eye gouging and other skulduggery which ultimately cost them the match. The Tigers vacated the field to salvos of oranges and stones having pulled off a famous 19–14 victory. This season's trip to Toulouse had brought more of the same, both during the game and at the final whistle, with Rowntree, Cockerill, Eric Miller and Neil Back sporting marks around the eyes.

COCKERILL: It's pretty cowardly. When you have got the ball they put their fingers in your eyes and if you don't let them have it they stick them in further! You get boots put on you and you get fisticuffs because it's a physical game, but that's a premeditated act, not a heat-of-the-moment thing. It's very dangerous. I'm not saying we're whiter than white but none of us do that sort of thing.

GARFORTH: We don't hand out the severe things the French do, gouging and things like that. We just hand out as good as we get – kick 'em, punch 'em – whatever it takes, really.

ROWNTREE: It's not such a grim underworld as it used to be.

COCKERILL: You can't get away with it. There are cameras everywhere. You've got to concentrate on playing. And there's the legal hassles of it all, too.

ROWNTREE: You've got to play hard, but keep within accepted boundaries. The French only resort to gouging when things are going wrong. It's not a question of intimidation. When they're in the shit is when they revert to old ways.

GARFORTH: When you match their ferocity up front, that's what they come back with, that's how they reply.

ROWNTREE: So when that's happening it's good.

GARFORTH: When they start doing that you know you're on top.

COCKERILL: Unfortunately, the refs can't see it much of the time because it's in the middle of rucks and mauls. Speaking personally, if I catch someone doing that to one of our players or to myself, I'll take the law into my own hands. If that means getting sent off or cited, so be it. I'll take the risk. Gouging is unacceptable. It's a big issue. It's worth standing up for.

Pau will mark the hundred and twenty-fourth occasion Rowntree, Cockerill and Garforth have packed down wearing the A, B, C letters denoting the Leicester front row. Emulating the legendary Pontypool front row of the 1970s that turned out for Wales (Faulkner, Windsor and Price – the marvellously dubbed 'Viet-Gwent') by doing the same for England, is the abiding dream. Garforth and Cockerill appearing in tandem is the best representation as yet, although they have constituted the Barbarians' front row on three occasions. The character of any club, great or small, is the sum of its members. Graham Rowntree: dependable, fair-minded and infinitely willing; Richard Cockerill: the loose cannon, primed by a swagger and a bluster, that conveniently protects a centre softer than most may imagine; Darren Garforth: a rock-like yeoman of the shires, the avuncular Pickwickian figure binding them together. Alternatively, some chastened opponents might spot a greater affinity with the principal characters in *The Godfather*: Garforth, the paterfamilias Don Corleone; Cockerill the hot-headed Sonny; and Rowntree the pragmatic Michael.

The association began at Sheffield in the opening fixture of the 1992–93 season after a 21-year-old 'Cockers' (originally a schoolboy loose-head) had joined the club from Coventry; their home début came the following Saturday against an England Fifteen in a game to celebrate 100 years of rugby at Welford Road. 'They'd had a training camp that weekend,' recalls Rowntree, 'and sent up a side. We gave them a hard time up front, even though the likes of Probyn and Moore were playing.' The youngest of the three at 26 (four months younger than Cockerill), 'Wig' is nevertheless the longest-serving Tiger, having played in the Youth Fifteen and making his first-team début in October 1990. 'I went to school with Dean Richards's cousin and everyone at school called me "Wig". It was all something to do with my dodgy haircut (or some say my ears – "Earwig"). Anyway, Dean got wind of it from him, so everyone calls me "Wig" now!' Rowntree won his first England cap as a temporary replacement for Jason Leonard in the 1995 Calcutta Cup and now has 15. Failing to make the Lions Test Fifteen in South Africa was all the more disappointing for being unexpected. 'There's a massive point to prove. A few reputations were dented, including mine. A lot of us experienced some tough rugby, we've learnt a lot and we want to use it. I'm very determined. When you get to the top of the pecking order and it's taken away, you do start to look at yourself and worry. You get a bit introverted. Now I'm seeing each game as an opportunity to impress the selectors. It's like aiming to win your first cap all over again.' Father-figure and 'sobering' influence (Dean Richards once declared his ambition was to be standing at the end of an evening's drinking alongside his tight-head) is 31-year-old Darren Garforth, who won his first cap as a seventy-eighth-minute replacement for Rowntree in the Welsh match last March, following no fewer than 17 appearances for the 'A' side; he subsequently played in all three of England's summer internationals against Argentina (welcoming Cockerill to the fold) and Australia. Garforth's transformation from soccer-playing centre-forward into a highly mobile, ball-handling tight-head prop (despite being diagnosed asthmatic last season) is part and parcel of Leicester folklore. At the time, 'Daz' was a scaffolder in his native Coventry. 'My football match was called off, and a minibus with all the lads was going off to a rugby game, so I got on that bus instead. I'd played full-back at school – Binley Park – but they took one look at me and said: "You're short and fat, you can play prop!"' Thus began a career with Coventry Saracens, Nuneaton and, eventually, in September 1991, the Tigers.

The combative trio endeared itself to the Welford Road crowd and pretty soon a banner extolling the virtues of 'The ABC Club' was in evidence on the terraces.

COCKERILL: Dunc has this philosophy that it doesn't matter who you are or what you've done in the past, it's all about getting stuck in. Our attitude is, and always has been, we'll play to the best of our ability and if they want to take us on they're welcome! We do our bit on the pitch and the crowd seem to like it. Off the pitch, it carries on. We're close-knit and we always look after each other. It's just spiralled from there, really. Graham trains hard and he always eats healthy food. He won't eat chips and he cuts the fat off his bacon! He's a bit of a 'keeny' – he likes talking to the coaches.
ROWNTREE: You can f***ing cut that out!
COCKERILL: He's worked hard and deserves where he's got. I think a lot of his international recognition has come from the Leicester front row as a whole. I never thought I'd play for England, never, because of the reputation people have given me. People thought I spoke too much and that I was a liability, giving away too many penalties. I never thought of myself as a Jack-the-lad off the field, maybe on it once or twice! But I proved to the management I could cope with international rugby. As soon as I got on in Argentina I could have cried. It was brilliant, the ambition of a lifetime achieved. You've worked all your career trying to get there, complained so much when you haven't and suddenly you're there! They put me in charge of all the scrummaging meetings, because my scrummaging is second to none and, whatever else they say about us at Leicester, they respect us for what we can do in the scrum. Daz has been unlucky not to have played a lot more times than he has, but it's pretty difficult when you've got one of the club props in there already because they're reluctant to pick two props from the same club and they shy away from picking the whole front row. Daz is the opposite to Graham. He's one of those naturally talented as a rugby player, naturally big and aggressive. He doesn't watch what he eats! He cuts the fat off his bacon and makes another sandwich out of the fat!

GARFORTH: Bollocks! Bob reckoned the way I could improve as a player was to lose a bit of body fat. He wasn't bothered about the weight, just the body fat. I've only lost about three kilos but my body fat has dropped from 24½ to 19½. I actually eat more than I did, a lot more pasta and I have skimmed milk. That's how I've done it. I haven't changed my diet dramatically, although my drinking is virtually non-existent now in comparison to when I started. My only drink is on a Saturday after the game, and then only three or four pints. A drink on a Sunday dinnertime is also out – I have to do some training on a Sunday otherwise I'll be knackered on Monday!

ROWNTREE: As Richard says, Darren is probably the most gifted rugby player out of the three of us. He's the oldest and keeps an eye on things. Richard is an immense competitor. There's no one really like him! He's a pain in the arse a lot of the time but there's no one more competitive and keen to do well. He keeps us all going, not just the front row but the whole pack. I sometimes wish he'd change the record before a game.

COCKERILL: But it's a classic, isn't it? You've always got to keep playing the classics! I'm not asked to do it – I just do it! A lot of it is for myself more than other people. Some people can sit quietly and think about the game. I find if I sit down and just sit there, my mind starts to wander and I drift away. If I talk, I wind myself up and, hopefully, it starts to wind some of the others up. There'd be no atmosphere if you'd got a lot of quiet people.

GARFORTH: It's not necessary for everyone. It's more for him, to get him in the right frame of mind.

ROWNTREE: Some people, like Dean, can just turn it on a few minutes before a match, other people you can't speak to half an hour before a kick-off.

COCKERILL: You want to enforce a few things that we need to be doing and thinking about. It's a physical game and you can't just go out and expect things to happen. You've got to get yourself 'up' for it. People do it in different ways. You've got to create atmosphere, create hatred for the people you're playing against. It just raises the importance of certain things. I get criticised for talking a lot on the pitch but I do that to keep myself going because you can drift in and out of games. It gets me involved, winds the opposition up and keeps me focused on the game.

GARFORTH: Graham summed Richard up. He is a great competitor, gets stuck in and enjoys it. Sometimes he becomes a little bit too much – I've had six years of it now! Usually we cope but occasionally when he goes a little bit too mad we have to have a quiet chat with him. But he rarely listens! Graham's done well for himself with England and the Lions. The hard work he's put in has really paid off – he probably trains and works the hardest out of the three of us. Another great competitor, though he hasn't got the mouth that Richard has – which is a good thing, really.

COCKERILL: We'd never cope with two of them! We'd fall out all the time.

ROWNTREE: Yes, that's right. We've got a bit of everything. Richard's the loud one, I'm the quiet one and Darren's probably in the middle.

Bearing the brunt of French spite is one thing but the recent indignities suffered at Franklin's Gardens was another cross altogether, particularly as Northampton had tried to entice all three members of the ABC Club away from Welford Road (reputedly a £300,000 transfer fee and £50,000 a man signing-on fee) during the summer; there was even talk of a straight swap involving Rowntree and Gregor Townsend. 'We contemplated it for a short time until the club intervened,' explains Cockerill. 'It's very difficult because we want to play for Leicester but you want your market value. You have to look after yourselves because careers are very short.' Wisely, the ABC Club was made 'an offer it couldn't refuse' and Rowntree, Cockerill and Garforth retained their stripes instead of trading them in for halos.

ROWNTREE: The reason we lost to the Saints the other week was simple. We trained too bloody hard that week! We played Sunday, travelled all day Monday and on Tuesday we did fitness testing and rugby training. The week just got out of hand. We had a meeting, changed a few things and it's worked. I wouldn't say we've been on the back foot a lot of the time. There have been a few occasions when we have been found out, but a lot has been made of it, noticeably in Toulouse. We've been together a long time and worked hard at our set pieces, but a lot of people have caught up. We are not head and shoulders above the rest any more. Teams have closed the gap by better personnel coming in and concentrating more on their scrummaging – look at Wasps, they have a full-time scrummage coach. A lot of the lads had a hard summer and that's caught up with us. We're still tinkering around, finding out what's best for us this season because no situation is the same. We're still finding our feet. The length of the training sessions, the amount we were trying to cram into one session, the things we were doing and when we were doing them in the week.

GARFORTH: Last year we were trying to do a lot of things in the week and get them all right – and were getting half of them wrong. This year we've concentrated on a few things a week and getting them right – and then moving on to something else the week after. Bob and Dunc seem much further in front in their coaching, a lot more developed in their coaching than English coaches. They're years ahead of us.

ROWNTREE: They're very professional. Everything is broken down into different components and they're very businesslike. I wouldn't say Dunc has changed our scrummaging, but he has made us individually aware of what we are doing with our feet and binds. He's improved little things to make the whole thing better.

COCKERILL: Bob and Dunc are very ruthless. You have to perform or you're under pressure straight away, especially with Bob. If you're not playing well, they'll find someone who is. Even if you're better than anyone else in the club and there's no one to fill your boots, they'll buy somebody who's better than you – regardless of whether you're a crowd favourite or a local lad. The club needs success to finance itself. Supporters like the local lads but they soon forget if Leicester are winning. They loved Jez Harris but then Joel arrived and Jez is forgotten about. Dunc is very knowledgeable on scrummaging. He goes through every little piece of the scrum – feet, body positions – and now we watch a video of the game every week there's no hiding. You can't say, 'No, that's not right,' because he'll say, 'Here it is on the video!'

ROWNTREE: We're now working on the little things so that, hopefully, the big picture will take care of itself.

COCKERILL: Everyone knows that when they play Leicester it's going to be a big scrummage game, so they lift themselves. Before, we were unknowns. Now they know what they're getting into, they know they're in for a tough time. So they train and get ready for it.

The blackboard and the VCR call. Just how 'ruthless' will Dwyer and Hall be? This week's video is certainly no video nasty. Cockerill can be optimistic. His ears are still ringing with the praise his coach bestowed upon him in the wake of the Bath game. Various members of the press corps placed the blame for the front-row shenanigans squarely at Cockerill's feet – or, should one say, mouth. 'Behaviour so tiresome and irritating as to make a rash appear as soothing as a massage,' wrote Alan Fraser in the *Daily Mail*; 'A spiteful, puerile display,' according to Mick Cleary in the *Daily Telegraph*. Bob Dwyer was having none of that and seized the opportunity to say so in his *Sports Mercury* column the following Saturday: 'We need more Cockerills in the game. He is a major contributor to the game, to youth development and to the Tigers' performance on the pitch. And, although at times his behaviour is a little more theatrical than I'd like, I don't want to do anything to detract from his positive, aggressive nature. Sean Fitzpatrick is a pain in the butt on the pitch but he's a great player and his abrasiveness has made him such. Like Fitzy, Richard's very abrasive, which a lot of people don't care for – but, then, they tend to be the opposition. Richard is cocky, pugnacious and a huge asset. If he goes outside the laws of the game he will be brought into line or pay the ultimate penalty. But, this is not the case. I want aggressive people to play the game fairly, with maximum impact and minimum transgression of the laws. And this is what we have got in Cockerill. I'd be happy if he could hand some of his attitude on to a few others.'

Cockerill actually took it upon himself to respond personally to a churlish piece from former England lock Paul Ackford in the *Telegraph* via the paper's letters column. 'The game has always had its characters,' he ended, 'and would be much poorer without them.' Chris Goddard also weighed in with some words in defence of a player he acknowledged was no angel yet is a credit to Leicester: 'Cockerill is one of the game's great characters. He plays with a smile and a snarl on his face. Often at the same time. And since when has winding up opponents been a hanging offence? It will be a sad day if ever the game becomes populated wholly by automatons.'

Sighs of relief all round: Dwyer is pleased with the Glasgow performance – 'And I'm not an easy taskmaster!' So, no trial by video this week. He asks for comments from the floor about the game, what went well and what went not so well. He knows what he wants to hear, of course, and such points are given predominant positions on the board, for example turnover reaction (Eric Miller), no let-up once ahead (Neil Back) and use of the ball going forward (Will Greenwood). 'Why was the forward drive better?' interjects Duncan Hall. We were tighter, is the common consensus. 'Remember what Jim Telfer has said in this respect,' adds Dwyer, 'you must be able to touch the ball with your hand as you go past.' He then commences to reinforce visually on the board by recourse to the old analogy of a magnet acting beneath iron filings laid out on a sheet of glass.

Muffled groans and murmurs of 'When do we get our pencils and paper' abound. 'The ball is the magnet and you lot are the bloody iron filings! Watch the alignment of the filings as the magnet moves. That's what you've got to do. What we do in training must be repeated on the field. We must avoid just doing it in training and then doing our own thing once we get on the field on a Saturday. Our width, depth and angles *must* be within half a metre or so of the training field.' Thereafter a lengthy discussion develops on the subject of defending against the sort of five-man lineout that had earned Glasgow a try. Dwyer concludes by drawing attention to the very deep in-goal area at the Stade Municipal du Hamaeu into which Pau habitually plant a succession of grubber kicks to great try-scoring effect.

Briefing complete, Dwyer introduces Fritz van Heerden, who had arrived just before lunch, 'after helping Western Province win the Currie Cup'. The Springbok lock's assimilation into the team is imperative since Matt Poole's ligament injury rules him out for six to eight weeks. There are fears, however, that the South African RFU, angry at losing the player, will invoke a 180-day qualification rule – a relic of the amateur age. 'Fritz's playing status should be resolved by the weekend,' announces Dwyer. 'I bloody well hope so!' implores an instantly recognisable voice. After being out of action for five weeks following a knee operation, Dean Richards ('looking as fit as a trout', according to Dwyer) sat on the bench for the Glasgow game. 'I'd be worried if someone came off with only two minutes gone,' he quipped beforehand. Needless to say, Sod's Law decreed 'someone' did come off after two minutes, namely Matt Poole. Playing almost the entire 80 minutes of the Welford Road romp against an increasingly dispirited Glasgow (even scoring a try, nearly felling the posts in the process) was a perfectly acceptable way of spending an afternoon, but a trip to Pau's Pyrenean bearpit was not exactly Deano's idea of a carefree day out in the mountains. Llanelli's visit in September had resulted in a bloodbath (for which both clubs were fined) and constituted a painful reminder of Leicester's own ill-tempered encounter with Pau last year. On that famous day, Bob Dwyer, unable to contain his elation, had paraded in front of the grandstand with fists clenched in victory, before pointing theatrically to the scoreboard. Subsequently, Pau had won 19 home matches on the trot.

'The bigger the challenge, the tougher the game and the more obstacles in our way, the more you feel your success when you win.

I can't wait to get to Pau. These are the kind of games sportsmen live for. I won't have to tell our players much they don't already know. Pau are a very strong team, their scrum destroyed Llanelli. We have put a lot of work on our scrummage to try and stop Pau playing the game their way, and we simply have to make sure our forwards are in top form and mentally ready for the match. We are expecting a volatile atmosphere after the events of last year. They will be waiting for us and instead of waiting for the match to be in full swing to reach full voice they will be ready from the moment we arrive. In such an atmosphere you have to be strong, aggressive and composed. This is an extremely difficult assignment. We must have great courage and put pressure on Pau and not let them play their game.'

The coach's optimism proved ill-founded. The gods made their presence felt even before the squad's chartered jet lifted off from East Midlands airport. First, in spite of obtaining clearance from the SARFU for van Heerden to play (and the player himself flying to Holland to collect a European Union work permit), European Rugby Cup refused permission. Dwyer was furious. 'I was assured by the RFU that Fritz was registered and eligible to play. I feel we have been entirely let down by the people who control the game because we went to a great deal of trouble to ensure that Fritz was eligible to play in the competition. We had done everything to satisfy the requirements. Peter Wheeler discussed it with a number of people and he was assured everything was okay.' Someone else not smiling was Deano, the reluctant lock! Next, international referee Clayton Thomas was forced to withdraw, to be replaced by his far less experienced countryman David Davies. Then, arriving at East Midlands airport, Michael Horak discovered he had forgotten his passport and Tim Barton-Knott, the club's travel agent, discovered there was no plane: the aircraft concerned had been held up at Gatwick and was still awaiting a slot to land. The hold-up at least enabled Horak to zoom home for his passport.

These ominous smoke signals were all too prophetic. The Tigers were never able to stamp any authority on a game which the home side won comfortably, 35–18. Just to rub salt into Dwyer's wounds, one of Pau's four tries resulted from a kick-and-chase into that cavernous in-goal area. 'I was disappointed in the game. We didn't manage to control it for a single minute. There's no doubt they were the better team, but the match didn't seem to be under anyone's control. It was an absolute farce – the referee had no idea. I wasn't sure at one stage whether the crowd or the opposition were reffing the game. The opposition cheated for four minutes in a row before the break. They broke the laws every single time the teams came together. Control of the sport is now so amateurish it's farcical. We could not even get a replacement ball when we wanted! The people running the sport don't seem to be able to enforce the regulations on the pitch. The whole culture surrounding the game is out of control.'

The scrummage, as anticipated, degenerated into an unholy mess. 'They were cheats!' declared an irate Rowntree. 'They kept standing up all the time.' Darren Garforth was at pains to explain: 'They're very good at what they do. They don't hit very well into the scrum, but when the weight comes on they almost stand up. If they concentrated on keeping their heads down, a lot of weight would come through, but they keep popping out of the top and that's no good for them and no good for us. There's not a lot you can do about it. You're relying on the ref to intervene. It's not as if they're pushing you backwards, they're pushing you up and out of the scrum.'

Cockerill was similarly unimpressed by the Pau tactics: 'They just stand you up which stops you doing what you want with your scrum. You can't wheel it and do what you want with it. The ref was a bit slack on that. Otherwise not much went on – it was a little tame. I think they learnt from last year and played more rugby. They concentrated on their game, were a lot more professional and stuck to playing rugby, which is reflected in the result.'

Thus, it was a very subdued Tigers party that departed Pau airport at 8 p.m., barely three hours after Mr Davies's final whistle. 'Well, it's only a game,' said Tim Barton-Knott to Bob Dwyer's wife, Ruth. 'No it's not!' she countered. 'It's bloody big business!' A semi-final place would have deposited a further £40,000 into the club coffers; and each finalist netted £115,000. Yes, Ruth Dwyer certainly had a point. So much for the bad news. 'The good news,' ventured her disgruntled husband, 'is that we don't have any more European matches this season!'

13

Hail Reg!

Cult figure, totem, talisman, icon, living legend, god. The Toon Army may idolise Alan Shearer and the Stretford End may have worshipped Eric Cantona but Welford Road trumps them both. Dean Richards has been a Tigers institution – usually with socks residing round his ankles, shirt flapping loose, bent over, muddied hands resting on muddied knees – ever since that far-off April day in 1982 when the 18-year-old prototype was rolled out to confront Neath at The Knoll. A flimsy refrain like 'Ooh-aah-Cantonaah' is reduced to a mere playground jingle set beside the stirring call-to-arms that is a full-throated Welford Road rendition of the 'Deeee-noooh!' anthem. To his team-mates, however, Richards is just plain old Reg. 'A few years back one of our centres, Ian Bates, came over to do some work on our house, and he spotted my efforts at building a barbecue in the garden. He nicknamed me "Reg" after one of the characters in Kenny Everett's TV show, the disaster-prone DIY expert Reg Prescott.'

Iconic status does not rest all that comfortably on the hod-carrying broad shoulders of a man whom Roald Dahl could have had in mind as he spun his tales of the Big Friendly Giant. After completing yet another Wednesday morning grind on the Oval Park weights, Richards, cradling a cup of hot coffee in one huge fist and clenching a fruit bun in the other, tries to explain in the soft voice only the teak-toughest of men seem to possess, how it feels to be feted like a living god by the Welford Road congregation.

'It's satisfying, enjoyable and faintly embarrassing at times, to hear the crowd chanting my name. When it first started to develop it was a little bit embarrassing because I'd never experienced anything like it before, but you get used to it. It's not such a great lift to you or anything like that, it's just very pleasant to know that people are aware of you. Sometimes you do feel embarrassed because it's a team sport and you get praised for doing something that has been a team effort. As for my appearance, I never thought as a 20- or 21-year-old that people would latch on to it quite as much as they did. We never had tape to tie up our socks at school, so when they fell down they stayed down. And I always wear my shirt outside my shorts for the same sort of reason – once it came out I couldn't be bothered to tuck it back in!'

Veneration, however, is not like some sort of regulation long-service medal, it does not arrive as a matter of course: it must be chiselled out by conspicuous conduct over a considerable period of time. 'When I first came to Leicester it was very difficult to get accepted, being a young boy vying for a position of someone who was already established. And not only vying for it but vying for it quite strongly. I hadn't played for the Youth, either. I just came in and said: "I want that spot and I'll have it." It takes a while to be accepted. It was very strange in those days to find people coming from any kind of distance – even though I was only coming ten to 15 miles. It took a season before people started to accept me for what I was. You have to earn respect, both on and off the field, and I worked on both sides. You can't put everything into your game and disrespect the club: equally, you can't put everything into the club and forget your playing. You try to reach a happy medium. Then it pays dividends and you go a long way. That's what happened in my case.'

'There's nothing really new to say about Dean, except to keep reiterating, because it deserves reiterating,' emphasises Peter Wheeler, 'that he's been such an important part and made such an important contribution to the club – and world rugby as well, which accentuates what he's done for the club.'

Any suspicion that Richards, or 'Deanosaurus Rex' as the *Daily Telegraph*'s Martin Johnson memorably – if somewhat cruelly (it's not a soubriquet to Richards's liking) – dubbed him, might find himself out of kilter with the more fluid, mobile style of play favoured by his new coach (not to mention more of the training with which he was never enamoured – 'It bores me: there's no competitive element') was not endorsed by Dwyer himself.

'Dean has fantastic skills, phenomenal co-ordination, great hand speed in taking the loose ball away from other people in the air or off the ground. I didn't realise he had this tremendous skill level until I got here. Added to his great knowledge of the game, it's this which makes him such a formidable competitor. It's why, I'm sure, he is able to dominate some games. He's one of those players who always seems to have the ball in his hands. I don't think there's ever been any problem for Dean to adapt to any sort of game physically. It's just whether he has had confidence in the players around him to play another sort of game. We've never had a discussion about Leicester's style of play. He knows what he's doing out there. His contribution is as an inspirational player with massive leadership qualities. I'm not big on captaincy, to be quite honest. I'm big on players showing leadership qualities. Any good team has about five or six of them. Dean has those qualities, as everyone knows. He's an impressive person.'

It is fair to say that Richards and one or two other senior players took some time to come to terms with the palace revolution of 1996 which saw Tony Russ and 'Dosser' Smith ousted in favour of the southern hemisphere connection.

'When there's so much of a change, a drastic change, it's a bit of a shock to the system and some of us rebel and some of us don't rebel. A fair number of senior players weren't sure what was going on but thought "We'll suck it and see". Tony Russ's departure was a surprise. I got on well with him for a long time and he did a very good job at the club. Dosser being pushed to one side was a big shock to the players. But a new broom . . .

'It is a great experience, though, having southern hemisphere coaches over here and being able to learn from them. Anybody who's experienced the amount of coaches I've experienced – some extremely good, some extremely bad – will tend to agree with the majority of coaches on 80 per cent of what they say, but there's always something you'll disagree about. And it doesn't matter if it's the best coach in the world or the worst coach in the world. Last season was the first season of professionalism and some slight amendments needed to be made for this year. For example, rest periods should be rest periods rather than given over to other things; they are just as valuable as actual training time. Through restructuring the training programme we've actually introduced far more rest-time but at no loss of activity. In June it was pretty intense but it's levelled off a lot now.'

Patriarchs like Richards are the unofficial, self-appointed custodians of the club's unique legacy and they are all acutely conscious of its possible erosion by the necessary demands of professionalism. 'It takes time to prove yourself as a person within the club, more so than as just a player, which I don't think is a bad thing. You prove your worth to the club, that you are dedicated, and aren't here just as a stepping-stone to somewhere else. The professional era has taken a bit of that side away from the club. Some may view it for its earning potential and not have the feeling for the club that was there before, which is a great shame. We older players still try and instil this family feeling and the sense of pride we have in the club. It's difficult when people haven't got this feeling and are at the club for just one reason. Professionalism was always going to change this sense of pride but it was a question of to what degree. It's minimalising this damage that we are trying to achieve.'

Despite his initial reservations, Richards has seen fit to adjust his oft-quoted anti-professionalism stance, although he is quick to counter any suggestion that he might regret professionalism's late arrival from the financial perspective. 'Financial security for my family would have been nice but *c'est la vie*. I wouldn't change anything at all. I would go as far as to say I'm very happy having played when I did. I wouldn't like to have been born a few years later. I'd have missed the enjoyment, for example, of playing with Peter Wheeler, Paul Dodge, Dusty Hare . . . I've never been motivated by money but, at the same time, having been given a sniff at playing professional rugby, I think the lifestyle of a professional sportsman is superb and I'd recommend it to anybody who gets the opportunity to do it.'

Even if an army of coaches, conditioners, nutritionists and dieticians are monitoring your every forkful or glassful? 'I'm completely teetotal before a game these days,' chuckles the man who was famous for a pint or two even before an international. 'We had a daughter four years ago and are expecting twins any day now, so I've really had to take a backward step! I still go and enjoy myself now and again, and do occasionally become ill-disciplined! But the nutritionists keep an eye on us now. It's all necessary, and provided everything is structured and people understand why it's being done, I feel it's all a push in the right direction. Not only does it lead to us becoming fitter, faster, stronger, but it leads to a healthier lifestyle – so there are two positives to it. Professionalism will change the way the game is enjoyed by top-level players. They will not be getting up to childish, harmless pranks, even if training every day means there's plenty of scope for practical jokes! Those days are gone and the type of humour will be different. The greatest change, I find, is the fact that you're more accountable than before. A few years ago if you weren't playing well and had a run of three games with things not going well it was easier to handle, but these days it's your career and source of income. If something's not right and I don't pull my finger out I may face a drop in my income, I may have to consider moving elsewhere or I could be sacked. Two years ago it was just a hobby.'

Richards's reward for devoting 15 years of his 'hobby' to Leicester Tigers is a testimonial season that features a variety of dinners and sporting functions, the highlight of which is a testimonial match at Welford Road on 24 November between his Invitation Fifteen and Australia's ACT Brumbies (a brumby is a wild Australian bronco), who were the beaten finalists in last May's Super 12; their coach is the former Tigers hooker Eddie Jones. Richards has twin priorities: 'I am keen to maintain the old traditions and have friends and old team-mates in my side. But I am aware of the strength of ACT – 14 of them have been included in various international squads in the last year – and the need to ensure we can match them. I'm determined it will be a real battle. I'm delighted so many players have agreed to come because it is very difficult these days with contractual obligations. It will be a full-blooded clash!'

Deano needs a crowd of 3,000 to 4,000 to break even; double that will see him do reasonably well out of the night. Ticket sales are sluggish, however, as fans are refusing to buy tickets from TicketMaster because of the £3 surcharge. A potentially embarrassing situation is averted when the club intervenes by deciding to absorb the surcharge internally; the *Mercury* also boosted hopes of a sizeable crowd by agreeing to sell tickets through its 56 news shops scattered around the county.

On the Thursday before the game the omens seem propitious: Nicky Richards gives birth to twin boys, Joseph (6lb 11oz) and William (5lb 3oz) , but the following Monday, alas, only 4,527 turn up at Welford Road. It is not only spectators who are *in absentia*. A substantial quota of the 'big' names who had agreed to participate (Humphreys, Young, Collins and Webster of Wales; Hull, Bayfield, Redman and Grayson of England; Halpin and Burke of Ireland) eventually cry off, causing Deano's decimated squad to be padded out with largely home-grown players. The match yields 109 points and includes 17 tries – four of which the Brumbies have on the board within 12 minutes of the start to race into a 26–0 lead. Deano's 'select' begin the second half trailing 38–12, but the introduction of seven fresh pairs of legs (notably the quicksilver variety belonging to Marika Vunibaka) enables it to outscore the visitors by five tries to two (two of them courtesy of Vunibaka) and claw its way back into contention with seven minutes left on the clock. The Brumbies, however, prove to be party-poopers; two further tries decide the match at 64–45.

Richards's every contribution is cheered to the echo and there is a nice touch at no-side. As that familiar trudge began taking him toward the dressing-room, Richards found his path blocked by Rory Underwood, who pushed him back toward the centre of the pitch where, looking characteristically reluctant and retiring, he took a bow and, equally characteristically, applauded the crowd for coming. The crowd's response was deafening. 'For a side which came together tonight – we didn't even train – I thought we played very well. I enjoyed it. It was a good, hard game and fair dos to the Brumbies, they played very well. I wasn't disappointed by the size of the crowd. It was a Monday night, after all. They were lovely and the support was tremendous.'

One half of the evening's celebration safely concluded, Richards moved on to the second: there was some serious wetting of babies' heads to be done. The clock had struck midnight before Deano and chums were obliged to vacate Welford Road and adjourn to alternative watering holes in the town, and it was 2.30 p.m. before Richards, under police escort from an off-duty pal, was finally reunited with his other family – the only one more precious to him than that which had just publicly thanked him for service above and beyond the call of duty.

14

Bench Fever

The November rain beats a pitter-pattering tattoo on the roof of Niall Malone's white Mazda MX5 and the windows are fast steaming over. He has pitched up early in the hope of getting his evening weight-training over and done with, but Oval Park is in darkness and his thoughts are directed toward contemplation of the limbo into which his Tigers career has seemingly become trapped.

'This is my fifth year at the club and I've always been on the fringes. It used to be that it wouldn't be that great a team and you'd be on the bench but, because they keep buying all the world-class players, it gets more and more difficult to get in. I don't hate being on the bench like some people do. I feel if you're on the bench you're part of the first-team thing, and I'd rather do that than play for the seconds. There's such a comedown from the first team – atmosphere and that – but the playing standard is not massively different, so, it's not because of playing standard that I don't like playing for the seconds, it's because all the focus is on the Firsts. The perfect scenario for me is to play for the Extras midweek and sit on the bench for the Firsts at the weekend – if I'm not in the Firsts!

'When the team's going through a really good spell of matches you realise the only chance you have of getting there is if somebody ahead of you plays badly. But it's pretty irrelevant how well you are playing in the Extras if the guy ahead of you is playing well. There's no way you'd want somebody to make a mistake or play badly to harm the team.

'During a game, if things are going badly for the team, you think, "If they put me on I could make a difference." If things are going really well, you think "I'd love to be on so I can join in with things."

'It's probably because I can cover so many positions that I'm on the bench so often. I think if you can move positions it's very difficult to get picked in any one of them. I always feel I'm third-choice centre and second-choice full-back, which means I'm not too far away from getting in the team. When Bob asked me to play in the centre last year I was amazed because I thought I was quite a good fly-half – why doesn't he think I'm any good at that? I quite enjoy playing centre now. But, the team almost picks itself these days, there are very rarely any surprise choices.

'There used to be only 15 to 17 likely to get into the Firsts and the coaches would always take you aside and give reasons if you weren't picked. They'd say things like: "We think you're playing really well at the minute but we've decided to leave you out this week and give somebody else a run." They'd usually say something that didn't fit in with the fact that you were being dropped! It's supposed to boost your confidence, but it's just flannel. It was a nice token, to know you were next in line rather than fifth or sixth in line, but I never used to like it. Now, the team is posted on the board or Bob announces it out on the pitch, he'll say: "This is number one to 15 – you go over there and everybody else grab a pad and we'll run into you."

'When Bob joined the club he said he didn't want to waste his time explaining to players why they weren't picked. He said if you're playing well you'll be picked for the first team and if you're not in the first team you should be a good enough player to realise why you're not playing well enough – you don't need me to state the obvious. A lot of people would prefer their egos to be pampered and something to be said, but I much prefer nothing to be said.'

Malone has enjoyed the honour of pulling on the emerald-green jersey of his native Ireland in three internationals and, up to the commencement of the 1997–98 season, had started 55 first-team games for the Tigers at fly-half, centre or full-back (scoring 151 points), most pertinently seven of the last nine matches of 1996–97. Malone, however, is well aware nothing is certain in the professional era, least of all a guaranteed spot in the firsts. His name was one of the nine on a transfer list allegedly circulated (denied by Bob Dwyer) to all first- and second-division clubs. Be that as it may, what can be said without fear of contradiction is that approaches from Waterloo and Wakefield were rebuffed and, reassured by Dwyer, Malone decided to stay put – only to see summer signings Michael Horak and Waisale Serevi further jeopardise his chances of regular first-team football. Of the 11 matches up to, and including, the defeat in

Pau, Malone had started only two (the Heineken European Cup away ties with Leinster and Milan), occupying the replacements bench for every one of the remaining nine – getting on three times. At the age of 25, Niall Malone found his career was at a crossroads.

Malone's frustrating predicament is mirrored by other talented fringe players likewise suffering from a nasty bout of 'bench fever' (a debilitating ailment resulting from irritating bench splinters being allowed to develop into virulent bench blisters!), whom more than one premiership club would be glad to have in its starting line-up. Scrum-half Jamie Hamilton, hooker Dorian West and centre James Overend may not have represented their countries in a full international (West and Overend have worn an England shirt at 'A' and Under-21 level respectively), but they do represent precisely the same keenly felt sense of unfulfilment. Indeed, West's recent fortunes were more frustrating than anybody's because he had sat on the bench for all 11 games and had got on just the once.

'It is frustrating,' admits Hamilton, who has started once and been on the bench for the other ten games. 'You don't really feel part of the team afterwards. Everybody will be chatting about the game and if you've not been involved you feel left out of it. On the whole I'd rather be on the bench than not, though if I was on the bench for six months without getting on, I'd rather be playing for the seconds. But I'm getting on in a fair few games so I'm not too frustrated. When I get my chance I will have to take it. Bob's not going to change his mind because I spit my dummy out. I don't like to see anyone get injured but every week I'd not be too upset if someone did get injured if it meant I could get on!'

James Overend, a 22-year-old Yorkshireman, wears his heart on his sleeve and like many Tykes tends toward plain speaking. 'It's all right when you're on the bench because you're a part of it – but you do want a lad to go down at times! The worst bit is when you're in the "twos", or when you think back to June and say: "Crikey, I've been training since June and I'm still where I was then!" You've put all this effort in and you're still where you were before. That's the most frustrating thing, I find. The team tends to be pinned on the board, and that's all you know about it, which is a bit unfortunate because you want to know where you stand, what's going on and where you go from there. That's the worst thing – man-management. I like to be told straight what the situation is, but you can't raise it with the coaches. Exercising discretion is the better path! I'd prefer more of a feedback. I missed most of last season after dislocating the same shoulder I dislocated in the Students World Cup, and I had to have it operated on. At the start of this season we all had a good crack of the whip. Basically, the first-team backs ran against the second-team backs. They mixed it around and you had a really good go. You thought you were a part of it. Then, about a month into the season, you're basically used as cannon fodder, which annoyed me to death. My skill level went down and I picked up a calf injury. I was out for a month. You think, "What am I doing here being used as a tackle bag? Am I here just to tackle somebody or to improve my rugby?" Now, I'm getting back into it and they're giving me a chance. But I don't think I'm ever going to displace "Pots" or Will. I'll live out the year and see what happens.'

Once he pulls his woollen bobble-hat down around his ears on a sharp morning, only a pipe and a can of spinach is required to transform the burly, jovial figure of Dorian West into a dead ringer for Robin Williams's stubble-chinned, jaw-jutting screen personification of the legendary Popeye. As befits a seasoned campaigner, West is more worldly-wise: 'A lot of people need talking to and reassuring that they're still in with a shout. I've been playing a long time now – I'm 30 – so I can work a lot of it out myself. I know when I'm going to get picked to play, but it's still nice to be told now and again that you're in with a chance or whatever. Last season I played quite a few games early on and I obviously got noticed: I was picked to play for England A. I don't seem to have had the opportunities this year, mainly because we've only had Saturday games and they've all been big games. They've had to pick their strongest team every week. I never think about anyone getting injured. You sit there thinking, "I hope he's going to give me a chance soon," but we're a professional club and if the team's doing well, we as individuals will do well. You never wish bad things on the team. All you do is keep trying and the better I play the better Cockers has to play – so it benefits the team. Cockers and me respect each other. Everyone has moments when things aren't going well on the pitch and sometimes things do boil over – we've come to blows a few times! But, generally, we get on all right.'

Inactivity has all manner of repercussions and Niall Malone, for one, has seen his international aspirations dealt a severe blow. Capped at the age of 21, two months after winning his Blue at Oxford in 1992, Malone became a fixture in Irish squads throughout the ensuing three seasons, yet he now finds himself surplus to any requirement. Selectors and coaches prefer to see prospective internationals being tested by regular first-team competition. Might it not be worth moving on? 'If anyone gave me an offer which I perceive to be better than I've got I might consider going. I've the same agent as John Liley and Steve Hackney, and he said, "Do you fancy going to Moseley as well?" But I'd rather stay here. These agents speak to clubs weekly and there's always a lot of talk. London Scottish came up in the summer looking for a fly-half, for instance. I can't imagine a club I'd be interested in joining, and I'm not good enough to be offered enough money to make the money more important than the place. I don't think anyone leaves here except for the money – unless it's at the end of their career and they don't fancy not getting picked. Perhaps that was what was in Rory's mind.'

One man who did leave Leicester in furtherance of international advancement was Jamie Hamilton. The scrum-half from Lincoln began his Tigers career in the now defunct Swifts (thirds) before making his first-team début at Nuneaton in December 1990. At the age of 26, however, and boasting a Scottish father, the blandishments of London Scottish in the summer of 1996 proved irresistible. Hamilton quickly discovered that the grass at the Richmond Athletic Ground is not so green as Welford Road's. 'In my last year at Leicester I got into the Scotland development squad, so that was part of the reason to go to Scottish. But it was one disaster after another. I joined along with Chris Tarbuck and when we got down there we found out they didn't have any money. We only got paid in the end because we threatened to sue them. Things didn't work out. I didn't get on with the director of rugby, John Steele, the former Northampton fly-half, for various reasons. Going to Scottish was a massive shock – the difference in facilities and the difference in overall standard of the players around you. The difference is vast and people don't realise this until they've left Leicester. With a team like the Tigers, which is so high profile, you get a lot of exposure, even if you're on the bench. You're seen by far more people. Everything's on a far bigger scale at a club like Leicester.'

To make matters worse, Hamilton tore a knee cartilage halfway through the 1996–97 season. A chat with Andy Key, and a subsequent phone call from Bob Dwyer, was all the prompting he needed to head back up the M1. Hamilton's London sabbatical, of course, coincided with the most far-reaching changes not only in the history of the game but also the Leicester club. What impact has the rapid influx of players and coaches had on Leicester's proud claim to a special sense of identity, that famed family ethos?

The scoreboard provides the headline and the skipper provides the details for Sky Sports, while the *Leicester Mercury*'s newshound Chris Goddard gets it down in black in white.

Litane Airport: 'Oz' takes custody of his errant passport from his coach. Relations between Healey and Dwyer were not always so cordial.

They who also serve: Helen Morrell, Keith Grainger and Andy Key
really do know what all those pieces of paper relate to!

Dorian West and James Overend test the Welford Road bench
for comfort.

See no evil, speak no evil, hear no evil? The ABC Club of Rowntree (top), Cockerill and Garforth torment a hapless photographer.

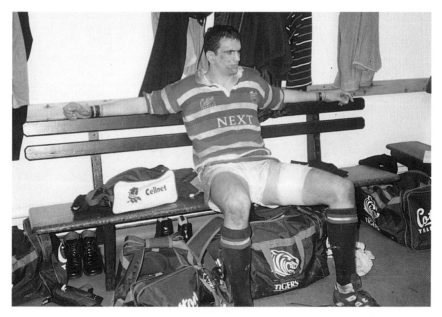

Harlequins have been vanquished: the skipper, muddied and bloodied, is left to unwind.

Derek Limmage attends to his 'lawn'.

Deano: Top Cat once more.

The men of power: the Leicester Board pose in the Barbarian Room.
Back row (L to R): Roy Jackson, Philip Smith, Peter Tom, Bob
Beason. Front row (L to R): Garry Adey, Nick Donald, David Matthews,
John Allen, David Jones, Peter Wheeler.

The pained expressions on the faces of Peter Wheeler and Dean
Richards at the press conference following Bob Dwyer's dismissal reflect
both the tricky situation and the tricky questions.

One for the West family album: Leicester's 58th England cap.

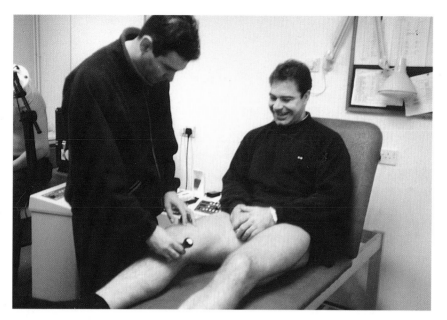

Mark Geeson administers to Matt Poole's troublesome knee, though 'Pooley' seems more concerned with protecting his dignity.

Leicester Youth 8 Gloucester Youth 6: scrum-half Chris Chapman waits as Josh Lowe (letter 'C') prepares to assist Chris Jones.

'The club has definitely changed in every respect. The family side of it has changed. We see each other every day. After a game you might have a few beers, but you just want to get home. It's still fairly tight, but not as tight as it used to be. Bob and Dunc have a totally different philosophy of how to play the game. They're also not afraid to put young guys in the side, which is a real southern hemisphere trait. The way we're trying to play the game now is more southern hemisphere based.'

Malone, Overend and West all bear witness to the enthusiasm and expertise of Dwyer and Hall. 'They're definitely very keen and committed to the game,' says West. 'They think of nothing else but rugby. When we come to training everything is planned out and we do things pretty quickly. Sometimes Bob gets carried away and keeps us out there for hours, but he's a perfectionist and highly committed, so he expects us to be. Duncan, for example, has made us aware of different techniques in the scrum and lineout – he knows a lot about everything.' As a back, Niall Malone is just the man to comment on Dwyer's input: 'I think Bob Dwyer is an amazingly astute coach and very good at expressing what he wants. The coaching used to be more heart-based rather than skill-based – "We're Leicester and we don't lose" sort of thing. The opposition wasn't so strong then and we used to win most of our games. Bob has improved a lot of players by the way he coaches. He's much more technical, and because we do so many sessions now, I wonder how we'd have kept our interest if we'd continued as before. We used to do total full contact, just bashing into each other, but we only trained twice a week and you needed to get some contact work in.'

And is Leicester's renowned *esprit de corps* alive and kicking despite all the changes and upheaval? Dorian West's first taste of the Tigers came as a flanker in the Youth, back in the mid-'80s. Limited opportunities subsequent to his first-team début in September 1988 sparked a move to Nottingham, then riding the crest of a wave. West spent five seasons at Beeston, was converted into a hooker (by former Leicester favourite Dusty Hare) and eventually assumed the captaincy. A policeman for 12 years, West is not a man to be trifled with, since he is firearm-trained and was once a member of the unit which responds to any incident involving 'shooters'. West still puts in two days a week with the police and will return full time once his professional rugby career finishes. He transferred back to Leicester for the beginning of the 1995–96 season, ultimately winning his players' tie (awarded for 20 games in the first team) some eight years after making his début. Possessed of this unique perspective, West's views merit due consideration: 'There's always been a core of players who've moved on from season to season, decade to decade, and provided valuable continuity. But Leicester's always been a "professional" club, and approached everything professionally. If you didn't want to play or keep yourself fit to a high standard, they got rid of you!'

James Overend concurs: 'The players haven't really changed that much – they've always been highly professional – and there's always been good *craic* among them. But in terms of management, things have altered a bit. Before, everyone always tended to be from Leicester. Bob and Duncan's training is very, very good and their game plans are always spot-on. It's a lot more professional than before, but whether that's because we are professional now, I don't know.'

Neither does Niall Malone see any cause for concern. With the likes of Stransky, Greenwood, Serevi and Horak arriving to threaten his livelihood, one might expect the Irishman to be actively seeking flaws in the system, but he isn't. 'I don't know if they've carefully selected who they've brought in but they all seem particularly nice people. As soon as names are mentioned in the paper everyone thinks: "God, I wonder what they're paying him?" and "Do we really need them? We're doing fine without them." But as soon as they come along, within one or two training sessions you forget they weren't always there and it doesn't matter whether they play well or not. Leicester always has recruited the best players, even without paying them. Players come for the exposure, the crowds, players don't come just for the money. That's why Leicester have been so good for year after year – because of their image, everyone wants to play for them. I always thought that highly paid players, foreigners, being brought in would cause a problem, but not at all. When we train we're squad-mates. If there were rivalries, for instance, you'd expect it to come out in fights between guys of the same position. Some guys train more roughly than others and if you get a big hit you do get a bit annoyed and may retaliate, but there's no sense scoring points off each other in training as the team is so fixed. It might be different if it changed every week. It's more likely to be a clash of personalities that causes trouble.'

The onset of the pre-Christmas series of internationals resulting from the visits of Australia, New Zealand, South Africa and Canada which creams off the top performers, bequeaths a gilt-edged opportunity for the 'bench boys' to parade their wares in the

Cheltenham & Gloucester Cup, the competition specifically designed to occupy the hiatus in the Premiership season. For their matches between 14 November and 5 December the Tigers are shorn of eight regulars (Rowntree, Cockerill, Garforth, Johnson, Miller, Back, Greenwood and Healey – who justifies Dwyer's claim by being capped as a wing) by the demands of national training camps; in addition, Horak, Lloyd and Moody are called up for Under-21 duty and, to cap it all, Martin Corry (who probably would have been in the England set-up anyway) is sidelined with a prolapsed disc in his neck. The heart is quite literally torn from the first team. For the bench boys, however, it's very much a case of seize the day. 'These four weeks,' says West, 'are a great opportunity to show you can still compete at first-team level. Perhaps when the big games come back afterwards, Bob will give us a bit more of a chance.'

For the opening match of the new competition, against Rotherham under the Welford Road floodlights on 14 November, Malone (at centre), Hamilton and West are each given their 'chance'; each score a try in the 60–19 cakewalk – which also marks the long-awaited début of Fritz van Heerden. A second elusive Tiger is spotted for the first time in the following Friday's friendly with Loughborough Students: Marika Vunibaka still has no work permit, but he is granted permission to play in non-competitive matches. 'The ironic thing is that he would already have played for Fiji and satisfied all the criteria had he not accepted an invitation from the British Barbarians,' observed an aggrieved Dwyer. 'So it is the British who have prevented him from gaining the criteria he needs to play in Britain. It doesn't make a lot of sense to me.'

Vunibaka and Serevi (now reunited with his family) have just featured prominently in the French Barbarians' 40–20 victory over South Africa and would be in tandem once more. There were no places, however, in what was a 'soft' fixture for Malone, Hamilton, Overend and West, all of whom had been involved in the Extras' far tougher clash with Bath in the Second-Fifteen championship (won 51–20) on the Tuesday. West and Overend did sit on the bench in case of emergency, but there was no need as the Students were slaughtered 71–7, Vunibaka notching a hat-trick of tries. West, Overend and Hamilton were reinstated for the final pair of Cheltenham & Gloucester ties with London Irish (won 18–16) and Exeter (won 50–20) , though Malone's contribution was limited to coming off the bench in the latter half when the 19-year-old Irish full-back Geordan Murphy (carving quite a reputation for himself since joining the club from Leinster Division One side Naas in the autumn) was injured in the thirty-eighth minute.

West expressed himself 'well pleased' with his three starts, so did Jamie Hamilton: 'The consistency of my general play was good and my running game went very well.' Overend also enjoyed his two outings: 'It's a lot easier if you're playing with good players. It's a step above what you're normally used to and it's a lot easier. I'm just waiting for my chance now. Hopefully, it'll come in the next few weeks.' Niall Malone, by contrast, was less upbeat: 'The opposition wasn't very good, so it's not as interesting playing in those sorts of games. People say it's nice to score so many points but it's not really. It's better to play against guys who are good so you have to play really well to beat them. It's nice to get a few games, but I've had no feedback at all so far. I think all the guys who've been away will slip straight back in.'

Dwyer may not have given much away to the players concerned, but their cards had been marked all right. 'I thought they all played really well. The Cheltenham & Gloucester was so valuable for us because we were able to get our reserves playing; and playing with a number of quality players. It brought them on so well. It's obvious what it's done for Dorian West's game; it's pretty obvious what a succession of games has done for Jamie Hamilton's game. Niall's game was beginning to suffer a bit, possibly through inactivity, and it has started to come back, too, because he's a very good rugby player. Jim Overend's game has come on leaps and bounds. Everything about his game has come on and, in fact, we're very impressed with him. He's gone a couple of rungs up the ladder. He missed half of last year and when he came back he'd not done the same rigorous training programme that the others had been able to do and, bearing in mind that was the first time we'd done that rigorous training programme, he was a fair bit behind. But he's really starting to impress and has definitely gone up a couple of rungs.'

When the Allied Dunbar Premiership resumed with the visit of Sale on 13 December (the first of five league games inside 18 days over the Christmas period), both Hamilton and West found themselves in the team in place of Serevi (who had broken a bone in his hand during Dean Richards's testimonial match) and Cockerill (resting a sore neck after international hostilities versus New Zealand). Overend's patience was asked to take a little more strain; his time would come. For Niall Malone, however, the tyranny of the bench beckoned for the eleventh soul-destroying occasion. Things were just not going his way – he had also pranged the Mazda.

15

Shere Khan

To those who don't know better Martin Johnson gives the distinct impression of being 6ft 6in of rolled-up barbed wire: frightening to contemplate, dangerous to approach and probably best avoided altogether. 'Johnno', it is true, does cut as daunting a figure off the park as on. He can, and does, put himself about a bit and, for sure, he will not waste two dozen words if two are sufficient. Johnson is a player in the Dean Richards mould, one who prefers to do his talking by deed on the pitch, a player who if you opened a vein would likely as not bleed red, white and green. In short, Martin Johnson is the kind of no-nonsense player, intuitive leader and what-you-see-is-what-you-get character Leicester Tigers are happy to follow toward the sound of the guns. Pussy cat he most definitely is not: Shere Khan he most indubitably is.

Far preferable, then, to lend an ear to those who know him best: his fellow Tigers. Since his début at the age of 18 versus the RAF on 14 February 1989, Johnson has packed down for the majority of his 166 appearances alongside Matt Poole, his perennial room-mate and closest friend in the club.

'He's a great room-mate – a bloke who keeps his mouth shut and doesn't snore very much! We've had great times rooming with each other and we're as relaxed with each other as you possibly could be without being members of the same family. We go back a long way, to playing against each other for Syston and Wigston at the age of 15 or 16. We played together for county teams and came up through the ranks together. We played together a few times in the Youth – not a lot because I was involved with England Colts and he was involved with England Schools. I was a year older and went up earlier: I had a season of playing Extras and the odd first-team game. I went out to Australia and he went off to New Zealand. When he came back, we linked up in the first team. We've toured together with Leicester and with England. The rest, as they say, is history.

'Martin was born and bred to be a world-class rugby player. His mum's a great athlete and his dad's always been a good sportsman at whatever he's put his hand to. The breeding's there for him to be a very good athlete. His tremendous stamina probably comes from his mum who's an ultra-distance runner – she's competed in the London Marathon and holds the world senior record. She has a resting heart-rate of just over 20. If you wanted to produce a rugby player, physically and mentally, at birth, that would be Martin.

'It's difficult to comment on him as a player without sounding sycophantic. I've played against, or with, most of the second rows England has produced in the last ten years and there's been no one to touch him. I don't know anyone who understands the game better than he does, from full-back to front row he knows the position and its role – even better than a lot of the coaches I've known. He reads the game so well, and I've never met anyone who's more passionate about actually winning and performing. Some people misconstrue that passion as aggression. He is, though, as hard as he looks! He'll never back away from anything. My girlfriend and sister both find him quite attractive – though I don't fancy him myself – so I suppose there's something else in those looks, but he has taken a kicking in his time. All the years I've been lying in the bed beside him I've never been tempted!

'People who perhaps come across as not very humorous in public are, to the people that know them, the most humorous people they know. Martin has an incredibly dry sense of humour. They say sarcasm is the lowest form of wit, but in Martin's case, he has a great ability with it and can be very amusing. He also has a great capacity for remembering jokes and quips he's come across over the years. His humour can be very Reeves and Mortimer, you don't know what he's getting at to begin with, but then find it very funny. We often call him "Statto" because on the bus we have a sports quiz book and there's nothing he can't answer. He'll bore the pants off you about American football and there was one occasion when we all had to be quiet because darts was on the TV. We even found out that he knows the periodic table for elements off by heart! There are hidden depths!'

Dean Richards has seen Johnson blossom from callow youth to

hardened campaigner. 'When Martin came back from New Zealand he hardly spoke, he was very quiet and unassuming, but he obviously had a lot of potential. One of his first games was Bath, away in the cup, and he played outstandingly well. We knew we'd got a rare talent on our hands: he'd returned a man instead of a lad. As a player he's one of the world's best two jumpers, if not the best. As a figurehead, his value to the Tigers is immense. You couldn't ask for anyone whose reputation in world rugby is as high as his. Everything he does has meaning, as opposed to someone who is just a lot of hot air. He's still learning the ropes of captaincy, but he is learning.'

Graham Rowntree speaks for everyone in the squad when he likens the present Shere Khan to his predecessor: 'He's just one of the lads, always has been. A lot of people have a lot of respect for him. He's been outstanding for a good few years now and the way he's taken on the captaincy has earned him even more. He is similar to Dean. He doesn't have to say a lot to get us going. All you have to do is follow his lead. Everyone knows he's fairly quiet. He can appear a bit miserable, but that's the way he is. He's not really that bad, it's just that if he hasn't got anything to say he won't say anything. People who know him think he's a good laugh; he can be the life and soul of the party when he's had a few. He hates losing – we all do – but him and Dean are worse than anyone. After the Welsh international last season, we went to Rory's testimonial game at Richmond the next day. Everyone was treating it as just a run-out but Johnno went round knocking seven bells out of everyone! That's the way he is.'

Duncan Hall has seen more than his fair share of world-class locks at close quarters – and has the lumps, bumps and bruises to prove it. 'I think Martin will go down as one of the greatest locks in world rugby. It's a shame they've brought in this new lifting law because it's detracted from his ability in the lineout. To his credit, he's now thinking a lot more about the game, he takes a lot of pressure off everyone, and as a leader he's a "do as I do, I'll lead the way, you follow me" kind of guy. I think you need guys you'll follow into the valley of death. He'll deserve everything he gets out of the game. He's a great asset for Leicester.'

Finally, neither Bob Dwyer nor Peter Wheeler underestimate Johnson's importance to the club in both his playing and figurehead capacities. 'We're a club that aspires to world-class standards and world-class players,' says the chief executive. 'What we also aspire to, and have done for over 100 years, is to be a local rugby club. It is important that we have people who are both world-class players and personalities, but also local guys who've been brought up to see the worth of perpetuating the values of a rugby club. You can bring world-class people in but they have to develop the feeling for the club and the community – and may well do so – but it takes some time compared to having been brought up all your life with it. Martin is a solid citizen in every sense. There's no danger of Martin's feet getting one centimetre off the ground. Like Dean, he keeps his feet firmly on the ground whatever accolades come his way.' Dwyer rates Johnson as: 'An excellent player who can get in any team in the world. He's pretty aggressive. I don't see him as a dirty player. Suggestions that he's done the odd outrageous thing I see as a long way from the truth. He's coming to terms with the captaincy role, he's growing into the role. He's a tough fellow, he shakes off injury, he plays through the pain. He's definitely a player's player, is Johnno.'

The man himself is fully aware of the club's rich heritage and the responsibilities it places on his shoulders. Captaincy of the Lions is the pinnacle of any player's career, yet, if you are a local lad who was educated in Market Harborough, played your early rugby with Wigston and came up through the Leicester Youth Fifteen, captaincy of the Tigers runs it mighty close. 'It is a big honour. The first time I did it, a few years ago when Dean didn't play, it was a big honour then, and it is now. It's a big responsibility, a long history with a lot of success in it. You've got to live up to it. The crowd is pretty expectant. Success for us is to win things, otherwise we're considered unsuccessful. It's a lot of pressure, but a nice pressure to have. It's completely different to the Lions, which is really just an eight-week job: you know how many games you've got, what your objective is – it's a short time-span. Captaincy of a club is a much bigger thing. You've got lots more day-to-day things to take care of, a lot more games and a lot longer season, an eight- to nine-month season to contend with. And Leicester, being such a high-profile club in the city and county, brings lots of additional responsibilities.'

As one might expect, Johnson's approach to the mechanics of captaincy is devoid of any frills or highbrow cod philosophies. 'If you're doing well it's a relatively easy job. The testing times are when things aren't going well, when you have to keep the guys together and keep their confidence up, or sort out any internal problems within the squad. It's no different from the job of being a professional player: if things are going well it's a great life. As captain you have to gauge the mood of the team and if that mood needs to be changed in order to do well, you've got to try and change it. Most of the time we're very keen to do well, so there's no need to be in there trying to motivate guys and psyche them up. At the moment we've got five games in two and a half weeks which will be very difficult for us all, and what we have to do is keep the confidence and morale high in case we do lose any games; then, I can keep them going. If they're too confident or complacent, you wake them up to how hard the game's going to be; if they're anxious, you try to relax them. It's getting to know the players as blokes. You have to get to play with guys for a bit to get to know them, captain or not. With guys like Wais and Fritz in the team, who are both fairly quiet sorts of blokes, it takes a while, but they've both played well so it's not really a problem. There's not been any real instances where people have had to be spoken to. When we lose, most of the time we know why, so there are no major panics. We've not lost two on the trot. If we had a run of two or three defeats it might be different. I leave the man-management to the coaches. I might pass on the fact that someone's lacking confidence or whatever, but often I find Bob's already noticed it and spoken to the player.'

Last season Johnson slogged through 48 matches for Leicester, England and the Lions, and wound up requiring surgery for a classic wear-and-tear groin condition before he was fit to commence this season's taxing schedule. 'You can feel stale mentally and tired physically. Sometimes the physical side is the easier one to fix. A couple of days light training will usually do the trick, but the mental side can be more difficult, the appetite for it, the hunger. With so many guys being away, not just South Africa, but Argentina as well, it was tough coming back straight away and being as eager as if they hadn't played. I don't think that's been our problem, really. We've been hot and cold early in the season but we've pulled off some good wins.'

If training and playing are not gruelling enough, there are the incessant demands of the media to be met. 'It all comes with the baggage. As captain you're representative of the team. There are times when you don't want to speak to people but you just have to front-up and do it. It pisses me off when the press just take the controversial angle on everything rather than take a fairer viewpoint. A lot of it is ill-informed. Austin's piece about his sex life, for instance. Most of it was tongue-in-cheek – and we take everything Austin says with a pinch of salt anyway. If his brain does turn to mush, well, that's an improvement! As for me making post-match speeches, frankly it doesn't really matter. You just get up and say what you have to say.'

Johnson is talking while he lies on one of Oval Park's massage tables enjoying a rub-down after the last training run prior to the Premiership away fixture with Richmond on 16 December. Time is precious: no point in burning daylight. Richmond are one of those clubs whose recent surge into the élite division was fuelled by the cheque-book, in their case the high-octane variety belonging to Ashley Levett, the 36-year-old Monaco-based metal trader, reputedly worth £45 million.

'While we will always regard the match against Bath in cup or league as a crossroads,' says Johnson, 'there will be no monopoly for us on the prizes. No team will dominate the Premiership this season because too many sides will be so difficult to beat, especially on their own grounds. In the past, the champions would expect to lose no more than two games – this season the title winners will probably lose twice as many. There is so much quality now because most clubs have improved their squads and possess match-winners who will find you out on a bad day.'

The rapid emergence of Richmond, Newcastle and, to a certain extent, even Saracens, as viable contenders for top domestic honours is probably the most articulate and persuasive testimony to the impact of professionalism. The natural pecking order is in a state of flux, as are the clubs themselves – Tigers not excluded. 'People say things have changed and of course they have,' says Johnson. 'Professionalism was inevitable. I know you read some letters in the *Mercury* from members saying that the club is different. I don't feel we've lost the atmosphere. If anything the team spirit has got better and better, year after year. You have to accept that players will now change clubs quicker than they used to. When I first started playing the team was virtually the same for five years. We had few changes. I think the new guys have been a breath of fresh air. You can get stale with the same people being here. You have to get used to changes of personnel. We lost a lot of players in the summer, and it can be a little disturbing to see guys who are part of the furniture leaving the club when they've still got a few years left in them. That's difficult. But the guys who've come in are all good players and have fitted in well. When Joel, for example, came in halfway through last season he was on a big contract and he had to play well and put the hard work into prove himself to the players on the field and prove he was worth his place. Getting used to new colleagues is part of being a professional player. But a lot of us have been here a long time and we all have huge pride in ourselves and the club.

'We've paid for some very experienced world-class players and if they've got thoughts on the game they're going to bring them out on the training field. The coaches are receptive to that. The guys who've been playing internationals recently, for instance, have learnt quite a bit from playing against the All Blacks this autumn. We try and bring the good things we've learnt back into the Leicester team. It will bring the best out of the guys. It's a tremendously talented team and we can get more from them. Rugby is changing all the time. Playing New Zealand this autumn was almost a different game to playing them four years ago. We've got to be able to adapt to this and come up with our variation on it that suits the players we've got at Leicester. A lot of our training is player-driven as well as coach-driven.

'Things have changed out of all recognition. Just look at Welford Road. A new stand, new clubhouse and at any time of the week you'll find a team of people working away, people streaming in and out as a result, because it's big business these days.'

Johnson's conviction that all Premiership sides will be difficult to beat on their home turf receives brutal confirmation on a bitterly cold Tuesday night at the Athletic Ground, just four days on from the resumption of the league programme after the round of autumn internationals. While the Tigers had been dismantling Sale to the tune of 55–15 the previous weekend, Richmond were visiting lowly Bristol and could only manage victory by a single point. The London club, however, had not tasted defeat on their own patch for two years and Johnson's Tigers discovered how Sale must have felt as Richmond sent them packing with a 32–15 drubbing.

It was a muted, ruminative journey back up the M1 late on Tuesday night, but at least the coming Saturday provided an opportunity to flush this reverse out of the system right away. Harlequins are the visitors on a raw, dank, marrow-chilling afternoon which sees the mist rolling across the Welford Road from the Rec. It might conceivably not be the kind of day the 'Fancy Dans' from London relish most. Someone has to pay for Tuesday!

Steam is rising from the forwards' shirts – and coming out of the ears of one or two – when they return to the dressing-room after the team's pitch warm-up. There are 20 minutes to kick-off. The room so wreaks with the pungent aroma of embrocation that it almost makes your eyes water. If adrenalin was possessed of a smell this would be it for certain. Johnson's team-talk is a model of pointed brevity. 'It's a cold, shitty day in Leicester. Let's rattle them, so eventually they'll f***ing not want to be here.' This brand of fiery invective is steak and Guinness to Garforth and Cockerill, who are already on the brink of climbing the walls. 'F***ing batter 'em up front, that's how we'll beat 'em!' thunders the prop. Never the shrinking violet, Cockers picks up the beat of the drum with some tub-thumping of his own: 'They haven't the f***ing balls for this! This is full f***ing blood and shit all the time today! Drive straight through the c***s!'

Johnson interrupts the torrent. 'Forwards, in the showers!' The skipper leads the way, back flagpole-straight, glare set in stone, brows not so much knitted as knotted, kit already sullied, eschewing any of the lock's namby-pamby protective headwear – all in all, a sight you'd definitely not want to see coming towards you in a dark alley. The skipper's words come through the shower-room door like crossbow bolts. 'We'd better be f***ing burning for this or it'll be Tuesday all over again. We're f***ing going to hurt the f***ers! It's a f***ing shitty day, just what we enjoy. It'll be fast and furious. We'd better be f***ing ready for it. Right?'

They stomp into rejoin the rest. It's 2.55 p.m., Bob Dwyer walks among them, patting some on the backside, eyeballing others as he dispenses parting advice and encouragement. 'If the forwards play like they did against Sale,' he shouts, 'Harlequins have wasted their time turning up! Aggression and enthusiasm! Let's be all over 'em! All over 'em! All over the pitch!' Two minutes to go. The whole team goes into a tight huddle, arms linked. Johnson administers his Churchillian *coup de grâce*: 'We don't lose at home. We don't lose to these f***ers! We HATE them more than most. Tunnel vision from all of us. It's US going forward, US knocking them back! RELISH IT! F***ING LOVE THE HITS! We've got the f***ing balls for the job. Let's get out there and F***ING DO IT!'

The team does go out and do it. It takes a bit of time and it is seldom pretty but the Tigers inexorably grind down the Quins' resistance in the tried, tested and trusted manner of yesteryear to win 27–3, scoring three tries. The first and third tries symbolise the nature of the contest quite perfectly: one a penalty-try awarded after Quins repeatedly drop a scrummage to avoid being bulldozed over their own line, and the other the result of a clinically executed lineout catch and drive.

Johnson was correct. Eventually Quins did not want to be at Welford Road. He brings his men through the back-slapping crowd to the inner sanctum of the dressing-room, helps himself to some of the hot, sweet tea being poured by Cliff Shephard into a row of plastic cups, and plonks himself down on a bench. The mood is one of quiet satisfaction rather than wild euphoria. The victory moves the Tigers up to third place in the Premiership behind the two unbeaten sides, Saracens and Newcastle, whom they meet inside five days after Christmas.

The skipper drains the last of his tea and stretches his arms out along the top of the bench in reflective pose, perhaps contemplating the impending announcement of his OBE in the New Year's Honours List – perhaps, though unlikely for such a down-to-earth individual: more likely, another Saturday gone, another job well done.

16

Limmage's Lawn

Derek Limmage cannot bring to mind the last occasion he enjoyed as many as three consecutive days off at any stage of the rugby season let alone over Christmas. But there is no Barbarians or Premiership fixture to preoccupy him this particular festive period: he can relax in his favourite armchair, sipping his favourite bitter and entertaining his four-year-old grandson, Zachary, as wife and daughter prepare Christmas lunch. Only one thing ever so slightly nags away at him, threatening to ruin his day. It's raining again. Limmage's thoughts briefly turn to that one and three-quarter acres of green sward between the Aylestone and Welford Roads which he has tended for the best part of 20 years. Billy Williams once had his Twickenham cabbage patch: Derek Limmage has his lawn on which he periodically allows Leicester Tigers to play a game of rugby.

Every single day for almost three weeks over the Christmas and New Year holiday the skies above Welford Road have deposited rain to some extent or another. Keeping the pitch playable in such circumstances poses the sternest test of the groundsman's art. 'Rain can be a help, though. After the game we had against Newcastle when it absolutely poured down and the pitch got rutted by all the scrummages, a bit of rain afterwards sort of levels it out and does half your work for you. We also have a machine called an outfield spiker which is worth its weight in gold. This pitch drains very well. If I can get on it two or three hours after a downpour with my spiker it'll dry up. The spiker propels itself along with spikes and a chain, but you have to walk behind it and lift it all the time. It's a bit of an animal because it tends to pull to one side, so I tend to go across the pitch rather than up and down as it's a shorter distance and the spiker won't pull so much. It takes me four and a half to five hours. I do this at least once a week, or as and when necessary. If it's raining Saturday morning I'd do it to remove surface water. The bottom of the Crumbie terrace is the worst part of the pitch, one or two metres in from the fence, where all the water collects from the terrace. It can get boggy there. I've got three strips of sand-banding down that touch-line which also helps get rid of the water pretty rapidly.

'On the whole, the pitch drains very, very well. Its foundations are unbelievable! I've seen what's underneath this pitch up to 19 feet down because we had a hole appear in it once. The sewer that runs from the old cattle market right across the centre of the pitch had collapsed and it just drained all the soil away over a period of years – so there was nothing but a crust on the top!'

It's Friday, 16 January, 24 hours before the televised premiership game against Wasps and Limmage now has another problem to contend with: the weather forecast is for overnight frost. He and his assistant, Cheryl Hill, are busy hauling huge protective sheets into position down the Crumbie touch-line. 'This is where the rain collects, if we don't cover this area it'll be as hard as rock here tomorrow. We've never lost a match to rain, one or two to frost and snow, though. We've 42 polythene sheets which we lay on the pitch, and they will keep out five degrees of frost – and if you've got a covering of grass it'll keep out six or seven because the grass acts as an air cushion between the sheet and the surface. Those sheets have paid for themselves four or five times over with the games that we've been able to play when other grounds had to cancel. The times it's snowed we've had all the people from the town come down – even little old ladies with their brooms and dustpans and brushes – to get the snow off the sheets, 400 to 500 of them.'

Derek Limmage is as short and stocky as his predecessor, Fred Cox, was long and lean. An exceedingly chirpy character never at a loss for words, his accent and patois instantly betray his Leicester pedigree: he hails from the 'navigation area' of Old Belgrave, 'near the old gasworks down Archdeacon Lane – pulled down now', and spent most of his youth on the Northfield Estate. Limmage attended Mundella School, along with future county cricketer Maurice Hallam ('so I always followed cricket a bit') and loved his football; when not turning out for Northfield United he could always be found at Filbert Street supporting 'City'. Rugby never held any fascination, that is until Jerry Day, Leicester's forthright and crusty honorary secretary from 1966 to 1982, experienced difficulty in finding a satisfactory successor to Fred Cox.

'I was a thermal-insulation and sheet-metal worker and got made redundant. I used to race pigeons in my spare time and got talking to a mate, Joe White, who was also in the pigeon game and worked for Jerry Day's chrome-plating firm. He told me there was a job going down at the Tigers as groundsman. I said to him: "I don't know anything about pitches or grounds," but Joe told me to give it a whirl because there were several people down there who'd tell me how to go on and show me the ropes. Anyway, I came down and Jerry asked me to start as soon as I could. I saw him on the Wednesday and started the following Monday. People like Robin Cowling and old Tom Berry and his sons – all farmers – helped me out and sorted any problems for me. I had some of the best people in the country to advise me because they were all farmers and knew what they were talking about. I had a good few teachers and it paid off.'

That was over 20 years ago and Limmage has gradually developed into a Tigers institution in his very own right. Indeed, so much so that he frequently found himself being thrown fully clothed into the plunge bath after notable victories and at the end of the season. Given half a chance, Limmage can get quite nostalgic and he'll happily wax lyrical about days of yore till the cows come home.

'I've been in that bath many a time, the last time three years ago, but you don't get the same rapport now, not since they started training elsewhere. I don't know half the players, I only know the first-team squad. I'd never let the Youth play on here! "That's Wembley Stadium," I used to tell them, "and when you're good enough you'll be in the first team and then you'll be able to play on it." Even Wembley's lost some of its glory nowadays because every Tom, Dick and Harry gets to play there. One day the Youth did play here, against Cardiff. They threw me in the bath afterwards but I stood up and I only got my socks and the bottoms of my trousers wet. So they threw me in again and I sat down in it and got wet from the waist down. I was still not wet enough, so they threw me in a third time and held me under! I was drowned! I've also been tied to a post and stripped naked! Everyone was taking pictures of me out of the clubhouse windows! We used to have a bit of fun!

'One day I'd taken some "slobber" from Graham Willars and I came back from collecting the buckets from the side of the pitch and saw him in the bath. So I thought: "I'll have you, Willars." I emptied the bucket and filled it with ice-cold water and poured it right over his head! Then I turned round and in the doorway was standing Graham Willars! It weren't him in the bath at all! It was Robin Cowling. So you can guess what they did to me. In the bath I went, fully clothed!

'On a Thursday I used to get in the bath on my own while everyone was training. One night I got out and all my clothes had gone! They'd put all my clothes in the middle of the pitch – and there was nine inches of snow on the ground! My shirt, trousers, socks, shoes were slap bang in the middle! Then they picked me up and stuck me outside, absolutely starkers! By the time I reached the middle I was dry! If you couldn't take the stick you were no good here. You'd got to be able to take as good as you gave. I used to look on this club as a family – and I still do. Not so much as I used to when we groomed all our own players but to me this club was family, which is why we had so much success.'

Some things at Welford Road may have changed in a major way but some have not. The one constant in Limmage's tenure is his pitch; its welfare and its preparation. Bearing in mind Welford Road's deserved reputation for being one of the best playing surfaces in the land, it comes as something of a shock to the system to hear Limmage confess to spending relatively little time on it during the course of a normal working week. 'I'm afraid the pitch gets the least attention to be quite honest. On Monday I've got all the kit to sort out, empty the skips, turn the shirts and socks the right way round for the laundry; all the baths and changing-rooms to scrub. That takes most of the day, even though I've got a girl cleaner who does the main changing-rooms and the corridors. Tuesday and Wednesday it's a matter of cleaning up all the stands – after a first-team match the amount of rubbish is unbelievable! It can take you two or three days to go around the three stands cleaning up. I like to get onto the pitch by Thursday, or a Wednesday if I can. I'll cut the grass or cut the lines in. Of course, you've got to work with nature all the time. If it's going to be a fine day Wednesday and going to rain on Thursday, you rearrange your scheme and go on the pitch Wednesday and clean on Thursday. You've got to work with the weather all the time. You can't really say you'll do this Monday or that Tuesday because it can completely alter. And then there's midweek games that throw your schedule out. You can never sit down and say you'll do this. When they used to train here two nights a week it used to be even more hectic! There's nothing here that's routine, every day's different. You never get bored, there's always something to do down here.'

Professional rugby not only demands more of its players but also its pitches, a prospect guaranteed to cloud Limmage's customary sunny disposition. 'I do worry about double-headers and so on. The RFU sent round a circular saying the standard of pitches in this country was terrible and they wanted the standard raised – good-quality pitches for good-quality games. They recommended 20–25 games on a pitch a year. I also went to a seminar where top men talked about wear and tear, and they were of the same opinion. They've got no chance here! We had nine games on this pitch in three weeks before it was even September!

'When you have a lot of early season games like that I leave the grass a little longer to save it: it would be two to three inches normally. Years ago when I first arrived the type of grass was different, it was a sort of meadow grass that was good for cattle, very, very broadleaf grass, like a bullrush type of thing. Over the years new grass seeds have come out and the surface is far better. We used to seed in the first weekend in May, now that's gone by the board because they're still playing! I use 60–80 tons of top dressing and then 6 cwt of seed. Afterwards, you spike 16 inches into the ground, which vibrates and breaks up all the impaction to promote good depth of root growth.'

Saturday morning dawns bright and fair. It's around 11 a.m. when Limmage drives through the gates in his Ford Escort Estate (sponsored by Eurodollar) anxious to lift those sheets and check that they have done their job properly. All is well: 'I don't have to open the gates any more as the office and shop are open at 9 a.m. I just try to get my bits and pieces done while it's still quiet. Put the kit out; put the flags out; put the club flag up; cut the oranges up; get the cups and teapots ready; fill the urn; get the sand ready for goalkicks. They're not hard jobs, just silly little jobs. I prepare five balls for a match. The goalkickers tend to come in and inspect them. I blow them up by 'feel', I haven't got a gauge, I just press the ends in, like you do to a melon. I've never had any complaints. It's only during the last few years that I've been able to watch the match. Previously I had to be five yards from the heat- and smoke-detector alarms in case they went off. There are three big panels of alarms outside the door of my room in the Crumbie Stand and I just had to sit there. Now, we've got this safety control tower on the ground and they've all been moved there. I stand on the steps in "N" Block and pop my head over the wall. I've still got to be available in case anyone gets hurt and they need me to let them into the medical room or call for an ambulance. I can't just wander off.'

By the time the day's *dramatis personae* assemble an hour or so before the 2 p.m. kick-off, Limmage is back in his den in the bowels of the Crumbie stand brewing tea with which to warm the cockles of the match officials: referee Steve Lander and his two touch judges, Steve Savage and Brian Suttle. Before the pre-Christmas game with Harlequins Messrs Pearson, Morrison and Reay were plied with sherry, sausage-rolls and mince pies! Every little helps!

Since that victory against Quins on 20 December in the second of their five-match Yuletide challenge, the Tigers had blown hot and cold. 'If we can get through without dropping one, we will have done very, very well,' Bob Dwyer said at the outset, prior to the Sale fixture. In the event, not one but two were dropped: Richmond before Christmas and Newcastle on 30 December. The game that, on paper, appeared the likeliest defeat – away to a Saracens side that had not suffered a home defeat since April – resulted in a 22–21 win thanks to a 30-metre drop-goal from Joel Stransky in the last minute of normal time.

The loss to Newcastle definitely rankled. One could make excuses (of sorts) for the setback at the Richmond Athletic Ground, but losing 25–19 to the Falcons really did stick in the craw. First, and foremost, the game was played under the Welford Road floodlights; secondly, Tigers had chances to win; and thirdly, some of those chances were torpedoed by refereeing decisions which so got up Bob Dwyer's nose that his post-match comments led to accusations in the press of whingeing and sour grapes. Up on Tyneside the local paper stated: 'There is nothing like a good loser and Bob Dwyer is nothing like a good loser!' Even the *Mercury* received letters calling Dwyer's attitude to book.

True to form, Dwyer was unrepentant. He admitted his side had let themselves down by making 'enough mistakes to lose two games' and that Newcastle had defended superbly and deserved to win but . . . several things bugged him about Brian Campsall's performance with the whistle. 'We were over the Newcastle line three times in the dying minutes and I don't understand why he didn't award us a try on the last occasion. He did a 360° circumnavigation of the maul for Newcastle's try, yet he immediately decided we had been held up. Neil Back said he was a metre over the line with the ball on the ground. It was a fairly important try, to the left of the posts with Joel attempting the conversion for a one-point lead. The try that Pat Lam scored when he charged down Joel's kick should never have been allowed – if you look at the video you can see Lam standing at least three yards offside. Apart from the tries, I had other beefs. In the opening minutes, Joel was hit heavily by a late tackle, which went unnoticed by the touch-judges and the referee. In the next five minutes Joel missed two relatively easy penalties which begs the question, was the illegal play a factor in unsettling him? I'm certain that his position as a key points scorer was a determining factor in that late tackle. One of our strong weapons in wet conditions is the driving maul to force fringing forwards into the pack to defend – thereby leaving space for our backs. Every single driving maul from a lineout was defended by the illegal tactic of collapsing it, but not one penalty resulted. It also allowed the fringing forwards to stay out and defend against our backs. Brian Campsall's failure to pick this up had a significant effect on the outcome. The win was a four-pointer for Newcastle. Instead of being two points closer to the leaders, we are two points further away. Come May this result could mean the difference between winners and also-rans. We're getting situations now where people's livelihoods are being put in jeopardy by the appointment of sub-standard officials and the arbitrary application of the laws. To me, the answer is easy: do what the law book says, don't do anything it doesn't say – then we'll all know where we are. Don't hide behind the word "interpretation", because the laws are written in English and we who speak English can understand them! Then, support the referee by allowing communication with touch-judges, appointing in-goal referees and utilising video replays whenever possible. Give the laws, the players and the game a chance!'

Dwyer really put the cat among the pigeons by subsequently airing all these grievances, and more beside (including the dreaded 'g' word, gamesmanship), in a *Sunday Times* article entitled, 'Newcastle push rules to the limit'. The response from Leicester's journalistic *bête noire*, the *Daily Telegraph*'s Paul Ackford, was swift and par for the course: 'Dwyer presses sour grapes . . . you can only take the moral high ground if you have nothing to hide and Dwyer's and Leicester's cupboards are as full of skeletons as those at any other top-class, competitive rugby outfit.' Ackford had been presented with a bone and he shook it for all he was worth.

Dwyer was having none of it. 'I could take the soft option and say nothing, but that's never been my way. Whether we win or lose, if someone seeks my views it's them he wants, not some watered-down version influenced by the probable reaction of other people. I gave full praise to Newcastle for their tactics and their implementation, but my comment that they practise tactics which could be described as "gamesmanship" stands. I totally reject any suggestion that any teams coached by me are coached to break the laws. And Paul Ackford didn't even see the game!'

Thus, a lot was at stake when Wasps came a-calling on 17 January. 'It's a must-win game for us,' admitted the coach. 'We must win at home, nothing else will do. The top two teams (Newcastle and Saracens) are sneaking away with the Premiership. They have points in the bank and if they maintain their form, one of them will become champions.' The Londoners' defence of the championship they had won so impressively last season had already come unstuck: only three wins from eight games compared to the Tigers' five. They were enduring a terrible run of injuries to key personnel and were now, on match day itself, to suffer the unkindest cut of all with the defection of inspirational captain Lawrence Dallaglio, who was nursing a bruised shoulder.

Not that Bob Dwyer's own Saturday morning started smoothly. 'Four players phoned in sick and I had to phone the second-team bus on the motorway, which was on its way to Wasps, to get Paul Gustard off the vehicle at a service station and into a cab back to Leicester. Joel reported in with blood poisoning, Eric Miller had a virus and both Martin Corry and Backy had a back problem.' Only Miller failed to make the starting line-up, however. Corry, playing out of his skin, lasted 60 minutes before giving way to Gustard; Neil Back ran and ran and ran for the full 80; and Stransky rattled up 25 points as Tigers walloped Wasps (flattered by two late tries) 45–21. The only blot on an otherwise marvellous afternoon's entertainment for the sell-out crowd was the sight of Richard Cockerill being stretchered off in the sixty-fifth minute with damage to his left knee – the indomitable hooker's first injury in six years. Anyone who doubts the affection in which Cockerill is held by the Welford Road regulars should have heard the reception the stricken hooker got on leaving the field.

Derek Limmage's day is not done, however. While mud-caked combatants wallow contentedly (well, the victors at least) in their bath, Limmage sets off through the gathering gloom on his post-match rounds. 'Besides the dressing-rooms, I've got 23 toilets to lock up! It'll be a good hour and a half before I can say "That'll do", and walk across to the clubhouse for a pint of beer and a cob. Some of our players you just can't get out of the bath!' Fortunately for Limmage, the players, despite being in the good spirits invariably associated with a crushing victory over sworn enemies, stop short of perpetrating those extreme high jinks of yesteryear.

To sighs of relief (or was it disappointment) from all Welford Road womenfolk, there are no reported sightings of a stark-naked Limmage tied to a goalpost.

17

Pooley's Fight for Fitness

Matt Poole has had quite a fight on his hands. It's now 11 weeks since he was forced to leave the field in the second minute of the Heineken European Cup match with Glasgow: 11 weeks of mounting frustration. Up in the Crumbie Stand that fateful opening day of November sat Fritz van Heerden, freshly arrived from South Africa, taking the opportunity of watching his new colleagues for the very first time. The Springbok lock, possessor of 13 caps, is the man Bob Dwyer has effectively signed to replace the 28-year-old Poole, who has been Martin Johnson's regular second-row partner for six seasons solid, and a first-choice for eight. Poole's painful predicament embellishes a scenario already becoming increasingly evident: the home-grown product – Roundhill College, Syston, Leicester Youth – giving way to the exotic – Roodeport School, Stellenbosch University, Western Province. Unable even to defend his jersey out on the pitch, 'Pooley' can do nothing other than twiddle his thumbs as he vegetates on one of Mark Geeson's treatment tables day after an infuriating day.

'Initially, the shock of signing someone of that quality takes a bit of getting over. Fritz is a very, very good player and I was under no illusions when Bob signed him. It's comforting for me to say it, but it's a squad game now. With all respect to the other lads in the club, Martin and I were the only second-rows and no one was pushing us. We couldn't have carried on playing 40-odd games a season. Dean's made no secret of the fact that he doesn't like playing second-row – in my opinion he's still got a lot to offer in the back row. Bob had to look for another second row and, in this era, if the money's available, there's no point in signing someone to fill in. It's better to sign someone with a long-term future with the club and someone with an outstanding record. Bob was lucky to get someone like Fritz. Putting my club hat on, he was a very good buy because he can play in the second row or back row. I remember playing for England on tour in South Africa in a midweek game against South Africa A and he was in the back row, and he subsequently got picked for the Test in the back row. Fritz offers the club an awful lot, and Bob and Dunc have said if I play as well as I can, there's no reason why I can't force him into playing in the back row. Even if that doesn't work out, it's a long season and injuries do occur, there's a lot of games to cram in and more than enough games to keep me happy on a rota basis or sitting on the bench. To be successful in this day and age, the club needs two or three quality players for every position. You can't expect to play every game. Look at soccer where millions of pounds sit on the bench – and our game is far more physical, giving more injuries. So you need stronger squads. Even Martin, who's in the top two or three locks in the world, may sit on the bench for a rest. You have to be positive about it. There's no reason to lose sleep over it. In a club like Leicester you can't expect to be number-one choice for ever. The saving grace is they've signed a guy who you rate as a player yourself, and is a thoroughly nice guy as well.

'The injury came in the first game Fritz saw. We had a laugh about it afterwards. He said to me: "You must have been trying too hard!" I got it straight from the kick-off, I just clattered into the guy, and having had a similar injury in both knees last year I knew immediately what I'd done. I tried to persevere, but it wasn't having it. It transpired that I'd torn the medial ligament in my right knee. During the whole course of this season I'd been plagued with torn abductor muscles, the groin muscles, and knowing it was going to be a minimum of six weeks to get the knee right, and the groin was causing me considerable discomfort – affecting the way I was training – I discussed things with the medical staff and decided to have that operated on as well. It turned out to be a more involved operation than first thought, as it was a worse tear than they thought and I'd torn my lower abdominal muscles as well. I had several layers of gauze inserted to strengthen them. That has taken considerably longer to put itself right than anticipated.

'Within 24 hours of the operation you have to walk for 20 minutes, which is the stipulation for leaving hospital. It was carried out at the Princess Grace in London by Gerry Gilmour of Harley Street. The groin operation is actually named after him. He's very specialised in this area and has done the same operation on Shearer, Asprilla and Johnno. Gilmour stresses six weeks as the ideal recovery period – Shearer made it in four – depending on the patient and the severity of the problem, it could be six months. He gives you a rehab programme to get you back in six weeks. After the first day, for two weeks you walk four times a day for 20 minutes. Then, you gradually progress into jogging the same amount of time. Then into more pace, twisting and turning, sit-ups (mild ones in my case because of the abdominal muscles). No weight-training in the first three weeks. In fact, I'm still not up to doing full weight-training. You must lower the weights and increase the reps rather than overload anything; I'd swim in the later stages, too. My problem was that some of the conditioning I should have been doing for the groin I wasn't capable of doing because of the knee. As soon as I started running again the knee started to swell up and I had to be very careful. I tend not to listen to everything I'm told and I do tend to overdo things – I've had one or two slapped wrists recently! The knee is the one that's really held me back. I had hoped to be available straight after Christmas, but when you come back you've got to be fit enough to come back at first-team level. The knee is just rest and recuperation, really. Last year I was out for six weeks. This tear is in a different spot, but it's probably an ongoing injury. The two injuries are healing at about the same time. It didn't help that the groin operation was on the left and the knee was on the right because as it was tender I over-compensated on my right, which probably delayed the recovery in the knee. It was well worth having the groin operation because the surgeon said there was no way I'd have finished the season without it. I'd got to the stage where I was only able to train in the sessions I was having to take part in to play. I was losing fitness and eventually I'd not have been fit enough to play at first-team level.

'I have a tendency to put weight on! My fighting weight would be about 18½ stones, ideal for a fit 21-year-old! But I've been known to finish a season at 20½–21 stones due to lay-offs. For some reason, awareness of diet on my part perhaps, and the calorie-burning from all the walking, I've actually lost almost two stones in weight – much to the amusement of the lads. It's made me feel a helluva lot healthier. I've obviously lost a bit of strength but I feel much sharper. I've still got muscle tone but I've reduced my bulk due to the weights programme I've been forced to do. I wish I'd taken bets on how much weight I was going to put on because I'd have made a fortune! I really watched my diet because I've only got to look at a plate of "bad" food and I'll put some weight on – particularly with the injury being around Christmas! It was a matter of willpower and very good advice from the club staff.

'The knees will probably always be a threat, but sportsmen only think in the short term and I want to play for another two or three years. It's up to the body! The mind is willing to go on till it's 60 but the body, unfortunately, has a mind of its own and does what it wants!'

The man shouldered with the burden of ensuring that every player's body is in a fit shape to respond to a 'willing' mind is club physiotherapist Mark Geeson, who heads a team of four part-timers and is further supported by the club's consultant physicians, Mike Allen and David Finlay.

'There is a whole battery of people behind the scenes. The support staff work day in, day out, week in, week out, month in, month out, aiming to provide the players with the back-up in order to perform for 80 minutes on a Saturday afternoon.' The size and cost of this massive undertaking is apparent from the amount of money Geeson spends per month on tape, bandage and strapping, those most basic of items found in any rugby player's kit-bag: £2,000! 'We put out four teams – 60 players – every Saturday. Then there's daily training, sometimes twice a day, when ankles, for example, may have to be taped and retaped. All in all, we are dealing with between 100 and 120 players a week.'

When it comes to hands-on experience in the footballing sphere (quite literally in this instance), the 39-year-old Geeson can boast a full set: association football with Kettering, Grimsby and Leicester City; American gridiron with Leicester Panthers; and, since 1993, the William Webb Ellis variety with the Tigers. 'The skill level in rugby is not so high as in soccer and rugby players don't recover anywhere near as quickly as soccer players do because of the bump and grind and stamina-sapping nature of the game, especially for the forwards. American footballers have protection, of course, and are not on the pitch so long as rugby players. To a degree I was headhunted. I worked at the Leicester Royal Infirmary where John Ford, then the club physio, was my boss. One summer there was a South African tour, John Ford was going to New Zealand with England Colts and there were some players left behind and they needed a physio to look after them. I was asked and it took off from there. I did one year at the Royal part-time and part-time here but, as soon as things went professional, I began to spend more time down here. It's seven days a week now, even down to an hour or two on Sunday morning. It can get quite pressurised.'

Geeson is inured to the sight of semi-clad athletes but, in addition, he, more than anyone else on the Tigers staff, is the person also most likely to see the players stripped bare emotionally. His treatment room at Oval Park not only serves as a hotbed for gossip, but also a wonderfully convenient psychiatric out-patients clinic for distressed rugby players. 'If you took 50 or 60 young blokes out of a factory you would come across exactly the same sort of characters that we're dealing with, from one end of the spectrum to the other, from the Dean Richards to the Austin Healeys. We just have to try to find the key to them all and do what's necessary, within professional parameters, to enable them to perform. The frequency with which Austin visits the treatment room, for example, is very much inversely proportional to how well he's doing in games – the better he's doing, the more we see of him. When he's under pressure and feels he needs to be performing he tends to get on with it. There are those on the medical team that feel he's not such a bad egg after all; there are two or three of the doctors who are convinced he's a very, very insecure person. And if you have this insecurity and lack of maturity you look for sympathy and go to the medical team. If you are attention-seeking – which Austin quite patently is at times – then the medical personnel are a nice sounding-board.

'Some players are particularly fussy about their well-being; some will play with injury; some are worried by injury and are unable to perform; some like treatment more than others; some like a little bit of fuss made of them and there are others you never ever see in the treatment room unless they have a major problem. It's down to mental approach.

'A lot of it is down to what a player is prepared to do. Everyone knows who tends to be in the treatment room most often: Craig, Will – they're nearly all backs. The stoics are Darren Garforth, Dean Richards, Martin Johnson, Neil Back, James Overend, Lewis Moody – it tends to be the forwards that only trouble you when it's a major problem. Some players you push and some you hold back because they're too keen for their own good sometimes. But with fitness levels and demands getting higher, players are less able to get away with playing at anything less than 100 per cent fitness than they were five or six years ago. The natural rate at which tissues heal is fairly set in stone and if ultrasound could really improve the rates of healing we'd be using it on major surgery and major trauma, not sprained ankles. Having said that, Neil Back, for example, does seem to heal incredibly quickly: his stitches are ready to come out in three to five days compared to six to eight. A lot of the increased physio-therapeutic input is as much due to the increased training regimes as what happens in the 80 minutes on Saturday, for example, the increase in injury linked to weight-training. There are more over-use injuries like Achilles tendonitis, for example, and some players have the neck, hip, ankle and knee joints of someone 20 to 30 years older.'

Geeson is speaking whilst alternately organising some heat for Poole's knee and an ice-filled boot for Stuart Potter, who has just this minute turned his ankle over in training. Both men, and they are the first to agree, have suffered more than their fair share of setbacks. Are there such things as injury-prone players? Geeson thinks not. 'What tends to happen is someone picks up an injury and in an attempt to rehabilitate quicker than they otherwise would, starts exercising in a way that's not natural for them. The classic is the guy that has the calf strain. We push them along as quickly as we possibly can to get them going again but, because their gait isn't quite normal, they put strain on other joints and muscles and limbs and they develop a secondary problem. If you're relatively careful with your rehab it shouldn't happen. Luck plays a part. Matt had two knee-ligament injuries last season on completely opposite sides, completely unrelated. He spent six weeks out with the left, came back and did his right. There is pressure sometimes to get a player fit. Common-sense instances really. With Will Greenwood out and Stuart going over on his ankle like this, Bob will say, "We really need Pots to be fit for Saturday." We do get pressure from the players, who want to be fit all the time. It's one of the inherent problems of paying appearance money and win bonuses: players are prepared, in certain circumstances, to mask an injury or not tell you about it. It's the other end of the spectrum to players who tend to be hypochondriacs.'

When a player is faced with as lengthy a period out of the game as Matt Poole, it helps enormously if he can approach the ordeal with an equable state of mind. Pooley is that sort of laid-back individual. Despite his near perfect proportions – 6ft 6in and 19st 6lb – for the job, Poole's detractors have frequently castigated him for being just as unflappable on the field. Unlike his bosom buddy, Martin Johnson, he does not look mean enough, let alone play mean enough, to thrive in the hatchet-man world that is the modern-day international second row. Is he the Joe Bugner of the rugby field, possessed of all the weaponry but reluctant to deploy it?

'I have been criticised over the years by coaches and the press for not being nasty enough, but it's a criticism I don't tend to take on board too much. I'm aggressive enough for what's required. The fact that I don't go round slapping players or banging their heads together doesn't add or detract from my game. These days the second row is meant to get around the field and "do the dog", as they say, the rough stuff and the powerhouse stuff. I'm pretty athletic for a second-row and I like to think that quality can be used far more for the team than me going round the field clogging opponents and copping yellow cards every two minutes. If I was a coach dealing with someone like me I'd try to look at the positive aspects an individual has in other areas. I'm probably a frustrated back! If I had a different build I'd be far happier playing in the backs than the forwards. Perhaps that comes across in the way that I've played. Up to the last couple of years I was playing to enjoy myself and played in the style I enjoyed. In my early years I was asked to pop up in the backs, for example. Perhaps I carried that on longer than I should. Possibly, that was selfish of me in certain respects if it didn't suit the team or the coaches. Perhaps my nickname says it all: "GQ", after the magazine *Gentleman's Quarterly*. One of the first things Fritz said to me was, "Pooley, you've got to be the best-dressed second-row I've ever seen!" I'm probably more interested in business. Rugby has to be the be-all and end-all these days, and that's an outlook I've not had. It's pretty late to change now.'

Had Poole 'packed a punch' commensurate with his physique it's more than probable that he and Johnson would have replicated their club partnership in the international arena. Poole holds England caps at Colts and Under-21 levels but has never featured in anything higher – not even the A side – in spite of twice touring with the senior side, to Argentina (1990) and South Africa (1994). 'I had two bites of the cherry and pretty much messed both of them up. If you're given chances like that and you don't take them, it takes a long while for the selectors to forgive and forget and bring you back into the fold. The first tour I was quite cocky, I suppose, as I'd gone straight from Under-21 to England. It was soon knocked out of me but it didn't start me off on a very good footing. Then I had a very bad case of the shits before one game but, because I didn't want to let anyone down and I wanted to prove myself, I went ahead and played – and had a shocker. In hindsight I should have dropped out. I learnt the lesson from that: you never play injured or ill because you are judged on that performance and no excuses are accepted by coaches and management. You took the shirt so you get judged by that performance. In South Africa I didn't use the lessons I'd learnt from Argentina. I was probably too easy-going and didn't force the issue. I tended to thank my lucky stars I was there and just enjoyed myself. I didn't push myself enough to get a Test spot. I didn't do my job as effectively as I could have done. It's such a disappointing aspect of my career. I just try to learn from those tours, but forget about them. They were two extremely tough tours and I'd had no England involvement beforehand. It's difficult to instantly perform on tours like that. I'd like to have been involved slightly before, or immediately after, just to show that when you're not in the pressure situation of touring I was capable of learning from them. But I never was subsequently involved.'

Disappointment on the international front, however, cannot dim Poole's joyful catalogue of memories on the club front. 'For every low point there are ten high points. The best memories have always been the bus on the way home from a Cup victory or something like that: the front five having a beer and gradually getting pissed. We really need to cling on to as much as we can of the old game, the tradition of amateurism and all the great times that brought about. The majority of the current crop of players know more of that era than the professional era and it's important that we pass that on to the younger guys coming through and they continue to enjoy the game as much as we did when it was amateur.

'The club has changed and progressed all the ten years I've been here, but it has changed out of sight in the last two compared to the previous eight. I think Leicester can cope with the pace of recent change, but it worries me whether the rest of the game can. We're in an outstanding position here – in finance, coaches, players, facilities and support staff – and I don't think any other team is close. You hear of salary cheques bouncing and all sorts of horrendous stories. Much as we're getting it right at Leicester we're still very much reliant on the opposition getting it right as well, and that's a worrying factor. These club backers have made money by being very, very good businessmen. At the end of the day they make business decisions and at the moment they're throwing good money after bad. Eventually they are going to call it a day. We've not got that problem. Everyone at Leicester has the club at heart and it's put us in a very healthy state.

'I'd like a role in the business and commercial aspect of the club when I cease playing. That would be fantastic for me. I'd like to go out at the top as a player. I've had enough windy, wet nights as a player not to want to be a coach! I'd prefer to go back to the business world; either the family firm – G&B Office Supplies – or the computer-related businesses I've set up. If I put the same amount of effort into them as I have rugby, hopefully they'll be successful.'

The Matt Pooles of rugby may well become a dying breed as the bright new dawn that is the professional game heralds the arrival of players who know nothing other than rugby and, more alarmingly, have no ready-made alternative career awaiting them when their particular sun eventually sinks below the horizon. 'We are starting to see the first professional rugby players coming through,' says Mark Geeson. 'People like Eric Miller, Austin Healey and Leon Lloyd have never really worked for a living. The money being thrown at them is quite considerable and they, of course, only see it in the short term. They don't see the long-term drawbacks. Players have always just rolled up the sleeves, gritted their teeth and got on with it. I see a lot of problems round the corner for those playing at the top level. They're going to get burnt out, they're not going to last much longer than five years. They are playing all winter long for their clubs and in the Five Nations – and then come the summer months when they might be thinking they can go away and have a break, they're asked to go away on tour. Martin Johnson came straight back from the Lions tour and had surgery on his groin and still made the start of the season. He got little in the way of a break. It's no good in the short term and long term one wonders what he will be like at the age of 40 to 45 with the battering and surgery he's had. There's going to be a classic conflict of interest between what international management sees as being ideal for a player and what we at Leicester see as ideal.'

Matt Poole's personal ordeal finally ends on 24 January when he makes his comeback in an Extras game against Leeds at Welford Road. 'It was great to be back. It's about five years since I played in the Extras and it's totally different. These guys were young and keen, and I didn't know any of their names apart from the odd one. Fortunately the game was at Welford Road, which was a welcome bonus. We won quite convincingly by about 40 points. I got over twice, but some little so-and-so managed to get under me and stopped me grounding it! The score and the opposition were pretty irrelevant to me. It was just about getting out and surviving a game and feeling pretty good throughout. The two problems were quite sore but I expected that – if I'd waited till all the soreness had gone completely I'd not get a game in this season. It was a quite enjoyable pain to tell the truth! Waking up bruised and battered on Sunday morning on this particular occasion was quite a relief. Surprisingly, my general fitness was better than I thought, not that you can really judge because it was a second-team game against weaker opposition. Had it been a first-team game I'd have been really shagged! This was a reasonable introduction; and the psychological barrier with the injury has been overcome. There are sterner tests to come.'

That was the good news. The bad news was Fritz van Heerden, after a sticky start, had begun firing on all cylinders, and to such effect that Bob Dwyer was given to exclaim: 'I knew he was good but I didn't think he was that good! He's as good as Johnno. There can't be too many better second-row pairings in the world at any level below Test level than Martin and Fritz.'

Looks like Pooley has another fight on his hands.

18

A Litter of Cubs

Saturday, 15 April 1972, was a milestone in the annals of Leicester Football Club; it was a historic day with far-reaching implications. It was the day Leicester Youth took the field for the first occasion. Hammering Nottingham 78–9 was deemed a promising start, but the success or failure of the enterprise could only ever be gauged by the resultant flow of players into the senior squad. Within three years of that initial outing five products of the Youth, in particular centre Paul Dodge and scrum-half Steve Kenney (still only 17 and just 19 respectively), began to make a name for themselves in the first team; within six years the Youth produced its first full international in the guise of Dodge. Since then the conveyor-belt has never ceased. Today, some 15 members of Bob Dwyer's senior squad have graduated from the Youth, including Martin Johnson, Matt Poole, Graham Rowntree, Jamie Hamilton and, most recently, Leon Lloyd and Lewis Moody.

The current Youth coach is none other than Paul Dodge himself, one-time England captain and British Lion, he of the silken hands and raking left-foot diagonal. After retiring in 1993, Dodge coached the club's now-defunct Under-21 side and assisted Dosser Smith with the firsts until bringing his Tigers career full circle by turning his attention to the Youth last season. 'We get players from the age of 16 up to 19 and hopefully pass them through to the Development Fifteen and onwards. We've still got strong links in the county, and the local club coaches approach us to look at any talented youngsters. In addition, Dusty Hare watches a lot of school games in the area. We do still rely on local lads. Bob Dwyer and I share the view that the Youth should be developing players to move up to the next level as quickly as the individual is capable. If you're good enough you should be in the Extras or Firsts – as Lewis Moody was last season, aged 18.'

Managing the Youth's affairs is their former coach (and first-team prop) Ray Needham. Twenty-five years in Leicester have done nothing to moderate Needham's flat West Riding vowels, although he has at least abandoned his infamous 'Rizla and baccy roll-ups' in favour of a more managerial-style cigar. 'At the start of the season we had something like 50 players training. After trials and the first few games we've settled on a squad of 28 who play week in and week out. We have several players, who just train on a Tuesday, that we're looking at for next season. Everyone is involved on a regular basis, though sometimes we pick our strongest side – we look at the strength or weakness of the opposition. You might see seven or eight changes from one week to the next. Results really aren't the be-all and end-all. Last year we had a far better side and lost 12 games. We're well over halfway through this season and have lost only four. The difference is last year we'd got one or two better individuals who were pushed up to Development and Extras. We're here to produce players for the senior squad. If they're good enough they go up, they don't stay with us just so we can win games. If we went through a season unbeaten and scored 1,000 points and conceded only 100 it would be a poor season because it meant we hadn't the players to push into a higher team.'

The third member of the triumvirate which guides the Youth is the wiry figure of Pete Lowe. The Londoner represents a departure from the norm. He was never on the Tigers playing roster and, indeed, never held any pretensions as a player during his stints with the likes of Barking and Lutterworth. 'I was a forward who played everywhere, social rugby really. I don't think top-quality players always make top-quality coaches. I know a lot of top senior players who are terrible coaches.' Coaching was Lowe's metier. He cut his teeth with local junior club Vipers by taking their Colts side to the county title twice in three seasons, and was subsequently invited down to Welford Road by Tony Russ. Dodge and Lowe dovetail nicely and each man has the unswerving respect and loyalty of their protégés. 'Dodgy is the best coach I've served under,' volunteers 17-year-old wing Gareth Jones. 'There's a lot of coaches who dictate to you and haven't done anything. Dodgy's done it, so you listen. Dodgy's the thoughtful one, Pete's the workhorse. He works us hard and is a good coach. They're a good combination.'

The Youth trains on Tuesdays and Thursdays at 6 p.m. alongside the Development Fifteen, under its coaches Kevin McDonald and Malcolm Foulkes-Arnold – both first-teamers in their day. The exuberance associated with so many teenagers suddenly being let off the leash after a day on the treadmill of school or work generates an atmosphere in marked contrast to that of Oval Park's daytime clientele. On a still January evening, as the floodlights peering through the mist lend proceedings an air of being viewed through a thin muslin cloth, the whooping and hollering evokes visions of club training nights the length and breadth of the country. Dodge finally calls a halt to the boisterous game of touch rugby which has been raging for some 20 minutes and hands the reins to Lowe for the sequence of orthodox ball-handling and close-quarter contact exercises that follow. Exhortation has now replaced larking about and enthusiasm levels are rising fast. 'You're too HIGH, Josh! DROP your SHOULDER!' barks Lowe, the Josh in question being his son, a prop who has already represented Midlands Colts. The drills are carbon copies of those performed by the senior squad. No accident, of course. Continuity of methods and objectives is the holy grail of the club's coaching hierachy. Easy enough to seek, however, more difficult to achieve.

'It would help every now and then if Bob came down and worked with us,' says Dodge, 'but he's got more on his plate at the top end. That's what he's paid by the club to do.' Lowe favours another strategy: 'It would be better if they took us up to them, if, say, one Tuesday a month the Youth and its coaches trained with the first team, mixing in with Johnno and the others. Our lads would get a lot out of that.'

The responsibility for coaching the coaches lies with Duncan Hall. Some might say he has not done enough in this regard. Hall does not duck the charge: 'Time's always a killer. The way we approached it last year was that in the second half of the season on Wednesday nights we had a special "development" squad and we got all the coaches along and worked on how we approach the basic skills development in specialised areas. We were trying to get the other coaches involved, plus 20 guys from the Youth and Development Fifteen who we thought had potential. What came out of it was a good filtering down of the way and the why we do things. Outside of that, it's a matter of talking to the junior coaches about why they're here: it's great to win all the games but we're here to improve the lower players and identify the couple who may, potentially, make the first team.

'How you play the game depends on what players you've got. The lower sides may not have the players to play how the first team play. Tight forwards, for example, don't just appear. They've got to be nurtured and brought through. Everywhere round the world people are searching for front-rowers. The art of front-row play is lost in a lot of corners. What we do want every player to do is pass and catch properly. If they can do that properly at least they can participate. The way the English guys pass the ball is most peculiar – they nearly throw themselves off balance to get the ball away. The general training and philosophy of playing the game is consistent throughout the club. Now we're having curtain-raisers you can check these things. I've probably got to do something else, but finding the time to get everyone together is a problem. Some can only come between six and nine of an evening; Sundays they've other things they want to do.

'The real dilemma for the club is what to do with the Development side, not the Youth. All the better players should be in the Extras at that stage. But those who are not first-team level – invaluable to the club as they may be as good blokes – should perhaps play their footie somewhere else now that we are dealing with a professional sport. Basically, it's the Firsts who get the kudos and the sponsorship; it's the Seconds that keep the pressure on the Firsts; and the best of the Youth that filter through.'

Hall can be spotted conversing with Dusty Hare and club director John Allen among a healthy crowd as the Youth warm up out on Oval Park's number one pitch prior to its fixture with Gloucester on 31 January. The side has a score to settle, having lost to the visitors 19–30 on the opening day of the season at Kingsholm. It is a wonderfully crisp winter afternoon, perfect for rugby: the pitch has some give in it after all the recent rain, a watery sun is just about holding its own and there's hardly sufficient a breeze to disturb the tops of the poplars at the industrial estate end of the ground. Hall sees an exciting contest between two evenly matched teams. Tigers have the best of things up front, especially in the scrums (Gloucester have lost five of their first-choice pack to an England Colts trial), but when the Gloucester backs do get the ball they show far greater cohesion and ingenuity. The tackling, from both sides, is frightening in its intensity and thunder-clapping ferocity. Gloucester strike first with a penalty from their fly-half, Marling schoolboy Alistair Bressington. It is the only score of the half. Tigers miss two kicks of their own but cannot complain about being behind: the Cherry and

Whites have looked exceedingly slick with the ball in hand and could easily have been a couple of tries to the good.

The second period continues in the same vein and Bressington soon slots his second penalty. As the match enters the final quarter, however, their exertions are beginning to catch up with the lighter and less-experienced Gloucester forwards. Tigers mount an attack down the left and force a lineout 15 metres from Gloucester's try-line. The throw goes to the tail and reaches scrum-half Chris Chapman who, instead of rifling the ball away to his fly-half, spins on his heels and darts back up a fatally unguarded touch-line to dive over in the corner. Fly-half John Boden misses the conversion: Tigers trail by one point. Gloucester spring back on to the offensive and, had they used their heads a bit more, they could have kept Tigers safely pinned down for the remainder of the match. But, to the chagrin of their animated coach, the ex-Lydney flanker Pat Kiely who has been combining the role of touch-judge with that of increasingly demented *eminence gris*, they continue to throw the ball about – inviting a thumping tackle or dropped pass in midfield. Well into stoppage time one such spilled pass leads to a chance for Tigers' left-wing Pete Williams, but he knocks on with the line at his mercy. Tigers hurl everything bar the kitchen sink into one last thrust, this time down the right touch-line. Any score secures victory. Kiely is running out of expletives to chuck at the referee as nearly eight minutes of 'extra time' now show on the clock. Mr Waterfield blows his whistle. But the dapperly kitted-out teacher from Leicester's Hamilton Community College has not blown to signal 'no-side': he's blown for a penalty against Gloucester for handling in the ruck. 'I f***ing knew it! We've lost!' mutters Kiely, running toward the posts for the kick. Up steps Boden. Over goes the kick. Up go the flags. Peep goes Waterfield's whistle. Pop goes Kiely's patience. Final score: 8–6 to the Tigers. Oh to be a fly on the wall in the referee's room during the ensuing five minutes when Kiely comes a-calling!

The two teams clap each other off the field in time-honoured fashion but while Glos head for the showers the victorious Youth have chores to perform, post-protectors and poles to be collected, before they can do likewise. John Boden, very much the team joker and Jeremy Beadle in residence, is beaming from ear to ear. 'I just didn't think I was going to miss. Usually, I take too long to kick them but this time I just stuck my head down and I knew it was going to go through. Everyone on the sidelines was calling "No pressure!" We ought to have scored more tries. That's been our trouble – when we

165

get into the twenty-two we panic a bit.' Boden's half-back partner, the blond-haired, fresh-faced Chris Chapman (a student at Wyggeston & Queen Elizabeth College) breathlessly recounts his own moment of glory: 'It was a spur of the moment thing. It was an off-the-top ball straight to me that was meant to go out to John. But the tail of the lineout had come forward and obstructed the pass. I checked, saw the gap and went for the line. It's my first season here. I came for training and the trials last summer. Hopefully, I can get into the Development Fifteen next year. I'd love to become a professional rugby player. If not, l think I'll join the police.'

Back in the clubhouse the two coaches give an immediate reaction to their side's latest display.

DODGE: We definitely deserved to win the game in the end. It was an important game for us to win because at this level we do get inconsistent opposition. Last week we went to Litchfield and put 50 points on them playing very poorly. Today was a better level for the players, and we could see them under a lot more pressure and how they reacted to it. From that point of view it was a very good game for us. We were a bit stronger in the scrum – I can only remember them pushing us back once.

LOWE: We had the nudge on them on every single scrum except one, which was static. They probably took the ball forward through the forwards better than we did, made it more available quicker.

DODGE: That was the disappointing part of our play. On several occasions we took the ball into contact and lost it.

LOWE: We were a lot stronger through the forwards. We had more options off our lineout and in the scrums we were solid and pushed them back. Our downfall was in the second phase where we tended to knock ball on or take the wrong option. Where they were better was breaking the tackle and making five to ten yards, whereas we made only two or three. The red mist sometimes comes down and then they all take the wrong option!

The one slight dampener on the team's extraordinarily 'professional' performance was its 'unprofessional' turnout. For instance, while Gloucester had warmed up looking the very epitome of unity, resplendent to a man in spanking new training suits provided by the club's sponsor, Eagle Star, the Tigers resembled Fred Karno's army in a motley assortment of gear. The contrast was equally noticeable in the match itself for the Youth were quite clearly wearing an old set of shirts with the name of last season's sponsor blotted out. That this sad state of affairs should be picked up comes as no surprise to Lowe. 'British Gas used to sponsor us, but now we've no one. We cannot understand, when the club's got a commercial manager, why he hasn't pushed someone down to us. Any sponsorship that comes into the club now makes its way to the top end.' The twin flagships of every English club, he agreed, are the first team and the Colts, so it's a crying shame to see one of Leicester's ships being spoilt for an 'apennyworth of tar. Nor could the team's post-match attire stand parity with Gloucester's mufti of blazer, collar and tie. Ray Needham pleads mitigating circumstances. Lighting up a cigar, he explains: 'We would have worn blazers and ties had we gone back to Welford Road after the game. This is only the second time we haven't. Our dress code is different to the first team. If it's a long away trip we may allow them to go "casual", but they always change into "number ones" after the match. These days the lads normally dress "expensively casual", so they actually like getting into collar and tie for a change. I think you have to maintain things like that because it helps the whole ethos. We have had kit this season – polos, fleeces, bags – which we didn't last year.'

Leaving aside the relatively minor kit considerations, the Youth appears to be in rude health – and yet there is apparently a question-mark over its future. Needham sees no reason why it should not continue unearthing gems to follow in the footsteps of Dodge, Johnson and Rowntree. 'There are 15 players in the senior squad who have come through the youth, and I think we can produce those players on a regular basis. Our loose-head prop today, Ben Buxton, is as good now as Graham Rowntree was at this stage and Marek Kwisiuk, our hooker, recently played for the Extras. Those two, plus John Boden, Chris Chapman and lock Chris Jones will all go up to Development next year. You can't push 15 through to the top every year because there isn't the room but if you can get a supply of home-grown players coming through, I think that's the way forward. When the next round of contracts come round, the professional players are not going to be paid what they're being paid at the minute because the club can't afford it! Home-grown players will be vital!'

How many of the current litter of Tiger cubs will make the grade is anyone's guess. But no young player's time, talent and enthusiasm for the game of rugby football is entirely wasted at the Tigers. Neither prop Terry Sigley nor wing Gareth Jones, who both failed to make the starting line-up for the Gloucester match, are under any illusions that their careers as Tigers could hit the buffers in the next year or so. Curtailed or not, its value in the modern game is not lost on either of them. 'If you've been at Leicester you can go to a lot of other clubs and they'll take you because of the training you've had here,' says Jones, before adding his reason: 'Leicester is the "Man U" of rugby.' It is hard to have phrased it any better.

19

Bob Bites the Bullet

The new year has not started kindly for Bob Dwyer. Tigers are dumped out of the Tetley's Bitter Cup at Saracens in the fifth round (by one point) and a league defeat at Gloucester, following on from the home loss to Newcastle, sees them kiss goodbye to any realistic hopes of being in the Premiership race come May. The club now trails leaders Newcastle by eight points. On top of all this, Dwyer's had to contend with plenty of ongoing fall-out from his adverse comments on the subjects of referees and Newcastle's gamesmanship. Sitting at his office desk, on the second floor of Livingston & Doughty's converted shoe factory amid all the cacophonous hurly-burly of the industrial estate at the back of Oval Park, there's no escaping the impression that Dwyer looks and sounds a trifle whacked. He appears a little pale around the gills and whereas he usually positively crackles in conversation, today sees him working with damp powder. According to quotes in the national dailies, Dwyer is 'completely disillusioned . . . sick of talking . . . out of ideas'. There has even been talk of him wanting to quit the club.

'It has crossed my mind a few times. I figure if a player is not producing the goods he should look elsewhere. And if a coach is not producing the goods he should look elsewhere. If the coach is doing everything right but the players are not responding there's two answers: change the players or change the coach. I get disappointed like everyone else. It was just the futility of our display at Gloucester. We played all the rugby but gave away an unbelievable number of penalties and then compounded the penalties by conceding an extra ten metres for a lack of urgency in retiring or arguing with the referee. Stupid!'

When a coach puts as much of himself into the job as Bob Dwyer does any body-blow strikes hard and deep. Asked how much of his waking day is consumed by rugby – thinking about it, coaching it, watching it, dwelling on it – Dwyer inhales long and slow, reaches for paper and pen, and proceeds to work it out. 'About 75 per cent, at least, I'd say – at least. I might not quite wake up thinking about rugby, but I'll be lying in bed thinking about it. I'm on the phone talking about rugby during 80 per cent of my showers, standing with my back under the water and my head out! I talk to Dusty Hare virtually every day like that! He thinks it's a good time to get me – I'm not having breakfast and I'm not in the office. I used to sleep like a log – but not the last ten years. My trouble is, as soon as I sit down during the day my eyes feel like anvils. Sometimes when I go to bed I've already been asleep for an hour and it's not easy to drop off.'

A typical Dwyer day tends to be so frantic that lunch, that is a sandwich, may occasionally be taken driving down the motorway en route to a meeting with a player's agent or, as on this precious 'day off', as late as teatime if the phone hasn't stopped ringing; it is not unknown for dinner to be a take-away picked up on the way home to Billesdon at 9.30 p.m. 'Now we've gone through it I feel tired just talking about it!'

The wounds inflicted at Saracens and Gloucester may need time to heal completely, but heal they will. 'I analyse my performance all the time and if I got to the stage where I thought I wasn't getting results and there was a better way to do things, like getting someone else to coach the team, I'd be happy to advise the club to get someone else. But I think it's fair to say that our progress has been both continuous and rapid. The level of general ball-skills is unrecognisable from when I arrived. We're much, much more dynamic this year, much more skilful. The thing we still lack is vision. We don't have a feel for how we can make space for other players, how one step in that direction can really make a big difference to a support player. They haven't clicked on to that yet. It's not quite in one ear and out the other, but there is a tendency for it to go in one ear and meet a barrier. Nor do we possess that mental toughness that enables us to adjust to situations during the game.

'All the "bottom" teams are coming up and passing the "top" teams. It's difficult to stay at the top, always has been. The top teams must look to improve – and that's what we've been concentrating on. It's no good winning unless you are constantly improving your performances. I think we are. The problem is consistency. You could not have wanted a better display than those against Glasgow and Sale. Like last year we blow hot and cold – the difference this season is that our hot's hotter and our cold's hotter as well!

'The reality of the situation was that we were always going to find it difficult to beat Saracens twice at Vicarage Road. I didn't think it was outside our ability but it was going to be hard. To beat a good side in a difficult environment twice in the same season is always going to be difficult. They were all over us like a rash! All we did was defend, defend, defend. Yet we did it with such courage, spirit and determination that we managed to restrict them to what some might consider a "lucky" win – and there was a possibility of them losing.

'My disillusionment at Gloucester came from the fact that we'd been able to do some things very, very well – we'd scored three good tries and the opposition had scored one average one we'd presented to them by throwing the ball to one of their players! Interspersed with the good play were a huge number of penalties – on five or six occasions giving away an extra ten metres for not being back the ten; once, even, 20, for talking to the referee twice. That sort of thing can't be part of a good rugby team.

'In order to make our season acceptable we have to do well in the league. Not necessarily win, but if we don't get to a minimum of third I'd say our season has been unsatisfactory. And there's more than three teams in it at the moment. Northampton are playing really well and Richmond, on occasions, are playing excellently. I think we have to win virtually all, if not all, of our remaining games to be in with a shout.

'As far as I'm concerned we are still on target for our two-year goal, which is to have in place a viable structure to enable us to provide an environment for players to reach their potential. People ask me if I'm staying for a third year. Well, I don't want to put all this in place and then leave!'

Since coming to Leicester, Dwyer has consistently demonstrated his reputation for being able to talk for Australia. He is a dab hand in the field of media relations, freely available for a soundbite here or an exposition there. Lately, however, he seems to have only succeeded in shooting himself in the foot. 'I don't try to protect myself, which is a bit of a problem; I'm not interested in protecting my job for the future. I'm interested in doing what I think has to be done now, regardless of what people think about it. If a referee makes an error I want to tell him about it. If a player plays badly I want to tell him so. I don't want to pretend he did when he didn't. I want the press to say good things about my team and I do everything I can to make sure they do. There is an element of manipulation on my part but not often consciously. It's certainly not a situation where I plot a course of action. But, gut reaction, rat-cunning or whatever, subconsciously influences what you do. Some are just honest personal responses to a straightforward question; others may be influences by normal human desires to find reasons other than yourself for your failures!'

Has the criticism of referees backfired on him and his team? 'Possibly. My experience, though, is that they do sit up and take notice. I take the view that, by and large, we don't get much from referees, so I doubt if it can be much worse! I see games every week where things are inherently wrong. It's not a case of being judgemental. Every week, for example, I see the tight-head break his bind and I've not seen it penalised. It happens ten or 12 times a match to Graham Rowntree and he ends up with nothing to push against. I'm paranoid about my players not breaking the laws of the game! We've had a huge amount of success. Neil Back used to break the laws all the time, the front row too. Yet we still suffer. If the front rows are penalised in a game, four out of five decisions will be against us. I expect refs to apply the laws of the game. Otherwise my players can justifiably say to me that I don't know what I'm talking about, that I'm outside the real world, that you are allowed to do this even though the law book says you can't. I get on pretty well with some referees – Ed Morrison, Tony Spreadbury, Steve Lander – they tell me the deficiencies in my team's performance and I tell them the deficiencies in their refereeing. If I said everything I think is 100 per cent accurate about referees I'd never be out of the newspapers! What I say about referees 50 per cent of the time relates to the relationship between the referee and the touch-judges – what they do together, how they react to one another. Maybe they need a microphone and ear-piece connection so we can make use of simple inexpensive technical equipment. But, if this is a society where accurate criticism – constructive or otherwise – is frowned upon, there's something wrong with the society.'

Coming to terms with the vagaries of refereeing is part and parcel of the coach's everyday life; Dwyer can handle that. Possibly more worrying, however, are the rumours emanating from both dressing-room and board room that one or two individuals would not lose any sleep if he were to leave. Peter Wheeler admitted that he was preparing a full review of the club's playing structure for a board meeting on 16

February which could have implications for Dwyer, notably the matter of whether the club would take up the option in his contract for a third year in the job. 'I'm looking for the next two to three years,' said the chief executive, 'I don't think there's any point in looking at just next year. We have been in the professional era 18 months and we have learned a lot. We need to take stock and look at what we want to do in the next two to three years. The review will look at Bob's position, what it is at the moment and what it might be. He could stay, his position could be the same, his position could change.'

The first player to break cover in support of Dwyer, and, in particular, play down any inflammatory talk of dressing-room unrest or the possibility of a players' *putsch*, was Joel Stransky – unquestionably Dwyer's staunchest ally at Oval Park. 'Bob has the full support of the players. There's always one or two guys not happy but you get that at any club. No one can get on perfectly with everyone else. I think a lot of the players are starting to understand his long-term plan and are getting to grips with it. The few that are not and don't want him here should be the blokes to go. Changing the game at Leicester was never going to be easy, it was never going to change overnight. Obviously we are not on a roll at the moment, but you can't blame the coach for that. The players have got to look at themselves and decide whether they are performing.' Perhaps Bob Dwyer had not been implementing the secret of man-management according to Scottish soccer's managerial wizard Jock Stein: 'Keep the six players who hate you away from the five who are undecided!'

The two players identified as the principal prima donnas at Oval were Will Greenwood and Austin Healey. According to the Oval Park grapevine, Greenwood's England caps were being won in progressively larger sizes. Oz, of course, was apt to run off at the mouth any time, any place, anywhere. The club's *enfant terrible* had openly referred to his coach in the media as the 'Führer', for example. Mention of Healey's name prompts another reflective intake of breath by Dwyer. 'Austin has gigantic mood swings. Just as we thought he was really maturing – we thought it was moving in with Louise, his girlfriend, and establishing a permanent relationship – he's off the rails again. It's a shame. With his head up he's a very good rugby player, with his head down he doesn't seem to have any instinctive feel for the game at all. He's not absolutely said thank you to me for moving him to the wing but he's given a bit of a clue that there was some value to it. I think secretly he is happy with the way he is going. He just wouldn't want anyone to know it.

'Myself and 50 per cent of the players consistently review our performances; but the other 50 per cent don't bother. There are some who waste my input. Perhaps they're being confrontational, though not openly so. I've seen some coaches who run their teams in an unbelievably dictatorial manner with a network of spies to discover everything that's going on. I choose not to do that. That's a reason for some of my success and the reason for some of my difficulties. I expect players to be mature and honest, and sometimes they're not. I say: "If you disagree with some of the things I'm doing, let's discuss them. I don't want a shouting match. I'm obstinate but I'm 100 per cent prepared to listen. I have changed my mind on occasions. I could be wishy-washy and every time you make suggestions I change my mind. But then we'd not know where we were, we'd be changing our minds every five minutes. We'll look at things, analyse them and agree how we're going to do them. Then we'll have no departure from that. What I don't want is for me to stand up and say things which are dismissed, because I might as well not bother. I try not to say things that don't have any value." The really mature guys, and generally speaking they're the best players, follow that line.

'I told Johnno and Joel recently that it's their job to sort out things like discontent, for example: one player saying something and another taking offence during a game, or Austin throwing the ball at Cockers during a game, etc. There's absolutely no place for it. I said: "You fix it or we'll get a captain and vice-captain who can." But Cockers, for instance, has his heart in the right place, he's a good guy. Of all the players, if you wanted someone to help a younger player Cockers is easily the best bloke in the club, better even than Joel and Fritz, which is saying something because they are good. He does shoot his mouth off and I have spoken to him about it a couple of times. He will listen. Cockers is a very reasonable bloke really, and his play has got better month by month since I first saw him. He has answered his critics in the best possible way – I hope he has a little brother somewhere!

'Neil Back was a bit surly when I arrived but it disappeared pretty quick. He gave the impression that he thought people were against him. I didn't try to kid him. The first thing I said to him was: "We don't really need a player who assaults the referee in our team." And he grunted. Then when he came back from his suspension – for knocking over Steve Lander at the end of the 1996 Cup Final – we picked him in every game and he said he felt like a rest. So I told him: "How do you think the others feel who've been playing the whole season when you've had bloody half of the season off for something imbecilic you've done and we've had to play without you!" Now he's possibly our best player, certainly right up there with Johnno, Joel and Fritz, very powerful in the drive, very constructive, possessing a good rugby mind and instinct. He doesn't say much but when he does, he's spot-on. He'd make a very good captain. I think he's terrific and I'm sure he appreciates the more professional approach to the game.'

The light outside is beginning to fade. Dwyer looks at his watch. Time he made his way round the corner to Oval Park for the evening session. Before he can utter 'I don't give a XXXX' in response, he is waylaid by Jo Hollis, the ice-cool, ash-blonde ('It'll be a different colour by Saturday!' she shrieks) head-turner who acts as the office Girl Friday. Until last summer Hollis had spent her entire life in Hong Kong, most recently as an assistant security manager for Cathay Pacific Airways with the responsibility for all anti-terrorist training and aircrew personal-safety programmes. Nowadays she endeavours to organise Dwyer and Hall. Apparently, someone has rung urgently wanting to speak with Dwyer before he leaves for training; he said he'd ring back. 'What time?' asks Dwyer. 'Supposedly half an hour ago!' says Hollis. It's like this every single day, she confides. Never a moment's peace for Bob Dwyer. And this is meant to be his day off.

Opportunity for one last irreverent question that is patently not going to get an answer: 'Exactly how much does Leicester pay you, Bob, for all this passionate and tireless labour?' He chuckles. 'A famous Australian rugby league coach always had his contract written to say he'd be paid one dollar more than the highest-paid player. He didn't care what it was, as long as it was one dollar more. Well, I don't get as much as the highest-paid player at Leicester, I can tell you! And, in actual fact, I took this job for £50,000 per annum less than I was offered in another job!'

Dwyer's salary remains a closely guarded secret, but however much Leicester is paying him – six figures or whatever – no one should be in any doubt that win, lose or draw; league champions, cup winners or also-rans, he earns every brass farthing of it.

20

Nobby Hits the Big Time but Pots Misses Out

The start to Bob Dwyer's new year may have read like a horror story but Dorian West's was pure Hans Christian Andersen. In the space of 21 days Nobby went from the Leicester bench to the England bench for the Five Nations opener against France, and eventually, at 4.20 p.m. on Saturday, 7 February, into the England side itself as a seventieth-minute replacement for Mark Regan. The inevitability of such an outcome was surely written in the stars, for what Leicester's replacement nonpareil doesn't know about dramatic mid-match entrances is not worth discussing.

'To be honest, I thought all week I was in with a chance of Clive putting me on tactically, because he'd changed hookers in the games against Australia and New Zealand before Christmas. I was nervous, but not any more than for a big game at Leicester. I always talk a lot before games, so there was no change there, but my cheeks were red and my hands were sweating, which is always a sign I'm nervous. "Ronnie" got injured a few times in the match and I was up and down like a yo-yo. When he got injured about five minutes into the second half I was told to get warmed up because he was struggling. I kept looking up into the stand to try and catch Clive's eye – but couldn't! Anyway, Ronnie seemed to get better and, in fact, I'd stopped warming up. Then we got a penalty with ten minutes to go. I watched Paul Grayson kick it and when we were running back I could see Ronnie walking with the physio, who was shaking his head as if to say "You're coming off". So, I just took my stuff off and ran straight onto the pitch – I wasn't going to give him a second chance!

'I didn't have a great deal to do. We were just trying to keep the game going at that stage, running the ball from side to side – it was a bit frantic, being behind and needing to score. I had three scrums and one lineout. I told Johnno in the week that if I was to come on he had to make sure it was thrown to him! Two of the scrums were normal enough but the third was very hard! The French just stood up and you could feel your ribs tingling. They were very strong, even at that late point in the game. I was always trying to get the ball in my hands. I picked it up off the floor once and took it forward, that's all I could manage. You always look at these games on the telly and wonder whether you're good enough to play in them, how fast and how hard they are. It's obviously a higher standard than the Premiership, but not that much different. Actually, it was just like going on for Leicester, with all your mates around you. I was chuffed to bits. It's got to be the best ten minutes of my career.'

West was now in the invidious position of being the only elated individual in an understandably crestfallen squad in the wake of a 24–17 defeat. 'I was desperate to celebrate. I just wanted to run around and jump up and down but I daren't because everyone was so down in the dumps. I was walking around trying to find someone who was going to be as happy as I was! A lot of people did come up to me and say "Congratulations!" because they knew it was a big day for me. They hid their disappointment when they spoke to me but you could see they were down when they were amongst themselves.'

West's international initiation continued on the team bus upon leaving the Stade de France and was completed – in something of a haze – at the traditional banquet held in the spectacular Salon Opéra of the Grand Hotel. 'First of all I had to go to the front of the bus and sing a song, as all first-caps have to do. I sang what I call "Peaches and Cream", because it's the shortest song I know: "You come on like a dream, peaches and cream, lips like strawberry wine, you're sixteen, you're beautiful, and you're mine!" I had to sing the lot before I could sit down. No one joined in. They gave me a lot of grief! I was struggling along in a sort of monotone! The dinner was men only, and I got my tie and cap there. I can't remember who presented it to me, I'd had a few by then! The custom is for a first-cap to have a drink with every member of the team when they come up to you during the evening. You drink down in one whatever they're having. By the end of the night you're out of your tree! It started with wine and beer but, apparently, I was getting a bit cocky, saying I could manage my drink more than most and I'd be all right – so I think they started me on half-pints of Pernod. I had a few of them and passed out! They could have been giving me anything, I'd not have known! I was carried to bed by the doctor, Terry Crystal, and the physio, Kevin Murphy.'

West became the fifty-eighth Tiger to be capped by England (Will Greenwood's anticipated début against Australia being number 57) and the club's seventy-first international all told (seven Irishmen, six Scots – but not one Welshman). His remarkable elevation had been triggered by the televised match with Sale on 13 December when he started only his fourth game of the season as a result of the neck injury sustained by Richard Cockerill in England's 26–26 draw with New Zealand the previous Saturday. Cockerill had forced himself into the England team during the drawn Test with Australia on 15 November, coming off the bench at half-time to shore up the front row after Bath youngster Andy Long had endured a torrid international baptism of fire. Cockerill kept his place for the three remaining pre-Christmas internationals with New Zealand (twice) and South Africa; grabbing national headlines after he stood chin-to-chin with his opposite number Norm Hewitt and eyeballed the All Black hooker while he conducted the 'Haka'. Overnight Cockers's mixture of defiance and discourtesy (no one but no one is meant to disrupt New Zealand's ritual display of intimidation) transformed him from bad boy to folk hero.

West played a blinder against Sale. Considerably more mobile than Cockerill, he popped up all over the park, scoring a try and garnering plaudit after plaudit from both television and newspapers alike: he was a 'revelation' according to Michael Austin in the *Sunday Times*. Not that such praise prevented an immediate return to the bench. A second prominent display in the 50–14 victory over Coventry in the fourth round of the Tetley's Bitter Cup, however, in which he crossed for two more tries and drew comments like 'impressive . . . ebullient . . . pushing Cockerill for his place in the team, reigning England hooker or not', clearly made an indelible impression on England coach Clive Woodward because West was called up for the élite squad's Bisham Abbey training session on 28 January as third hooker behind Cockerill and Mark Regan. The final twist developed as it became obvious that the knee Cockerill wrenched against Sale had not mended sufficiently for him to be considered for England's opening game in the Five Nations. West was one step away from the big time and the realisation that boyish dreams can come true – even at the ripe old age of 30.

West's promotion to the the élite squad for the one match was worth £3,000 (play or not), but money is valueless beside the aura of that silver-tassled red cap. Eventually it will be framed and, almost certainly, end up in the house of West's father, Colin, a proud Welshman: 'He's chuffed to bits, but I think he'd sooner it was a Welsh cap!' Before then, West intends having his seven-month-old daughter, Harriet, photographed wearing it. Hopefully, she'll not be so camera-shy as her father who, despite all manner of enticements, couldn't be persuaded to pose in cap and jersey outside the privacy of a sealed-off dressing-room in case he's spotted by one of his team-mates. 'A lot of the lads have been giving me grief all week. Most of the team here have played international rugby, so they know what it's like, they're all prepared to take the mickey. If you happen to wear a T-shirt with anything to do with England on it, for instance, you're in trouble!'

When the next batch of England squads (to play Wales) were announced West found himself seemingly relegated to fifth in the pecking order, namely second string in the 'A' side. If that turnabout left West somewhat bemused, he knew full well what to expect from Bob Dwyer, whose habitual greeting to returning international stars is: 'I've got a bag of nails here to make sure you're feet stay on the ground!' With Cockerill fit to resume for the Premiership game with London Irish, West once more took his seat in the dug-out. Dame Fortune, however, was not finished with West just yet. Woodward's team to play Wales at Twickenham on 21 February recalled Cockerill (and dropped Darren Garforth) but also included West on the bench. 'The two young lads in the squad, Long and Chuter, were only along for the experience. I was still in the top three with Cockers and Regan. On the Monday, Clive decided to put me on the bench.'

For another 30-year-old Tiger, however, the international dream was rudely shattered within days of it being entertained, the fairy tale over before he could say 'Once upon a time . . . ' No fewer than nine Leicester representatives were included in the 30 called to Bisham Abbey on 28 January. Seven of them were regulars: Healey, Greenwood, Rowntree, Cockerill, Garforth, Johnson and Back. But, if Dorian West's name raised a few eyebrows, the identity of Tiger number nine was a real bolt from the blue – Stuart Potter.

For the greater part of the 1990s Stuart Potter has been one of the most consistent centres in the country, jousting with the best the game has to offer – Pieter Muller, Danie Gerber and Andre Venter of South Africa, Jason Little of Australia and Walter Little of New

Zealand, not to mention all the premier centres from the Five Nations. He has represented England A on no fewer than 18 occasions (most recently against the All Blacks at Welford Road on 2 December), touring Canada and Australia with them in 1993; the following summer he accompanied the senior squad to South Africa. But, thanks largely to the Carling–Guscott–de Glanville axis, he has never been able to force his way into the full international side – indeed, he's never even got so close as the bench.

'At the time I wasn't so upset at not getting picked because Carling and Guscott were a very good centre pairing. It had to take a couple of injuries for me to be there or thereabouts; and Damien Hopley was also in the running. I knew I was close but I knew there'd have to be a couple of injuries for me to get in. Then, a couple of years ago, I missed a lot of England A games through injury and the following summer I wasn't selected again. I thought that's it, I'm not being looked at. The New Zealand game in December was the first time I've been involved with the A squad for the last two seasons. I do feel more confident now about playing for England. Before, I was too young and I used to wonder whether, if I got in, I'd be too nervous. At my age now, I take things more in my stride. I'd play a better game now. But it will bug me for the rest of my life if I never get a full cap.'

The news that Clive Woodward had recruited 'Pots' for the Bisham Abbey get-together, as a result of some outstanding club performances that had recently secured one of Leicester's Player of the Month awards (sponsored by local jeweller George Tarratt: the prize was an Omega Seamaster chronometer), could not have been greeted more warmly by the centre's peers at Oval Park. Yet, no sooner was Pots in, than he was out. A thigh strain picked up in the Tetley's Bitter Cup defeat at Saracens on 24 January looked like ruling him out of the game for at least a fortnight.

'I knew straight away I'd not be training with England on the following Wednesday. I'd been going strong all the season till the last month. I've had my knocks at just the wrong time of the season. This one was a flexor tear. I got it sprinting away: someone grabbed my foot in the process of me pulling forward. It could be six weeks. But it's not too serious, I've got quite a bit of movement still. There should be fewer problems these days because all the training and recovery sessions probably better tune your body into meeting these demands. But I've actually had more!'

In fact, Potter attributes his current rich seam of form to the impact of the professional game and the not unrelated input of Bob Dwyer switching him to outside-centre alongside Will Greenwood. 'I respect everything Bob does. He's brought a lot of new ideas into the team and a lot of them work. He's a very straight-talking coach, which I like, straight to the point, no messing around. He tells you what he thinks and I react to that. The handling and passing drills he's introduced have helped me, I'm sure; and the different way of defending. We used to drift across to the next man, now we go straight up to the man until he's passed and then drift out. It stops the attack coming inside you. Now they've only one way to go, it's a lot easier. I prefer outside-centre because I've got more space to get some speed up and look around for the pass. I'm more comfortable in that role. I used to enjoy playing with Ian Bates and then Lawrence Boyle but my partner changed a lot after that. Without doubt Will is the best I've played with. I toured Australia with Will and England A, and I could see then he was a good player. It's great to have a partner who can do things. I used to be the only playmaker and the opposition knew that. Will is capable of making all sorts of breaks and if you get with him you're the man outside who gets the pass. Now that we've gelled we have many more options. Joel makes a lot of space for us. He'll take the ball right up to the defence and if there's nothing on for us he'll take the tackle. The strongest part of my play is to change gear and accelerate outside my man – a straightforward "miss-one" going wide and pass to the full-back. The professional era has improved everyone. I know I've improved in ball skills just by the exercises we do in training. As we're doing them all week it becomes second nature. Before, you only had two training sessions to do ball skills and that area of your game suffered accordingly. I used to work in an office, so training once or twice a day was a shock to start with and I didn't enjoy it at first because I couldn't get into the routine. The hour-and-a-quarter drive from my home in Litchfield took its toll, but I'm used to it nowadays.'

Potter's strengths have not been lost on Bob Dwyer. 'Pots is a lot better player than most people give him credit for. He's not a total answer to a maiden's prayer but he's got a lot of good qualities and he's a good fella. He has the desired amount of humility which I think is a really important characteristic. A lot of people think arrogance is important: I think humility is. That way you don't lose track of the opposition's ability – "The guy I'm marking has got qualities. I might be able to take advantage of that deficiency but I've got to watch out for that." Pots has got excellent power, he's probably the most powerful runner in the club – in mid-stride Pots is absolutely airborne, he's doing broad-jumps every stride, he's so far off the ground.'

Potter returned to the fray in late February and, despite picking up another injury (a twisted ankle), he finished the season on the highest possible note by making the England touring party for the summer trip to Australia, New Zealand and South Africa. Other Tigers on the plane were Austin Healey, Graham Rowntree, Neil Back, Richard Cockerill and rising star Lewis Moody, still only 19 and restricted to just 15 starts in a Tigers jersey – but already capped at Under-21 level and included in the 'A' squad. 'Clive phoned and asked how the ankle was,' says Potter. 'I told him it was on the mend and he said: "That's all I want to know." I wasn't aware I was going until the party was announced. I thought I might just be in contention for "standby". It's probably my last major tour – and my last chance of a cap.'

Unfortunately, any possibility of the Leicester centre partnership of Potter and Greenwood donning the white of England in harness was scuppered when Greenwood dropped out of the party in order to have surgery on his troublesome shoulder. Nor did Martin Johnson tour. After much discussion he stayed put for a second groin operation and some much needed R&R.

It was now Dorian West's turn to endure the swings and roundabouts of international rugby. Although England's solitary replacement not to get on the field against Wales, he did replace Cockerill for the final few seconds of the Scotland game to win his second cap and avoid the tag of being a 'one-cap wonder'. By the close of the Five Nations the two Tigers hookers had established themselves as the men in possession, but Clive Woodward wished to 'blood' younger front-rowers against the might of the southern hemisphere on their own turf. Instead, West, along with another old greybeard Darren Garforth (who had appeared in seven of the season's eight internationals) was invited to tour Argentina with the Barbarians.

P.S. Sport has a habit of being a great leveller. If Lady Luck had been cruel to West (and Garforth) she finally shone her torch on Stuart Potter. During England's international with Australia on 6 June, Pots made a brief two-minute appearance as a temporary replacement to gain that elusive, much cherished first cap.

21

Bob and Dunc Walk the Plank

'Mate, we're no longer needed.'

It was around 10.30 p.m. on Monday, 16 February, when Duncan Hall, having a cup of tea prior to turning in for the night, picked up the receiver in the lounge of his Thurnby bungalow to hear Bob Dwyer's voice relay the decision reached by Leicester's board of directors some two hours earlier. By a crushing majority of nine–nil (with one abstention) the ten-man board had decided against exercising the club's option to extend Dwyer's and Hall's contracts by a further 12 months. Dean Richards was to assume responsibility for first-team affairs with immediate effect.

'You can always sniff a bit of trouble about the place,' Hall reflected the following afternoon between mouthfuls of teatime fruit cake, 'but I really didn't see it coming because I was too busy doing my job and not with the "heavies". I'd been busy looking around for players and preparing for the Cheltenham & Gloucester game with London Irish, because that competition had been very much my responsibility.'

If Duncan Hall was dumbfounded, Bob Dwyer was almost dumbstruck. 'It came right up and hit me on the back of the head, really. The previous Thursday, Peter Wheeler and I had discussed various aspects of the report I'd submitted to the board on restructuring the playing side over sandwiches and a cup of tea at the Belmont Hotel in De Montfort Street. I'd been to two board meetings to progress that report, and had made a new one, which was quite extensive. Peter must have rang me around 7.30 p.m., before the meeting had ended. He just said: "I'm afraid I've got some bad news for you." He came across to our house at 9 p.m. and stayed an hour or so. He'd not had dinner, so Ruth made him a curry!' Ruth Dywer eventually swallowed a sleeping tablet and went to bed. Her husband had a restless night. At 4 a.m. he slid out of bed and played cards until dawn.

The two Australians had been swept away by a tide of events that had gathered the speed and momentum of a tsunami over the weekend of the home Premiership fixture with London Irish on 14 February. Dwyer purports not to read the papers. Just as well. Despite a piece by Chris Goddard, in which he drew attention to both the flaws in some players and Martin Johnson's captaincy, and applauded Dwyer and Hall for having done a 'fabulous job, working their socks off and preparing the team meticulously', the *Mercury* had received an increasing number of letters from dissatisfied supporters eager to castigate Dwyer for inadequate man-management and dwindling self-motivation. Then, right on cue, came a training-ground bust-up with Austin Healey on the Friday (the thirteenth, no less), which saw Dwyer's patience – hardly before time – finally snap.

Dwyer was fine-tuning the support lines of his runners: Healey's running arc was swinging too wide. 'When Joel straightens there, you've got to stay with him, give him a shorter pass, protect us against the intercept,' the coach pleaded. 'It's impossible for me to do it that quickly on my line,' insisted the winger. 'Yes you can,' protested Dwyer. 'The two of you are running concentric circles, and if Joel can do it on a tighter ten-metre circle you should be able to on a 30-metre circle. If he can do it so can you.' Healey remained obdurate: 'I can't do it. There's no need to discuss it any further.' That put the tin lid on it. 'Well, if you can't do it any better,' snapped Dwyer, 'you might as well grab the pads off Mitch (Read) and let him have a go!'

Dwyer picks up the story: 'Martin Johnson came up to the office later on and said there was no alternative but to leave Austin out, and that he'd been unbearable even before training started. I rang Peter to tell him, and he said Austin had already been into see him and was very contrite. Peter suggested putting him on the bench as the supporters liked seeing him. Austin's future at the club had been raised more than once because he was an unstable influence. In the more recent past I'd received an emissary from a deputation of the players who said things would turn around without Austin. I'd discussed it with Peter and he'd said: "If you think he's a disruptive influence, transfer him;" Peter discussed it with Andy Key and he said: "Get shot of him." In fact, Peter and I had been working tentatively with another coach on a possible swap that involved an international scrum-half.'

Healey was relegated to the bench with a diplomatic 'minor calf strain', but the story had spread like wildfire through the Welford Road press corps well before kick-off on the Saturday. The Irish were duly dispatched (34–19) – without the need for Healey's intervention. The Tigers, however, were dull and listless, and Dwyer's agitation was soon bared for all to see and hear.

His every response to Nick Mullins during an interview for BBC Radio 5's *Sports Report* was as if soaked in petrol – 'Questions like that give me the willies!' he fumed when asked if Leicester had anything still to play for. When the board convened on the Monday to discuss the club's playing structure, the negative images of Saturday – on and off the field – were undeniably still fresh in the memory and might conceivably assume persuasive testimony in any uncommitted minds.

Had Bob Dwyer complained recently to his doctor of a strange, tingling sensation between the shoulder blades it would not have surprised the neutral observer of goings-on within the club. Without a shadow of a doubt, Dwyer had inadvertently placed a number of potentially lethal daggers in the hands of any conspirators itching for the chance to rip Caesar's toga to shreds. A cursory glance at the composition of the board is sufficient to gain some idea of the possible opposition ranged against Dwyer.

Five of the board were erstwhile playing stalwarts of the club, Leicester men to their bootlaces and committee men upgraded to directorial status when the club became a plc. The chairman is Peter Tom (130 first-team appearances), also chairman of Aggregate Industries; David Matthews, a farmer, is a Tigers legend, holding the club record of 502 appearances and also a former captain and coach; another ex-number eight, Garry Adey, the incumbent club president, runs the family firm of Adey Steel in Loughborough and wore a first-team shirt on 381 occasions; prop Bob Beason, who played 203 games prior to becoming club treasurer and president (1985–87), likewise runs his own business; and John Allen, one-time captain, treasurer and hon secretary – until resigning upon the advent of professionalism with which he disagreed – notched up 457 appearances as a scrum-half and is now a senior partner in the Grant Thornton firm of chartered accountants. Lastly, there was chief executive Peter Wheeler, Prince Charming incarnate but, when needs must, also capable of impersonating the Prince of Darkness.

Also sporting Tiger stripes is Roy Jackson who, though never a player with the club, has built up an impressive CV on the commercial side over the last decade or so; he runs Cavalier Reproductions Ltd. Completing the board were David Jones, managing director of Next (the club's main sponsor); Nick Donald, a senior executive with HSBC – the investment bank that assisted with the club's share-issue – and, in consequence, held 10.4 per cent of the shares and 76 per cent of the voting rights on the board; and Philip Smith, the club's financial director. None of the last three named boast any intimate knowledge of rugby football whatsoever. 'I was a very poor centre at school, at King's, Worcester,' explains David Jones. 'I bring two things to the board. I am on the inside making certain that Next gets the benefit of its sponsorship. Secondly, my experience of running a public company for the last 20-odd years means I can help the Tigers get through the process of change now that they are a quoted company. I find it quite fascinating sitting here talking with people who've played rugby for Leicester for many, many years. We've all got a big responsibility to make certain that the new format of the club is run for the benefit of the shareholders and that we achieve the objectives of the prospectus.' One would confidently expect Jones, Donald and Smith to lean toward the views of the seven Tigers on any matters of playing policy.

The 'Magnificent Seven' – two of whom (Matthews and Adey) Dwyer reckoned were against him for some time – are all used to calling the shots in their business lives. They were appointed directors to carry the club torch into the unlit territory of the professional era, they are guardians of the flame. Bob Beason expands: 'What we're doing is assuring the continuation of the game of rugby football. We're not in it for profit or any other matters except playing rugby football. For all of us here, playing rugby football means playing it at Leicester, and Leicester being an ace team. It's the only reason we spend our time here. We're here to put out the best first team, the best rugby team in Europe. Success on the field provides the income to continue the success on the field. It's only a few marketing institutions like Man United that manage to make the off-the-field activities provide more revenue than the on-the-field activities. If rugby clubs don't take the money at the gate, if they don't earn the money by playing the game properly, they won't survive. What we did when we structured the board was to ensure that we had what we thought was a reasonable number of experienced past players, with experience of running the club anyway, to maintain – hopefully in the long term, but certainly in the short term – the continuity of rugby football as being of paramount importance.'

David Matthews receives the baton: 'The increase in our administrative overheads has grown enormously. If we're successful on the park we're in a strong position to raise finance, and if we're not producing the goods the local populace will vote with its feet. We retain a greater degree of tradition here than at the majority of clubs because the majority of them are individually owned, and one individual can wag the tail. We haven't allowed that to happen. Our members are still wagging the tail and we hope that that can continue for as long as possible. Evolution to me is not a problem. I'm a farmer and I remember the horse days! You learn to live with change. But you retain to the best of your ability the best of the past.'

Garry Adey reinforces the point concerning the value of heritage: 'You don't keep the past as part of the future for the sake of it. You keep the past as part of the future if it's worth being part of the future. There's lots of qualities in the past that we want to try and retain.'

These, then, were the men who entered the Barbarian Room at the Welford Road clubhouse to sit in judgement on Bob Dwyer, one of the world's foremost coaches and rugby brains, with whom only Ian McGeechan remotely stood parity in the British Isles; a man whose passionate involvement with, and dedication to, the game of rugby football transcended any inclination toward parochialism. Dwyer is a rugby intellectual if ever there was. He was no great shakes as a player. Many fine players, however, develop comparatively little overview of the game's broader canon beyond their particular position. Someone like Bob Dwyer can come across as a smart alec – and no one likes a smart alec, least of all successful middle-aged men reluctant to lose face through being shown up for their failure to appreciate rugby's finer points. Tolerated if things seem to be going well, brash and outspoken individuals, like Dwyer, leave themselves wide open to the assassin's knife once things are perceived to be going wrong, however temporarily. Only their consciences and confessors know for sure whether the ten directors, especially the Tigers contingent, endorsed the opinion of the noted nineteenth-century writer Charles Colton, who said: 'Proud men are the greatest lovers of humility – in others.'

In addition, Dwyer, by definition, was a mercenary. He was doing the job for money, not love of Leicester Football Club. The circumstances of his appointment in a professional world, unfortunately, denied Dwyer any opportunity to earn his stripes like the good-egg club-man who did so through year after year of selfless, unpaid toil on behalf of Leicester. He was an outsider and he knew he was likely to remain an outsider. Nevertheless, back home in Billesdon at 'The Wicks' – named in honour of Randwick – Dwyer had some grounds for believing he had weathered the storm which had raged ever more angrily in the aftermath of the Newcastle defeat.

Morale among the squad had, the Healey incident apart, been good. Even so, reports appeared in the press suggesting Dywer might be on his way. He reponded: 'Guys were astonished to think I might be quitting, the reason being that they were reading into it that I was deserting a sinking ship! I said I thought I was doing the honourable thing and offering myself up as a sacrifice! I had a chat to them and told them the real story. I said that if things are not going well people are entitled to look at the coach as well as the players. I said that as far as I was concerned we were in it together. There's no coach and players, there's just a team. Our satisfaction as coaches comes from their performances, so we are in a really difficult position because we don't have direct control over our satisfaction, whereas for the players their satisfaction, to a much greater degree, is in their own hands. We must strive to help them play well. We work together to achieve a goal – which is performance. All the rumours were disconcerting. There were lots and lots of changes going on at the club. People don't like change. Sometimes they have to find a target for their anger at the changes they don't agree with. I have to say, it was very reasonable that I went to Peter Wheeler and said: "Look, things I try to instil into players, such as discipline and attitudes on and off the pitch, don't seem to be getting through. Why don't you ask around the place and see why the message is not getting through, because the teaching is not good enough or whether the players haven't cottoned on to it."' Wheeler did so: the players, he reported to Dywer, are fully supportive.

As far as Dwyer was concerned, negotiations had already been in progress (for three months) with regard to a new two-year contract. 'We'd had brief discussions on my "continuing role" in a less demanding position, without the responsibility of coaching. I put to the board a plan of succession which brought new coaches into the first team, a family tree with names on it. Duncan would only stay for one more year, maximum. Next year we'd move someone into his role, and when I moved that person would take mine and someone would replace him – John Wells and Joel Stransky were the two people suggested. Although not part of my initial proposal, Andy Key was to move to Oval Park to undertake the paperwork side of the coaching business because I'd always got a lot on my desk – although it never kept me away from my coaching duties. Andy's level of management at Welford Road was not thought necessary. My report was different to Peter Wheeler's. The basis of Peter's was saving money in administration, at both Oval Park and Welford Road. My report was directed toward producing a consistently successful team; talent identification and development; at minimum cost for maximum benefit.'

The literal truth of what went on inside the Barbarian Room between 4 p.m. and 8.30 p.m. on Monday, 16 February 1998, is never likely to be revealed. The gist of the debate, however, is not so easily concealed. Wheeler had been asked by the board to prepare a report that would provide all the necessary information on which a decision could be made to enable the club to achieve its playing objectives. The basis of the report was Dwyer's own initiative, previously submitted to the board and expanded in late January. Over a ten-day period Wheeler had confidential discussions on the subject with over 20 players, coaches and directors, from inside and outside the club whose opinions and confidence he could trust. The outcome was a proposed new structure splitting the responsibilities of the director of rugby into two: a first-team coach and a rugby manager, who would oversee matters of administration and the development programme. Wheeler detailed five different options to fulfil the need: four included Dwyer and one did not. Wheeler discussed all five eventualities with Dwyer and told him, furthermore, that his recommendation to the board might not include him. As it transpired, Wheeler's final report carried no recommendation from the chief executive. Continuing with Dwyer, the report argued, offered stability, planned progression, known professionalism and experience. Weighing against these factors was the failure to achieve the coach's minimum playing criteria during the current season: Dwyer's honest 'I've run out of ideas' reaction after the Gloucester game (a press conference from which the Tigers' press officer, Stuart Farmer, had tried to shield him); the instances of ill-discipline, both on and off the pitch; the possible blocking of succession in the coaching structure if both Dwyer's and Hall's contracts were extended; a slowness in establishing the development programme; and some selection 'idiosyncrasies', such as Waisale Severi at scrum-half.

'He's a wonderful bloke to have around, with some very special skills,' conceded Wheeler, 'but the big games expose fundamental weaknesses, and in those sorts of games we've seen he's not an international scrum-half in all aspects of the scrum-half's game. In my view, we should have him on the bench all the time and play him when somebody's injured – principally Joel.' Dwyer had been seeking an international scrum-half and hoped he'd found his man: Richmond's live-wire Argentinian Augustin Pichot.

On the question of playing performance the issue appeared clear-cut. 'The minimum criteria we seek to achieve, as Bob had proposed,' explains Wheeler, 'is the quarter-final of the European Cup, semi-final of the Tetley's Bitter Cup and a top four place in the Premiership. But, we are seeking to achieve maximums: to be in with a shout in two out of the three and to be playing in a style that's exciting, with quality young players coming through. What progress had we made down our three-year plan? We know where we are in terms of time, but how far down that three-year path are we? Are we on track? Are we ahead of track? Can we still reach those targets? It's not clear where we are down the three-year road. The standard of play across the board has increased and it's more difficult to win nowadays.'

As far as the minimum criteria were concerned Dwyer was in no position to disagree. They were his criteria – and one of the targets had not been met. 'Those criteria were to measure our on-field performance throughout the season, not to assess coaching performance. I think it's misleading and dishonest to do so. But I'm absolutely, totally mindful of the fact that for people who are not very close to the scene it's impossible for them to make a judgement on the success of the season, except for it to be based on the amount of games you win and the amount of silverware you win. But, since the advent of professionalism, Leicester can no longer regard an appearance in the Cup final or first or second place in the league as of right. The playing-field is a lot more level now. Other teams have assembled impressive squads – Newcastle, Saracens, Richmond. It will require a miracle for us to win the Premiership now, but that doesn't mean you throw in the towel. I'm not suggesting we don't have good players, we do. But the reality is that there are now a lot of very good, even world-class, players in our competitions and it requires great mental toughness and a lot of ability to stay at the top. It is always more difficult to stay at the top than to get there. For a team like Leicester, every match represents an opportunity for an opponent to knock us off our throne. It was always like this, but the big difference now is that a greater number of clubs have the ability to go with the determination to achieve this feat. I'm not saying things are going badly but I would have liked to have made more progress at this stage. I would have liked to see us doing more consistently the things I want us to do, even though the standard of our players and their performances has improved almost beyond recognition in 18 months. Nonetheless, I stand by what I said after the Gloucester defeat – at the moment we are not good enough.'

In reply to all this, an exasperated Leicester director might justifiably point out that Dwyer's players can hardly be 'not good enough' when 16 of them are full internationals, including eight of the current England squad. 'It has become a hobby-horse of mine,' responds Dwyer, 'but the totally interesting statistic for me is that the two sides doing well in the Premiership are the two who do not carry a large England squad contingent. The squad that we've been providing players to has not been winning many games, so perhaps we've got the best of an average bunch. Our biggest problem this year came when guys returned from the Lions tour who thought they'd found the answer to the world's rugby problems. It's pretty obvious that that's not the case. In the Tests they had everything going for them, in that the opposition didn't have a kicker; the midweek team had some terrific performances, but against mediocre opposition. And yet they came back saying this is the secret of the game! It's proved well-nigh impossible to get some of them back into the way we want to play the game.'

Ah, the 'prima donna' factor, initially pinpointed by Dean Richards: 'There are too many of them and they need a good hiding!' Step forward Healey, Greenwood and, allegedly, after his inauspicious contribution as a second-half substitute at Gloucester, even Eric Miller. 'No, there's not a vindictive bone in Eric's body,' counters Dwyer. 'He was trying too hard. He got carried away with the result instead of concentrating on performance. His mind was so much in turmoil about what he wanted to achieve when he came on at Gloucester that he was a disaster. He conceded penalties, got yellow-carded and threw a pass direct to the opposition all in the space of 25 minutes! As for Will, I got a letter from his father some time ago that said "Will's position is due entirely to you." Will's improvement from an irregular Harlequins first-teamer to, at his best, a quality international player has been influenced by our coaching staff. Players have come to me and said that if Austin went

Will would be a changed man. People think that maybe Campese is similar to Austin, but I can tell you, Campo's a joy compared to Austin Healey! There's just no comparison!'

No player seems further from a prima donna than Dean Richards, yet here was another son of Leicester whose nose had been put out of joint by the Australian invasion. It was an open secret at Oval Park that Deano was no great fan of Bob Dwyer, 'all flash and no bash' as he was wont to describe him; nor, more inexplicably, did he warm to Duncan Hall. From being the man who ruled the roost, Richards was effectively pensioned off once his stint as captain ended in May 1997. During the current campaign his only three starts were in his despised position of lock; indeed, Dwyer was said to have wanted Richards to skipper the Extras for the season. 'No, that's just not true,' says Dwyer. 'We always pick a team before the captain. I realise it's not possible to be in love with a person who is overseeing the end of your rugby career. I'd tried to be sympathetic as it was none of Dean's doing, and I'd had several chats with him on how I might help, both inside and outside the game – mostly outside when he retired.'

Richards was one of the senior players consulted by Peter Wheeler during the course of compiling his report. If 'player power' was to exercise any influence on the board's thinking, however, it should surely have been in favour of Dwyer's retention not dismissal, since those canvassed by Wheeler had expressed strong support. Subsequently Wheeler was not so sure: 'It depends on which players you ask and when you asked them. No one will want to say anything against Bob now that he's gone, even if they are glad. At the time, I'd say around 35 per cent were strongly pro Bob, 20–25 per cent were against and the rest were decidedly neutral. I also spoke with other people whose opinions I respected, people like Clive Woodward and Les Cusworth, but this was on a wide range of issues in the report, such as restructuring and lines of succession, rather than about Bob himself.' Who knows, perhaps Deano's influence – as in his pomp – was worth half a dozen players.

'I honestly don't know whether my sacking might have been the need to find a place for Dean Richards. I'd spoken to the club about Dean and the part I thought he had to play in the club's future. I just didn't see him as a coach. I had no real vibes that Dean might have been working against me, but a number of things have come to light since my sacking to indicate that he was making comments behind my back.'

Were there other – largely unspoken – considerations that might possibly have soured Dwyer's relationship with the board? The Australian's high media profile, as exemplified by the furore over referees and Newcastle's gamesmanship, brought unwelcome attention to the club (nothing new, however: it was not that long ago Neil Back assaulted a referee); hanging the Sword of Damocles over a sacred cow like the Youth Fifteen was not guaranteed to win friends and influence people within the Tigers cabal; nor was elbowing aside Dosser Smith, another Son of the Soar. Money, of course, is said to be at the root of much Machiavellian activity and Leicester's flotation had not gone nearly so well as hoped, only around a third of the 4.4 million shares being taken up to raise just over £1.8 million (London Irish reputedly raised £2.9 million during the previous off-season).

'From a financial point of view we have to take stock of the fact that we have gone out of the three competitions, and the effect of that on the rest of this year and next year,' admitted Wheeler. 'We also have to balance the books. We have not got a rich individual underwriting any losses. The share issue raised over £1.8 million – we don't owe anybody anything and that money is now in the bank earning interest. But the share issue was a little disappointing in the end. Maybe we raised our sights too high on the back of not wanting to put a ceiling on something that might be exceeded. It was fairly close to Christmas when we did get the share issue out, Leicester City shares had just been floated, and had dropped, and there was outcry in the press from some owners of other clubs saying how much money they were losing. Against that backdrop, the investment market was pretty flat at the time. We were disappointed but what we got was enough to finance our business plan.' Money, insisted the chief executive, was not an issue in the debate.

So, with the depressing picture of the London Irish performance vividly etched in the mind's eye and Dwyer's own depressingly candid 'I've run out of ideas' words still ringing in their ears, the board reached its decision. Of the five options presented in Peter Wheeler's report, they plumped for the cheapest, which was also the single one excluding Bob Dwyer.

The following morning the relevant announcement, signed by Peter Tom, was released to the media, who were invited to attend a press conference timed for 6.30 p.m. that evening. The news made the lead story on local TV lunchtime bulletins, and as assorted members of the fourth estate, local and national, begin to assemble in the Presidents Lounge at Welford Road, several sets of eyes are busy scanning the front and back pages of the *Mercury* which scream: 'Dwyer Out! Bombshell as Deano takes over as coach'. Wheeler and Richards are already under siege for interviews. Behind the bar, Helen Morrell is dispensing the odd drink to one or two directors who, it must be said, have clearly come to bury Caesar not praise him, judging by their jovial demeanour; four of the board – David Jones, Philip Smith, Nick Donald and David Matthews – are in absentia. At 6.30 p.m. prompt the club's press officer, Stuart Farmer, calls for attention and introduces Peter Wheeler and Dean Richards: 'Peter will make a short statement and then he and Dean will take questions. There will be opportunities to do some radio and television work after that's been concluded.'

PETER WHEELER: I think most of you will have seen the statement, which simply said that the board of directors at their meeting last night decided not to take up the option to extend Bob Dwyer's and Duncan Hall's contracts by 12 months, and that the club had appointed Dean Richards to be in charge of team affairs with immediate effect. It also went on to say that we are grateful to Bob and Duncan for what they have done for the club since they've been here, in establishing the coaching and playing structure and standards, and leading the club into the professional era. To give you more background to the decision: the board asked me to look at the option that we had to extend Bob's and Duncan's contracts, not just in relation to the 12 months that we had the option for, but also to take the opportunity – 18 months, close to 20 months into the professional era – to ask if we'd got the structure of our playing and coaching right, and what should we be doing with it going into the next two to three years rather than the 12 months. That report was presented to the board on Monday, and I think what the board felt was that it was likely in the next nine to 12 months that we were going to need to make a change as we looked to the succession as regards Bob and Duncan and, probably, if that change needed to be made in that time-scale, it perhaps ought to be made now. The timing of the report was instigated by the option in the contracts and, coinciding with the run of results that weren't favourable, probably didn't help the situation as far as Bob and Duncan were concerned. That really formed the background, and once the club had decided that probably a change was going to be made it ought to be sooner rather than later. It was then a question of saying what we shall do in the interim and it was felt Dean would be the right person to be in charge of first-team affairs, to put in place over the next few days a coaching structure and personnel that would take us forward to the end of this season and into the future. The decision was not made on any financial grounds, but was made on the basis of achieving the objectives of the playing side of the club, which is ultimately to be the best rugby club in Europe, and to attain our minimum objective, which would be finishing in the top four in the Allied Dunbar Premiership. Any change that we made had to give us a better chance of achieving those objectives. That gives you a better background to the decision-making. I would reiterate at this point that we believe the appointment of Bob and Duncan 18 months ago was the right decision and that what they have done for the club during that time has been invaluable in taking us through a very difficult period for any club in this professional era and has established us as one of the top professional clubs. We are very grateful for their contributions to that. I'll be happy to answer any questions.

Q1: How long is Dean's appointment for?
PW: Dean has a contract which expires, I think, 30 June 1999.
Q2: You said that the changes had to be made in the next nine to 12 months. Why was that likely anyway?
PW: If you were looking at extending for 12 months and looking at how the club was going to go forward from the coaching point of view, and Bob's aspirations of what he wanted to do in the next two to three years, I think we felt the driving force of the coaching structure was probably going to need to start to take over from Bob during that period of time.
Q3: There has been all sorts of talk about rifts and clashes of personalities, e.g. Austin Healey. Was 'player power' a factor in Bob's demise?
PW: No. Dean and I have seen the international players in London today to let them know the situation and we've also met with all the other players before this press conference. I think it's true to say there is some surprise among the players and there was no element of 'player power' that influenced the board's decision. There was the highly publicised incident with Austin Healey on Friday which was just coincidental to the timing of this. It's probably fair to say that that sort of thing happens once a week with Austin anyway [laughter].
Q4: What will Dean's title be?

PW: He's responsible for team affairs. That means he will be responsible for the coaching, training, preparation and development of the first and second teams. As regards a title, we've not agreed on that. The title is the least important aspect of it. Over the next two to three days, as we put the structure formally in place, that may emerge.

Q5: Who will coach the backs? We've heard of Joel Stransky, even Brian Ashton.

PW: The final structure and the people within it will be in place by the weekend. This situation is less than 24 hours old and there's nothing more we can say about personnel at this stage, but as soon as those decisions are made an announcement will be forthcoming.

Q6: Is Dean's position an interim appointment or could it be longer term?

PW: I think the board would feel that there is an opportunity here. Dean is somebody who the club has been very proud of, right through from his youth to his dotage [laughter], and someone that's put the Leicester name all over the world. Every challenge that's been put in front of him from a rugby point of view he's accepted, and probably exceeded, people's expectations. I think what we're looking for him to do is to do that in the short term and we will monitor it for the long term. We'd hope, and wouldn't be surprised, if it continued. I would re-emphasise what I said, and that is one of the things Bob did was attract quality, ambitious internationals and world-class players to Leicester and the reasons for those players coming here must be continued. We must be known throughout the rugby world as a place where ambitious players will want to come so that they can realise their potential. We will do everything we can to make sure the coaching structure and the personnel within it reflect that.

Q7: Dean, in your coaching role, are you still available for selection?

DR: Hopefully, yes. But with the amount of young players that are coming through, and with the calibre of players coming through, I'm pretty sure I'll find it very difficult to slot myself in. I'd hope not to be able to find myself a place in the side but should I be required I will be available.

Q8: Is this job the culmination of everything you've wanted?

DR: I was quite shocked initially but to say that I feel honoured to have been offered the job would be an understatement. I think any player who has been at Leicester the vast amount of time I have, and understands what Leicester is all about, will realise the job is very important and that I certainly look at it as one of the most important at the club for some time. I am extremely honoured to be asked to take it on.

Q9: What are your immediate objectives?

DR: From a playing point of view, I think we've got to improve on our position in the league. It's difficult to say because, as Peter has said, Bob has done so many good things for the club and he's left us with a structure that is extremely good. It's going to be a very difficult act for me to follow. I just hope that the players will pull together, which I'm sure they will, and our goal is to win every game. Hopefully, with the way that we can play and the players we have got, we will do it.

Q10: Peter, you got Bob in the first place to get away from playing the sort of rugby you were playing under Dean as captain and now you've gone back to Dean as coach. A little bit strange, isn't it?

PW: No. I think if you directed that question at Dean he would say probably – possibly – at the time you're referring to we had a very strong pack and that we probably didn't have the quality of three-quarters that we have now, and that the practicalities of the situation forced a certain style on the team. If you look at the quality we have across the backline now I think you would look to try to expand the width of the game to encompass the skills and abilities of the players.

Q11: After the European Cup defeat I asked you if Bob's position was safe and you more or less said to me: 'Don't be stupid!'

PW: I say that to you all the time [laughter].

Q12: That was two months ago and now you've sacked him.

PW: A lot of things have happened in the last two to three months. The option to extend the contracts came up. Then I was asked by the board to do a full report on the playing structure and the people in it. Bob himself was frustrated by some of the play in games and results. He made that clear himself and I think other people have as well. Really, it was a question of looking longer term than just the next nine to 12 months.

Q13: What was Bob's reaction when you spoke to him?

PW: I've been in fairly detailed conversations with Bob over the last few weeks. He played a fairly full part in putting together the report and we've been through all of the different options, this being one of them. Having said that, he was disappointed.

Q14: Was the board's decision unanimous?

PW: The board's decision was by a majority.

Q15: What was the vote?

PW: I don't think we want to get into that. I prepared the report, which the board then discussed, and I stated to Bob that I'm quite happy for him and Duncan to see it

Q16: Were you behind him, did you want him to stay?

PW: I put forward, as was my responsibility, the different options that were available, some of which included Bob and one of which didn't. Then I took a full part in the board's discussion.

Q17: What was your recommendation?

PW: I didn't make a recommendation.

Q18: Do you feel disappointed as it was you that brought Bob in?

PW: I do feel disappointed because you feel disappointed when this sort of thing happens to anybody. I regard Bob as a friend and someone whom I've shared plenty of intense moments and an awful lot of work over the past 18 months; a man who came from the other side of the world to the club, in some ways because I wanted him to. I believe he's enhanced the reputation and the history of this club; and I believe he will go on to enhance the reputations of many other clubs in the future. I'm sure his phone today will be red-hot with clubs around the world who he can go to and help from where they are now to the next stage. He's done that for us and I think he's done that extremely well for us.

Q19: Is it indicative of how quickly success is going to be demanded because the game has gone professional?

PW: We've gone almost two seasons. I don't think we've been hasty. There was a period of difficulty last year toward the end of the season when he had a number of defeats over a period of time. We certainly didn't look short term and say this guy's not been successful. We knew that it was going to take a minimum of this period of time to start showing the changes we were looking for in order to reach our goals. I think one of the considerations at the moment, which we would ask ourselves, is to say: 'Do we believe the club at this stage is on an improving path to reaching the objectives? Some might say we were, but we've slipped a bit and it is toppling now. Do we have any guarantee that it will improve again before the end of this season or will it continue on that path?' Those were some of the judgements the board had to take into consideration.

Q20: When you compiled your report whose input did you seek?

PW: In the last ten days I sought several people's views, had conversations and meetings with around 15–20 players, players who I regard as senior players whose opinions I'd respect; with other people within the club and outside the club on a confidential basis. I did detail in the report who had had some input.

Q21: How long did the meeting last?

PW: From 4 p.m. to 8.30 p.m., which was almost exclusively on the playing report.

Q22: What was the opinion of the senior players on Bob's departure?

PW: The players these days are professional and they're working with people six to seven days a week and all day long. They respect each other as individuals and have experienced very intense occasions. It's always a sad occasion when somebody you're close to and spend a lot of time with and who you respect as a person moves on. I can't imagine that there are many players – perhaps the odd one or two – who wouldn't be anything other than disappointed and sad to see him go from that emotional point of view. There may be some who didn't see eye to eye with him on some of his coaching philosophy but you get that anywhere. There was never anything there in my belief that would have caused difficulty. So I think the players have been very good in all of this. They've been very supportive of both the coaching and the club as a whole.

Q23: In your short reign as chief executive three coaches have gone: Tony Russ, Ian Smith moved sideways, and now Bob Dwyer. Rather a lot in a short time.

PW: I think you've got two different positions there. Really it's just Tony Russ and Bob Dwyer. One came at the beginning and one has come, so to say, at the end – now. I think the committee made the decision with Tony Russ on what was best for the club going into the professional era and I think that decision and Bob's appointment was totally right. What has happened during that time has proved that. We hope the only reason the board made the decision last night was in the best interests of the club going forward. It was nothing to do with personalities, personal gain or anything. It was really to say, 'what is in the best interests of the club going forward?' – and they made that decision. It is not a decision that is black and white because I'm sure it could be said that each option could have been successful. It's really been a decision to say which one had more chance of being successful over a shorter space of time and in what manner.

Peter Wheeler reached for a proffered pint of bitter: he richly deserved it. 'What a marvel,' said Bob Beason admiringly. 'I don't know how he does it! Whatever he's paid it wants doubling!' Wheeler's oratory (unaided by notes) and coolness under fire may not have rivalled Mark Antony's on that torch-lit night in Rome's forum but it was a *tour de force* nonetheless.

The Leicester club was back in Leicester hands, opined the press. According to Stephen Jones in the *Sunday Times*, Dwyer's sacking revealed the club as 'not so much outgoing as parish pump parochial', and he went on to quote one former, anonymous Tiger as saying: 'I told Bob when he first arrived not to trust anyone because the Leicester "mafia" would get him in the end.' In the *Daily Telegraph* Mick Cleary wrote: 'Leicester are a close-knit club and there were those who were unhappy with Dwyer's manner and the way he brought in players from outside. Dwyer, an engaging, outspoken character, has an easy manner – until you cross him. Then he lets rip. Not in a malicious or gratuitous way but with force and emotion. It's called honesty. And it took those at Welford Road by surprise when he arrived.'

In the *Mercury* Chris Goddard recalled something Tony Russ had told him after his summary dismissal in 1996: 'Even after five years, he said, he still did not feel part of the Leicester family.' Wheeler, in fact, grew increasingly disenchanted with the local newshound's relentless pursuit of the 'truth'; he even framed a letter to the *Mercury* setting the record straight but eventually thought better of sending it. He denounced any talk of a Leicester 'mafia' out to 'get' Dwyer as 'utter rubbish'. As he phrased it: 'We have no problems with outsiders at Leicester. There was some baggage regarding Dosser Smith's treatment re: Bob, as far as two or three directors were concerned – which may have had some subconscious influence on them – but not everyone on the board felt like that.'

Throughout the week both fans and players – particularly in the light of the 'player power' accusations flying around – had their say: 'I was surprised. Bob's tenure has been very positive. He's one of the best coaches I've worked with – Dunc as well. What's happened says a lot about pressure and expectation. If there were individual clashes it's up to those involved to explain what they were about. But there's obviously people who didn't want him to stay.' (Martin Johnson); 'I was shocked. Bob is not only a friend of mine but a great coach. He has so much to offer and now he's gone. It's a huge disappointment. I believe that a lot of the players feel that way. There are people saying most of the players don't feel that way, but I believe they do. The ones I've spoken to are stunned. I certainly don't want to leave – I've been very happy here until now and this major calamity. If things don't work out some might want to look at their situation.'

(Joel Stransky); 'Bob's departure has nothing to do with the players. I am disappointed and surprised. Bob was good for Leicester in a number of ways and I am not aware of much criticism being aimed in his direction. He is a very, very good coach.' (Richard Cockerill); 'Everyone was aware there were a few problems but they were shocked. Bob brought my game on no end this year.' (Stuart Potter); 'Bob spoke to us the week before and made it clear there was a chance he could leave. So it wasn't a shock when it came, papers were full of it, but it was still a bit of an upset. I was in Italy at the time so I don't know what it was about. I feel sorry for the way it happened. All the players agree the way it was done was pretty strange.' (Fritz van Heerden); 'I learnt a lot under Bob and Duncan, especially Dunc being the forwards coach. Bob gave me a lot of chances because he likes to put the youngsters in. I owe him a fantastic amount.' (Lewis Moody). As for Austin Healey, butter had no chance of melting in his mouth (though he later poured forth his antipathy in May's *Rugby World*): 'I probably aired my opinions on the training ground too regularly and that's got to be the fault of the player not the coach. One or two differences of opinion are not worth building up into a grudge. I don't think a professional board of directors like Leicester's would make a big issue of a slight disagreement. Bob revived my international career and I respected him as a coach and a person.' Words were harder to find for Waisale Serevi: his tears said all that was needed to be said.

As was their wont, and privilege, the fans who wrote into the *Mercury* went straight for the jugular, be it Dwyer's ('no alternative but to get rid . . . we had simply lost the plot . . . probably a pain in the backside') or the board's ('shocking decision . . . nothing short of disgraceful . . . a major error of judgement'). Nor did Healey escape censure ('a glory boy . . . petulant . . . doubtful whether he will ever have the loyalty and commitment to be a true Tiger . . . it is such players who should be axed not the coach . . . superstars who openly badmouth their coach do not impress the terraces . . . he should keep his mouth shut'). In point of fact, Healey had been told in no uncertain manner that his Leicester career hung by a thread: one more tantrum and he was out.

Peter Wheeler's role in Dwyer's removal courted most attention. Having brought Dwyer to Leicester, how much of a fight did he put up to keep him? In voting with the majority was it not a case of 'Et tu Brute'? Speaking privately, a week after the event as the clamour was beginning to die down, he confided that as late as the evening before the board meeting he was still of the opinion Dwyer's services would be retained. 'I've examined my role over the past week, and going into the meeting I don't think I could have done more to secure Bob's plan of succession, even though I had some reservations which he and I had spoken about. I suppose I could have said: "If you remove Bob I'm going to resign", but I didn't because I didn't feel that strongly about it. I had been persuaded by some of the arguments. A particular line of succession may have looked attractive to Bob because it gave him another few years, but I felt the decision had to be made in the interests of the club and not to suit any one individual's own plan. I had some reservations about his long-term plan of succession, for example Joel retiring in a year to become coach. Perhaps he might not want to retire.'

Dwyer remained mystified. He had been left in no doubt that his proposals were enthusiastically received. 'Then, one of the directors leaked to the *Mercury* that I didn't have 100 per cent support on the board, and I was sacked. I was desperate to know why and asked Peter Wheeler to give me a reason. I might not have agreed with it but at least I would have been aware of their thought process. But I never got one. The closest I got to a reasonable answer was Peter saying: "I hope one day I can tell you the full story." To get sacked over the phone with no explanation was distressing to put it mildly. Professionalism has seen many changes but I don't accept that it should equate to a lack of morality. It's obvious, in retrospect, that people in high places at the club rarely said what they thought.'

'It was all very painful for me as I regard Bob as a good friend,' continued Wheeler. 'I don't believe that anyone other than Bob could have set up a professional club coaching structure and regime as he did between June and September 1996. The programmes he put in place changed the physique, attitude and skill levels of the players involved. It has been an exciting, sometimes frightening, time to be involved in professional rugby and I cannot think of anybody I would rather have had alongside me. There was some unease that Duncan's desire to return to Australia in a year's time might mean an offer arriving that caused him to leave us before Christmas. This could stifle, or delay, the development of one of our prospective coaches as the succession plan evolved. Bob's potential role in 12 months' time was also not so clear as possible successors started to take over the coaching reins. It became clearer that Bob and Duncan's departure from the club was not the question, but the timing of their departure was. This had to be controlled by the club and not to suit any individual's comings and goings. Once a line of succession could be seen – and it was Bob's own line involving John Wells and Joel Stransky – what had we got to lose by implementing it now? They've three months to cut their teeth and not so much at stake. Player-coaches are doing well at present – looking at Newcastle and Saracens – and we'll review things at the end of the season. It's my responsibility to keep abreast of the situation regarding availability of world-class coaches who would add to our potential in case the coaching team required heavyweight presence.'

So, in the words of Shakespeare, 'If it were done, twere well it were done quickly.'

Amid all the talk and counter-talk, however, one searched in vain for any outright condemnation of Dwyer's coaching. The only two pertinent criticisms that surfaced came from a director between sips of his pint: 'Healey is an international scrum-half but he can't pass – why wasn't he given individual coaching? And we used to be the best scrummagers and the best maulers in the country – now we're crap!' The second charge was only to be expected from a former Tigers forward (but consider the recent influx of quality forwards into the domestic game); the first is totally refuted by Dwyer: 'Austin had heaps of work done on him last season by Steve Kenney, the club's then scrum-half coach. But there ought not to be a need for individual skills coaching at this level. As Carwyn James said of the Llanelli scrum-half after Randwick had played them in 1973: "He should go away and learn his trade and come back when he's ready!" I try to do the individual coaching in the team situation because I know that there is no such thing as a team or a team game – it's only a collection of what individuals do, a sum total of individual actions and reactions. Austin finally decided he didn't want to play scrum-half, not that he said as much in words. When he did play scrum-half he was not always in the position a scrum-half should be. He had the idea he could play anywhere on the pitch but, in reality, one has to maintain your position. In the Saracens league game which we lost by a point, he went out to the right wing for the 22-metre kick-out after his stupid attempt at a field goal. When we won the ball from the kick he was still out on the right wing and there was no scrum-half when the ball came out! His biggest problem is he could never make the instinctive decisions required of a scrum-half. And he's a much better wing anyway. We did have problems at scrum-half: Gary Becconsall was unfit all season with a shoulder problem; then Jamie

Hamilton was injured, just as he was starting to play well; and Wais isn't the complete scrum-half – yet. I know Austin has played scrum-half for England and the Lions and Wais has some shortcomings, but I don't care what anyone tells me, Wais is a better scrum-half than Austin Healey.'

As the media tumbled out of the clubhouse after Tuesday's press conference, Dwyer watched from a vantage point in the Alliance & Leicester Stand. He had come to see the Extras, including Hamilton and Serevi at half-back, play host to their opposite numbers from Saracens. His spirits were momentarily lifted by a conversation with the visitors' coach, South Africa's World Cup winning captain, Francois Pienaar. 'He said to me: "If you go to coach Super 12, I want to be in your team." That can't be bad, can it?' When a coach of Dwyer's proven track record is on the market his name is linked with every coaching job that becomes available. Within 24 hours of his dismissal London Irish had been in touch. 'I told them I was not in a position to accept the job. Legally and factually my contract has been terminated because the heart of the contract is for me to undertake certain duties and responsibilities, which have been taken away from me. I was told that Deano was taking over straight away. But the club says my contract has not been terminated, I'm still employed by them, and they'll continue to pay me each month. I'll listen to any coaching offers just like I'd always listen to offers of players. Super 12 is the best job in the world because of the season's short duration and the high quality of the players. The likely prospect, though, is that I'll stay over here.'

Wherever Bob Dwyer lands he will not have Duncan Hall for company. The next stop for Hall is head coach. 'I said I'd be prepared to stay for one more year with Bob but if he got a job for a couple of years I wouldn't be prepared to go as his assistant. You can't be an assistant forever. Bob appreciates that. I feel a bit let down, I can't deny it. I took a punt. If you don't take a punt and learn from it you are not going to get anywhere.' Annie Hall pours her husband a cup of tea. 'Don't the board know what this man has been *doing* for them?' she asks with the emotional rhetoric of a wife who cannot begin to understand why her husband has been so roughly treated. In 15 years of marriage the Halls have moved no fewer than 13 times; move number 14 will uproot Gabrielle and Tobias from St Luke's School, only just around the corner. Tobias is presently burning energy on his roller-blades. Gabrielle it is, however, who enters the kitchen wounded: blood pours from her knee after an impromptu game of football. 'Life goes on,' says Dunc, heading off in search of some plasters.

So, the Australian dalliance was over. The very qualities that comprised Bob Dwyer's strengths constituted his Achilles heel. He is erudite, passionate, honest and coruscatingly forthright when it comes to the subject of rugby union football. To outsiders who knew no better, however, he was too erudite, too passionate, too honest for some people's tastes at Welford Road. By the same token, in removing Dwyer (and Hall) so mercilessly, the Leicester elders demonstrated the continuation of those very qualities which have elevated the Leicester club above the run-of-the-mill and kept it there during periods of adversity: a healthy respect for ties that bind; due deference to a united front; and strict adherence to the ethos of club before individual. 'The sadness was,' said Peter Wheeler, 'it affected two families.'

'Some of the letters of support I've received from Tigers fans have really impressed me,' wrote Bob Dwyer in the last of his weekly columns for the *Sports Mercury*. 'The accuracy of the comment, the assessment of our performances and the realisation of the coaching input behind those performances has been such that perhaps some of those fans should be on the board instead of some of the others.'

Dwyer's sacking coincided with St Valentine's Day. He received 14 cards and a bunch of red roses. Some people loved him to the very last.

22

We Play It with a Will

March winds brought no cheer to Leicester supporters reared on the inexorability of springtime excess in one competition or another. Despite the steady hand of Dean Richards on the tiller and the presence of John Wells and Joel Stransky as trusty first-mates, the good ship Leicester Tigers seemed to be veering toward the rocks, all chances of any silverware dashed in the most comprehensive manner after being blasted out of the Cheltenham & Gloucester Cup at the semi-final stage. Deprived to a greater extent than their opponents by international calls, illness and injury (both Stransky and Matt Poole turned out even though flu-stricken), a patched-up Fifteen lost 53–15 to Gloucester. The fruits of the professional game were, temporarily at least, beyond reach.

More alarmingly, so too were the traditional joys associated with the amateur era as bequeathed by the annual fixture with the Barbarians. For so long the high spot of the club's season in its Christmas slot, the fixture had become a casualty of professional demands by being shunted elsewhere in the calendar. Of the first 78 matches in the series five only had been rearranged due to bad weather, yet the eightieth clash succumbed to the pressures of the professional era, just as the seventy-ninth had in 1997. Just 7,314 spectators, the lowest crowd in living memory, braved the elements on the evening of Tuesday, 17 March, to watch what was effectively a Tigers second Fifteen put to the sword by a record 73–19 scoreline by a decidedly unglamorous Barbarians selection stripped of any current Five Nations participants. A backline, for instance, comprising Mallinder (England), Cuttita (Italy), Simone (Argentina), Robinson (Cambridge University), Hoskin (Manchester), Taumalolo

(Tonga) and Scully (Wakefield) did not warm the cockles of the heart in the same way as, say, the 1975 line up of J.P.R. Williams (Wales/British Lions), David Duckham (England/British Lions), Mike Gibson (Ireland/British Lions), Ray Gravell (Wales), Bosco Tikoisuva (Fiji), Phil Bennett (Wales/British Lions) and Gareth Edwards (Wales/British Lions) which epitomises the halcyon years of Tigers–Barbarians conflict.

Generation after generation of Welford Road habitues had come to savour this final Yuletide feast. In 1948, for example, 17,000 saw a star-studded Barbarian side featuring 14 internationals and the one traditional non-cap, pipped 9–8 thanks to a try from the Leicester skipper Peter Jerwood in the dying seconds. Another full house of more recent vintage marvelled at David Duckham's five tries in the visitors' 35–0 romp in the Golden Jubilee fixture of 1969. And even into the 1980s the Leicester legions were still accustomed to being treated to only the finest fare in a Barbarian shirt, wizards like Jonathan Davies, David Campese, Serge Blanco, Philippe Sella . . .

'The age of professionalism has been unkind to the Barbarians,' admits Peter Wheeler, Leicester's most frequent Barbarian with 14 appearances. 'Playing against the Barbarians gives us all a nice, warm, cosy feeling of days gone by when life was much simpler, when we did things only for enjoyment – and nothing was more enjoyable than playing with, or against, the Barbarians. Anybody that has been involved at Leicester, either as a player or a member, can have nothing but good memories about our Christmas encounters. It's only a few years ago that we would play what virtually amounted to a British Lions side in front of a capacity crowd – in those days the only one of the season. It was the highlight of any player's career, particularly if he wasn't an international. It seems such a shame that in such a short space of time all that has changed.'

Since the cessation of fixtures with Hartlepool Rovers and West Hartlepool in 1902, the visit to Welford Road has constituted the Barbarians' one and only regular confrontation with an English club. The first encounter, on 28 December 1909, came about after Fettes-Lorettonians had dropped out of Leicester's annual four-match Christmas festival the previous year; an invitation to fill the vacant date in future was extended to the Barbarians, and the already famous nomadic club duly made Leicester its third and final port of call on its 1909 Christmas tour. Having lost to both Cardiff and Newport during the sodden south-Wales leg of its travels, the Baa-baas arrived at Welford Road just in time to witness what eventually became an all too familiar scene – the sight of the straw, shrewdly laid in anticipation of frost, being removed by the groundsman and an army of volunteers. The Tigers had seen off Cinderford on 24 December, Birkenhead Park on 27 December and Penarth on 28 December, but they had to settle for a 9–9 draw with the Baa-baas in front of a 10,000 crowd. The Barbarians winter tour ceased in 1921; the Tigers' own holiday jamboree was cut to two games soon after the Second World War, and finally reduced to the Baa-baas only in 1965.

Leicester has not only provided a welcome oasis for its nomadic guests; it has also provided 73 players down the years, starting with W.H. Carey (a forward) in the Barbarians' inaugural fixture against Hartlepool Rovers on 27 December 1890. Twelve of the current playing staff are Barbarians, Niall Malone bringing up the round dozen in the Remembrance Match with the Combined Services earlier in the season (Richards, Wells, Back, Johnson, Potter, Rowntree, Cockerill, Garforth, Poole, Freshwater and Lloyd are the others). No surprise, then, that Leicester cemented this most special and precious of relationships by opening a 'Barbarian Room' in December 1992 in honour of its annual visitors.

'I don't know of any other club that has dedicated a room to the Barbarians,' says Tudor Thomas, the doyen of Leicester alickadoos, that largely unheralded species of devoted clubmen who give far more to their club than they can ever receive. 'They've got a room they can call their own. They're still a nomadic club but when they come to Leicester they can say: "That's our little room." You need a pillow sometimes to put your head down. They bring their memorabilia to us. They could fill ten cabinets if they wanted! They've just brought me two more jerseys to keep updating their display.'

Thomas is justifiably concerned that this most prized of appointments is in mortal danger of forfeiting its allure. 'The fixture has become a victim of the professional era, which saddens me. We've got to have a thorough look at the rugby situation today and, hopefully, if the RFU and the Premiership clubs get their act together and we develop a structured season, in which the clubs will have a say in how many games they're going to play and when they're going to play them, there is a possibility of a two- or three-week break at Christmas time that will enable us to put this Barbarians fixture back to its rightful place. That's what we want and what the Barbarians want. The structured season is paramount. The New Zealanders are laughing at all our fixtures! These lads playing today will be burnt out by the time they're 27, 28, 29 if something is not done to help them.

'I think in this age of professionalism the players themselves actually need to be reminded of the "good old days", when rugby was free from any worries. I may be wrong, but I feel the big players need this kind of game to express themselves from time to time. What the players don't need is the Barbarians game between two league fixtures where promotion and relegation could be involved. The players do need a little bit of a break, but if they could keep the old engine and the legs turning over by coming onto the field on Boxing Day – with a rest either side – they could get the enjoyment factor back into their game.'

Tudor Thomas has dedicated nearly all his rugby life to the Tigers. Now in his seventieth year, the patriotically christened Welshman from the village of Penycae, near Wrexham, played centre for the University of Bangor, RAF Midlands and, upon coming to teach at Leicester's New Parks School, the Swifts. 'I played only 15 games for the Swifts and managed one try – against Birstall, I think – before I retired at the age of 45! But, my only real sport was hockey. I was carded for an international trial but, unfortunately, my father died and that had to go by the board.' In retirement, Thomas (for 12 years headmaster of the city's Westcotes School) became in turn team secretary of the Swifts, Extras and finally, in 1978, the Firsts, a role he continued to perform until becoming club president in 1993. When the prospect of professionalism led to John Allen relinquishing the post of club secretary, Thomas held the fort on an interim basis until the board assumed responsibility in late 1997. 'I'm now the secretary and treasurer of the Leicester FC Association, a new body formed when the board came in. It represents the members until such time as we get a director nominated to the board.'

To the majority of Welford Road regulars, however, the mellifluous vocal chords of Tudor Thomas are more familiar than the face, for it is he who mans the public address system on match days, frequently lacing his pithy announcements with slices of Celtic wit. 'I was horrendous to start with, hopeless! I've developed a little more confidence now, but if I say anything at all funny it's spontaneous. I never ever prepare funny things to say because if you're not naturally a humorous person you cannot make yourself so. I try to be myself and if a quip comes up, so be it.'

The traditions and heritage of the game mean an awful lot to any son of Wales steeped in rugby lore and Thomas is no exception. In his eyes rugby over Christmas is synonymous with the Barbarians at Leicester. 'Even if the Tigers and Barbarians were at full strength in February or March, that festive occasion, that enjoyment, that fun part of rugby from the spectators' point of view could not be recreated. Whenever we've had to cancel the game because of the ground being unfit and brought it to a later date it was never the same. People used to use the Barbarians as a wonderful end to the year and a wonderful start to the new year. It was something that was unique. For as long as I can remember, right from when I was a boy, the day after Boxing Day at Welford Road was Baa-baas day. It was something special; it was something no other club in the whole of the country had got. People came from all over the country just for the occasion and it was a festive occasion. It was just what was wanted after Christmas and from that point of view moving the game is a big, big loss.

'The anticipation in Leicester was always wonderful as you waited for the publication of the Baa-baas team in the *Mercury*, and once they saw some of the names, the public knew it was going to be a marvellous occasion. The build-up was always hard, hard work! We would put straw on the ground three weeks beforehand and get it off on the morning of the match. Nine times out of ten – until recently when we've had the covers – we were still clearing straw as the players arrived. Even when I was team secretary and I had to see to the needs of the players in the changing-room I'd be attending to them still wearing my dirty pullover and my wellingtons because I'd not had time to change. To see how the game united the city, how mums and dads, children and grandparents, all came down to help in their own little way was terrific. Hundreds, thousands even, of people became members of the club because that was the only way they could get a ticket for the Baa-baas. The game of rugby is very competitive these days, but although the Baa-baas is also competitive it is a game that is really about fulfilment and enjoyment – and this word enjoyment could quite easily disappear from the world of rugby football in the professional era.'

Thomas's sentiments are echoed by the Leicester players who, to a man, hold nothing but the fondest memories of the big Christmas party. 'When I first arrived,' says Darren Garforth, 'everything was about playing against the Barbarians at Christmas. Things have changed a little bit since then, but it's always a great honour. You have a little bit of fun after the game and it's always a game to look forward to. You knew that you would be playing against some of the great players from around the world.' Graham Rowntree is in complete agreement: 'It was the one game of the season that the result didn't really matter. There was no pressure on you; we really looked forward to it; it was part of Christmas.' Attitudes on the field invariably reflected the seasonal spirit, as Dean Richards recalls: 'We had this move involving Les Cusworth, Paul Dodge and Clive Woodward where one would pass the ball, one would put the ball on the ground and the other would run over it and flick it between his legs to someone coming in on the burst – a totally outrageous move but it encompasses what the game was, and is, all about. Prior to the advent of leagues, the Barbarians game was, unquestionably for a Tigers player, the highlight of the season. There were still cup matches but if you were not selected for the Baa-baas you were devastated.'

Much as Richards hated having to take the decision, his team for the eightieth renewal contained not a single automatic first-choice player: international calls ruled a dozen players out of contention and with the Cheltenham & Gloucester semi-final also four days away, Joel Stransky and Fritz Van Heerden were rested; assured crowd-pleasers on an occasion such as this, Serevi and Vunibaka, were at home with the Fijian sevens squad preparing for yet another successful assault on the Hong Kong tournament. 'Given the opportunity I'd be turning out myself,' said Richards. 'But I'm knackered!' Only Niall Malone and Jamie Hamilton at half-back, the second-row pairing of Neil Fletcher and Matt Poole, Will Johnson at number eight and Geordan Murphy at full-back provided any real link with the first team. The Barbarians themselves fielded just one home international (Mallinder); plus capped players from Italy (two), Argentina (two), the Czech Republic, Tonga and Western Samoa. In the *Mercury*'s preview headlined 'Sad decline of Baa-baas bash' Chris Goddard lamented: 'The annual Barbarians knees-up has been on borrowed time for some while but judging by the teams for tonight's clash it has now passed its sell-by date. Suggestions that it might muddle along in its present form are probably wishful thinking because it is losing all the ingredients that made it special, the festive atmosphere, glamorous internationals and the feeling that a real humdinger of a contest was in the offing. Fixtures, however, don't survive on sentiment and the Baa-baas appear to be heading the same way as the dodo.'

Stars and spectators may have been in short supply but tries and fireworks were not: Tudor Thomas announced 15 try-scorers – ten of them Barbarians – as the visitors let rip from all parts of the field to such effect that at one stage they looked capable of eclipsing their greatest-ever haul, the 86 accumulated at Newport in 1990. Tongan fly-half Siua Taumalolo (unable to hold down a regular place at Ebbw Vale) racked up 33 points in the one match – surpassing by five points the record career total standing to any individual Barbarian.

'The people who came to see the game were thrilled with what they saw', reported Tudor Thomas. 'They saw world-class rugby and went away happy. The fact that we didn't compete was no fault of our own because we had league and cup fixtures to look for. I've heard players being asked whether the fixture will survive and they say "Yes" because they want it to survive. It's fraught with problems, there's no doubt. It's got a lot of things against it: big matches, touring teams, European Cup and so on. But, people don't give in to problems, they try to solve them. After what the Baa-baas have done for Leicester we will be in debt to them forever. I'd be stupid to say it will carry on forever. The Baa-baas and Tigers are associated with excellence and if you devalue the teams you are taking away excellence from the occasion. But I said to Micky Steele-Bodger, the Barbarians president, after the game: "Look at the players now. They're all talking, they're all laughing. They're all professionals yet they need this occasion." The evening was as full of fun as always. The after-dinner speeches are always entertaining. The presidents of the two clubs speak and then the two captains. Peter Wheeler is an absolutely brilliant after-dinner speaker, so his speeches were always wonderful; Les Cusworth ended his with a poem; and Willie Anderson was a great speaker for the Barbarians. There's an awful lot of mickey-taking in the speeches, and you only do that if you've got the utmost respect for each other. That respect entitles them to take the mickey. As opponents they've knocked seven bells out of each other, as companions in the clubhouse they are the best of friends. That is rugby football and that's why if we can still enjoy rugby football on Boxing Day or the day after Boxing Day, the things we've cherished and treasured over the years will remain a part of this great game of ours – good rugby, good companionship, good friendship, entertainment and enjoyment. The Baa-baas represent everything that is good about rugby, people who have contributed so much to their clubs, so much to the game of rugby football – and that's what sport is all about.'

That more carefree age evoked by the Barbarians club song – 'For the rugby game we do not train, we play it with a will' – has long since vanished. Nevertheless, rugby will be a poorer and grimmer experience for both player and spectator alike should the day ever dawn when the Barbarians spirit is expunged from the game.

23

New Brooms

The fallout from Bob Dwyer's explosive departure was taking an age to clear. No sooner than the dust began to settle it was being stirred up again. While the club endeavoured to look forward certain individuals outside the club were determined to look back.

Chief among them was John Barrell, a debenture holder and shareholder, intent on forcing a special general meeting to extract some answers from the board, most specifically why it chose the only option of five in Peter Wheeler's report that did not include Dwyer; Barrell also harboured growing fears concerning HSBC's influence on the board since it held 10.4 per cent of the shares and 76 per cent of the voting rights. The club, argued Barrell, could be vulnerable to the 'intervention' of a 'millionaire figure' if the bank decided to sell its holding – either to another financial institution or an individual – which it was allowed to do without reference to the Leicester board. Although 350 members supported Barrell's campaign they only held 1 per cent of the shares, some way short of the 10 per cent necessary to activate an EGM. Barrell said, 'We have not had an explanation from the chairman and we still expect one at the AGM on 28 July.' Like local businessman Dominic Tonner, who distributed 2,000 leaflets before the home game against Richmond on 28 March, Barrell was unimpressed by Peter Tom's contribution to the club's March newsletter in which the only additional clue as to Dwyer's removal – for readers between the lines – was the comment: 'No individual, my colleagues on the board included, can elevate themselves above and beyond the long-term interests of the club. No one can.' Needless to say, Chris Goddard knew a good story when he smelt one and remained doggedly on the scent. 'Tigers keep mum', he wrote after Tom refused to shed any more light on the subject. All Goddard could elicit from Tom was that there were 'differences between the southern and northern hemispheres in the way people treat each other . . . English people don't necessarily react to criticism in the same way as southern hemisphere people.' Goddard summed up the mood of the malcontents on 7 April, in a boldly displayed opinion piece imploring the board to 'End this stinking affair – Now!'

Then, with the heat at last beginning to abate, the May issue of *Rugby News* carried an interview with Tony Russ, in which the club's first director of coaching – sacked in 1996 to make way for Dwyer – really twisted the knife: 'They have become very good at mishandling difficult situations and have completely lost that club feeling they had before. Why not just wait until the end of the season and then say you don't want to take up the option? Peter Wheeler and the management committee [sic] look stupid and they have come out of this with a lack of respect. They haven't explained why they did what they did. If a coach deserves to go, then fair enough and the world should be told, but just for a couple of bad matches? I have to think there's a reason none of us know about. There's got to be something going on. Leicester is a very insular town club and that has probably been its strength and weakness. Traditionally, pretty well everyone comes if not from Leicester then certainly the Midlands. You were playing for the town. In those days the players were extremely powerful. People like Dean Richards and Les Cusworth before him would have been very dominant figures in the club. Dwyer rattled a few cages. He changed all that . . . but when things started going against him player power reared its head again. That is bad management in my book. When player power rears its head you get rid of the players not the coach.'

To rework, ever so slightly, the immortal phrase of Miss Mandy Rice-Davies, 'A sacked coach would say that, wouldn't he?'

If the new brooms wielded by Richards, Wells and Stransky were meant to sweep clean, then morale was in need of urgent restorative work. It frequently does whenever the seasonal run-in looms without the comforter of trophies to play for, and February's ructions merely served to exacerbate the malaise. The new stewardship arranged a night out, – go-karting followed by dinner – to lighten the mood. The reverie was but the spoonful of sugar, however. Richards immediately imposed a new dress code, reinstating blazers and ties for all away fixtures instead of the club's leisurewear, and mooted the introduction of a fines system to combat ill-discipline on the field.

The Tigers may well have smartened up their act off the field but they failed to do so where it counted. Indeed, they demonstrated even less savvy than they had under Dwyer. For the first time in 15 years a Tiger was sent off: Martin Corry in the return match with Northampton on 7 March. Then, to cap it all, a second player was shown the red card on 4 May – Will Greenwood at Newcastle. Amid all this mayhem games were being lost. The first ten Premiership matches played under the new regime yielded only four victories which saw the Tigers slip to fifth place, 13 points behind the leaders (with one game in hand); Dwyer had left them at eight points adrift. As for Waisale Serevi, he did not feature in a single game. Admittedly, Serevi was away for a while with the Fijian sevens squad but his disappearance from the scene spoke more eloquently than any words. Stuart Barnes, never one to miss an opportunity, rubbed salt into the wounds: 'Leicester appear to have turned a corner since the shock dismissal of Bob Dwyer . . . ', he wrote in the *Daily Telegraph*, 'into a one-way street. The Australian did not have them in rugby's fast lane but at least they were on the motorway. The only saving grace is that Leicester are not moving fast enough to be hurtling towards self-destruction.'

So the Leicester faithful had much food for thought as they trooped into a drizzly Welford Road on Sunday, 10 May, for the final home game of the season against Premiership strugglers Bristol. An hour before kick-off isolated knots of die-hard fans on the Crumbie Terrace are all too eager to pass judgement on an eventful nine months. 'They've played very well at home but rubbish away', states 13-year-old Ben Blount unequivocally, before grandfather Brian puts things into a more measured perspective born of age and experience: 'That's because they haven't got this Leicester crowd behind them. I think we lift them, I'm sure we do. I don't know why Dwyer went. I think it was bad. I couldn't understand why it was done and the way it was done. We like Deano, of course, but I was a big fan of Bob.' Further along the boundary fence student Jill Horsley, from Blaby, offers a different view of the deposed coach: 'Bob would never get on my Christmas-card list because I disagreed with a lot of things he did, like some of his chopping and changing – although what I did like about him was that he took every player at face value, whoever they were, and judged them on whether they could do the job.' Standing next to her is Fred Richardson, a season-ticket-holder for 30 years, who gives his verdict between thoughtful sucks on his pipe:

'I'm disappointed with the board. There seems to be a lot of wrangling among the directors, it's not all happy families, and this reflects on the playing side. It was disappointing that Bob Dwyer never got the chance to do a couple of years, or three really, because you can't do what you want to do in that space of time. You can't change things round in a few months. Now I've noticed we've started to go backwards in the style of play, into the old Dean Richards mould, taking the ball in – but these days they're being turned over and losing it! Things have got to start at management level up above: good feeling, good family, support all the way down. I feel that's gone at the moment. If it's right at the top it reflects all the way down.'

Up in the Tigers Bar, Keith Moore and Stuart Siddle, both decked out in replica Tigers jerseys, throw in their two-penn'orth. 'The competition is more difficult now,' says Moore. 'All the other clubs have come up in the world. I was sorry to see Bob Dwyer go. With hindsight, he maybe was doing the right things.' At the mention of the Australian's name, Moore's sidekick adopts a pained expression and begins quaffing his pint. Siddle confesses to mixed feelings on the subject of Bob Dwyer: 'At the time I thought Dwyer's dismissal was the right thing. I was down at Kingsholm for the Gloucester game and was actually shouting at him, "You're over here and you're overpaid!" Looking at it now, I think Dwyer had that little touch to bring the whole lot together, which at the moment we've lost. It was a negative response by the club. Maybe he should have been kept on till the end of the season. Maybe we've lost our way. Dean Richards is a great asset, but we need a head coach that knows the business – I'd like to see someone like Ian McGeechan. But, at the end of the day, I'm a firm supporter. I'll be here next year!'

Loyalty and stoicism of this order cannot cheaply be bought. It also comes in handy during the kind of match that ensues, a drab encounter characterised by a conspicuous lack of continuity or cohesive teamwork; were it not for a typically virtuoso display from Joel Stransky, who weighed in with 19 points (two tries, three conversions, one penalty) the 34–25 scoreline would have looked distinctly threadbare. Initially, Bristol's sole objective seemed damage-limitation, a stratagem loudly pinpointed by one of their travelling band of supporters as fly-half Mark Armstrong prepared to take the penalty that might bring them level at three-apiece just eight minutes into the match. 'Ref!' rang out a well-oiled West Country voice, shattering the dead silence Welford Road customarily affords any visiting goalkicker, 'if he gets this, blow the whistle – we'll take the draw!' It has to be said that without the vociferous interjection of the dozen or so Bristolians in the 8,678 crowd (the lowest Premiership gate of the season) there would have been precious little noise or atmosphere in the ground.

With only the London Irish fixture at Sunbury left to play, the future of the club's three-pronged solution to its coaching dilemma lay very much on the line. Fresh from the final Oval Park session of the campaign, Richards, Wells and Stransky plonk themselves down at a table to contemplate one final round of questions. Freshness, however, is not a concept exactly relevant to this particular conversation. All three men have a jaded, end-of-term look about them and, in truth, their words seem equally laboured and lacking any real spark or vitality. The season has been a long slog by any standard, an arduous journey guaranteed to exact a price irrespective of the additional burdens suddenly thrust upon them in February. For the last three months their every move has been under the microscope. How have they come to terms with being pitched in at the deep end? What green shoots of recovery are coming through which can be taken into next season? And if they have been on 'trial' what is the verdict likely to be?

A persistent ankle injury has severely restricted John Wells's activities for most of the season and he had been coaching the Extras forwards rather than playing, all of which gave him the opportunity to view the palace revolution of 16 February from a slightly different angle. 'It would have been easier to keep Bob than to get rid of him. He did a lot of good for the club, but I think he struggled in the last six months which put a lot of pressure on him. I think a lot of what was said in the papers about Leicester being a parochial club is possibly true. It took me about five years to get "into" the place. Perhaps he was never quite accepted because he was an outsider. As a club there seems to be a renewed vigour and renewed spirit about the place. Everyone seems a little more at ease, a little bit happier, a few more jokes are being cracked.

'It's noticeable that Andy Robinson at Bath, Rob Andrew and Dean Ryan at Newcastle, Richard Hill at Gloucester and Francois Pienaar at Saracens have all been successful at some point in the season and all of them are close to the playing side, either because they're playing or have just finished playing, so they have a rapport with the players because they're young enough, or their style of management is such that they can develop a rapport. Dean has helped enormously on the social side and has brought the spirit back into the club.

'We've tried to make training more concise with what we think is more structure to every session, so the players turn up knowing exactly what they're going to do and exactly what time they're going to finish. It helps players focus and approach the session in a far better frame of mind than if they were unsure of the session's length because it depended on the whim of an individual. All this may not have translated into the way that we've played but there's a much more relaxed atmosphere. Once you get people working for you they're more likely to sell themselves for you. Also, there's been a greater degree of commitment shown in the games since we've been in charge – and we've had to play some big games. Even against Newcastle when we lost we were the better side for 40–45 minutes. It's the little things that have been letting the side down all season that have let us down again. If we can take this passion and commitment into next season we'll move forward rapidly.'

Wells shovels a spoonful of cornflakes into his mouth, ponders as he chews and then concludes: 'I think we've come through a sticky period quite well. But I think the ball is rolling in the right direction now and we can start next season with the players not only fit physically but fit mentally. I think a fit, fresh Tigers team will do a lot of damage.'

Richards, meanwhile, between fielding numerous calls on his mobile phone, has had his head buried in the current issue of *Inside Rugby*. Once dragged into the conversation he instantly acknowledges the observation that his new role has seen him poacher-turned-gamekeeper. 'Anyone who knows me will tell you that management isn't exactly my forte, and at your own club people know your idiosyncrasies! At a new club you have new people and you can set your stall out a lot easier. I used to lead from the front in socialising, but not training! So now when I'm trying to get people to do things I disliked they are looking at me and saying: "Well, you never did it!"

'But if I don't produce the goods, if I don't gain the respect of the players I could be sacked. Being respected as a player gives me a foot in the door but this is a totally different role. I hope the honesty I have with the players will stand me in good stead, so they'll still accept me as one of the "boys". The feedback that the players get from the coaches has improved a great deal. I disagree with not telling players why they've been dropped or not considered. If they are to develop as players they need to be told what to work on. We are trying to give player-appraisals at the moment, sitting down with them to discuss if they've played well, how they can improve themselves; or if they've played badly, why they've played badly and how we can help them get the best out of themselves. There is a lot John, Joel and I can learn. We are going to make mistakes. But between us we have a nice balance.'

Joel Stransky was brought to Leicester by Bob Dwyer and he remained the Australian's most true-blue supporter right to the bitter end. Wads of smart money insisted Stransky would follow Dwyer out of Welford Road, most probably in the direction of Saracens to link up with his former Springbok captain Francois Pienaar. An approach was made but Stransky turned it down. Yes, he had aspirations to coach, all right, but he was on record as believing it would be a tough assignment to combine the roles of coach and fly-half. The call had come too soon, at least sooner than he had anticipated. It was, however, an offer he could not pass up. 'I have been fortunate to come out smelling of roses. The opportunity did not come in the circumstances I would have preferred but I have to make the most of it. I don't think that at the age of 30 I'd want to move elsewhere and have to start all over again. I'm a Bob fan but much as his departure was an unpleasant situation and I did not agree with it, we have to get on with it. I feel I've got two more years left to play and maybe from that point of view the job did come a mite too soon. It's not easy playing and coaching. You have to make decisions from a management point of view and it means analysing and judging your friends – and trying to detach your emotions is never easy. It's difficult detaching yourself when you have to be firm, or taking a stance other people are not going to like. I see myself from the perspective of being a player first and then a coach, not the other way round. It's a fine line but I still like to think if you're playing you've got to be one of the "boys" – and then detach yourself to be part of management. I do know there's a lot more thinking now. I lie awake in bed at night thinking about players and teams.

'The spirit has been good, but it was at times when Bob and Duncan were here. Rapport has been much easier for us because being players we understand the mentality of the players and their feelings a lot easier than Bob and Duncan did. Bearing in mind the circumstances, the fact that we weren't going well, the fact that we had a lot of injuries. I think we've done pretty all right for three blokes with very little experience and if it has been a "trial" I'd say we've passed it.'

The Tigers trounced a depleted London Irish (resting players for the relegation play-off) by a score of 55–16, thereby consolidating fourth place in the Premiership. Joel Stransky's 15 points raised his seasonal total to 459 and eased him past John Liley's club record of 446 set in 1995–96. The Premiership programme fell into two neat halves: under the auspices of Richards, Wells and Stransky the side had won five of its 11 matches (and drawn two) compared to the seven of 11 under Dwyer and Hall – who, to be fair, had benefitted from seven home games not four. For any number of reasons – good, bad and indifferent – the 1997–98 season was as eventful for Leicester Tigers as any of the 108 that had preceded it. The club is floated as a plc; sacks its coach; wins zilch. The fans say hail and farewell to Deano and Wellsy, while warming to young guns like Lewis Moody, Paul Gustard and Geordan Murphy. Yet things could have ended up so differently. Conceding a last-minute try at home to Toulouse in the Heineken European Cup ensured a hazardous trip to Pau for the quarter-final instead of a comfortable tie with Harlequins at Welford Road; Neil Back being denied a match-winning score by referee Brian Campsall in the dying moments of the titanic floodlit clash with Premiership pace-setters Newcastle; Michael Lynagh's penalty sailing between the posts three minutes from time at Saracens which put Tigers out of the Tetley's Bitter Cup by a single point; Will Greenwood's pass direct to an opponent which gift-wrapped Gloucester seven points and the match at Kingsholm, a loss that contributed as much impetus as any other factor to the 'dump Dwyer' bandwagon. By such flips of the cards was the 1997–98 season ultimately consigned to the record books as being unsuccessful.

What's done is done, however. The words crying, spilt and milk may come to mind but they must never be allowed to cross the lips. Onwards and upwards is the cry. A mood of optimism permeates the Tigers' lair. Richards, Wells and Stransky receive a two-year deal; senior players pledge their troth by renewing contracts; and, contrary to the harbingers of doom, new players are queuing up to be part of the new Welford Road set-up. England and British Lion full-back Tim Stimpson and 22-times capped Canadian wing Dave Lougheed signed on the dotted line even before the last ball of the 1997–98 season has been kicked – to be followed, so the tea leaves say, by an Australian back (Pat Howard) and a New Zealand front-rower. Pre-season training for the 1998–99 season commences on Monday, 29 June, just six weeks away. Professional rugby truly is 'a man's, man's, man's world'.